PREJUDICE
AND
PLUM BRANDY

PREJUDICE
AND
PLUM BRANDY

Tales of a Balkan Stringer

Alec Russell

MICHAEL JOSEPH
LONDON

To my Balkan friends
and most of all
domnisoarei S. *cu mult drag*

MICHAEL JOSEPH LTD

Published by the Penguin Group
27 Wrights Lane, London W8 5TZ
Viking Penguin Inc., 375 Hudson Street, New York, New York 10014, USA
Penguin Books Australia Ltd, Ringwood, Victoria, Australia
Penguin Books Canada Ltd, 10 Alcorn Avenue, Toronto, Ontario, Canada M4V 3B2
Penguin Books (NZ) Ltd, 182–190 Wairau Road, Auckland 10, New Zealand

Penguin Books Ltd, Registered Offices: Harmondsworth, Middlesex, England

First published in Great Britain 1993

Copyright © Alec Russell 1993

Typeset by Datix International Ltd, Bungay, Suffolk
Set in 12 on 13 pt Ehrhardt
Printed in England by Clays Ltd, St Ives plc

A CIP catalogue record for this book is available from the British Library

ISBN 0 7181 3698 5

The moral right of the author has been asserted

Contents

Acknowledgements

One of the more memorable lessons of my time in the Balkans came in a tactful memo from my office in London explaining that 'More is less'. This is a rule I feel entitled for once to break, although it would take at least another chapter to record fully my debt to those who have helped, guided and advised me over the last three years. Some, like the young Romanian who plucked Bill Mcpherson and I from the miners' cudgels in Bucharest in June 1990, or the two Bosnians who in August 1992 guided Maggie O'Kane and I to the edge of Serb-held territory, are anonymous. Others, like the doctor on the road through Slovenia, are not, but would rather remain so. I can only say let no one disdain Balkan hospitality or bravery.

To Charlotte Eagar and Perdy Fraser who badgered me into joining them on a plane to Bucharest, much against my better judgement, I apologise for my reservations. You were right. To Pat Prentice who picked up the phone on the eve of my departure and offered spontaneous encouragement, I owe my connection with the *Telegraph* and a new and congenial way of life. To Nigel Wade, my foreign editor, who enlisted me over the telephone, kept faith through months of wordy and unusable copy and then fired me off around the Balkans, I owe a job, countless hints in writing style and an incomparable excuse for roaming around the world.

The eyes and ears of foreign correspondents are their interpreters. To Mihai Radu, whose diligence and intuition in the early days in Bucharest far exceeded mine, Luli Popescu who became Romanian teacher as well as translator, Davor Huić whose laconic humour enlivened many a dismal day on the Croatian battlefields, Vlatka Mihelić, Dragan Čicić, Tamara Levak, Zoran Jovanović and all the others who were willing to take to the road, usually for a hopelessly inadequate sum of money, I owe most of my understanding of the region. You are among the true heroes of the Balkan beat.

Camaraderie and companionship often lightened the worst the Balkans could provide. The pivotal role played by fellow Bucharest stringers and travelling companions in Yugoslavia should be clear. I would particularly like to mention Alison Mutler, Bucharest's correspondent *par excellence* and the 'uncles', the old pros Robert Fox and Patrick Bishop, who time and again gave object lessons in foreign corresponding. In Belgrade Dessa Trevisan, rightly known as the doyenne of the Balkan press corps, steered me through Serbia's all-embracing propaganda. Michael Montgomery was unstintingly generous with his encyclopaedic knowledge. Bill Mcpherson has been a fount of advice and support. So too the bureaux of the international news agencies, Reuters, the Associated Press and Agence France Presse, in Bucharest, Belgrade and Zagreb, helped me out with facts and figures on countless occasions, in particular Michel Conrath, Calin Neacşu, Peter Humphrey, Adrian and Roxanna Dascalu, Nada Borić and Zoran Radosavlievic.

Meanwhile back in London, on the foreign desk, Paul Hill, Patsy Dryden and Theresa Jeffery breathed calm reassurance down the phone line while resolving a myriad of logistical arrangements with unfailingly chirpy humour. It cannot be easy dealing with the precious demands of correspondents day in, day out on the telephone. The switchboard traced me to the most desolate spots and the copy-takers took down and often rearranged my words on crackling phone lines, invariably on deadline. Without this back-up few of my dispatches would have made it into print.

As for the book itself, written in Bucharest, London and Johannesburg, between and sometimes during stints in Yugoslavia, it has, I fear, proved an editor's nightmare, arriving irregularly in half-finished chunks, while deadlines have passed with the monotony of Bosnian ceasefires. I received only support from Jenny Dereham, who encouraged me to write it in the first place, and from Alexander Stilwell who has coped with daily rearrangements, corrections and endless excuses. His editorial hints have proved invaluable, delicately reminding me when Balkan arcana are a little too arcane, curbing my obsession with medieval Romanian kings, reining in redundant phrases.

Mihai Catargi read through fledgling chapters with painstaking attention to detail. Lucy Broke, Virginia Marsh, Caroline Russell and Mark Almond picked up on points of tone and style. Monica Botez proved herself an expert in Romanian poetry and myth. Michael Montgomery highlighted some of the more glaring Yugoslav errors but I retain sole responsibility for all judgements and analysis. As I rummaged through mounds of old notebooks, struggling to convert memories and thoughts to paper, Nat and Katie Page offered surely the warmest hospitality in Bucharest and at the Premiera, Doctor Teodor Olteanu gave a taste of the old Paris of the East. The *Telegraph* turned a blind eye when for a couple of months in early 1993 no news was coming from their man in Romania.

To my parents and family, who have had to endure a succession of agonising silences, often broken only by alarmist radio bulletins, I can never adequately repay their unquestioning support. Not once did they query my fixation with covering the Yugoslav war. Not once did they ask why I insisted on breaching sieges. Now I have ceased to be a stringer, I will try to be more circumspect.

But my greatest debt by far is to Sophie. In January 1990 I left London, promising I would be back by the weekend. Eleven months later Sophie moved to Bucharest to start work in Romania. Within a fortnight I disappeared to Turkey. The day I was due to return I was re-routed via Slovenia. Throughout this catalogue of failed rendezvous, all I received was encouragement that covering the latest Balkan crisis was the right thing to be doing. It seems almost incidental to add that she read and rearranged the tortuous first drafts of chapters with an undeserved devotion to detail.

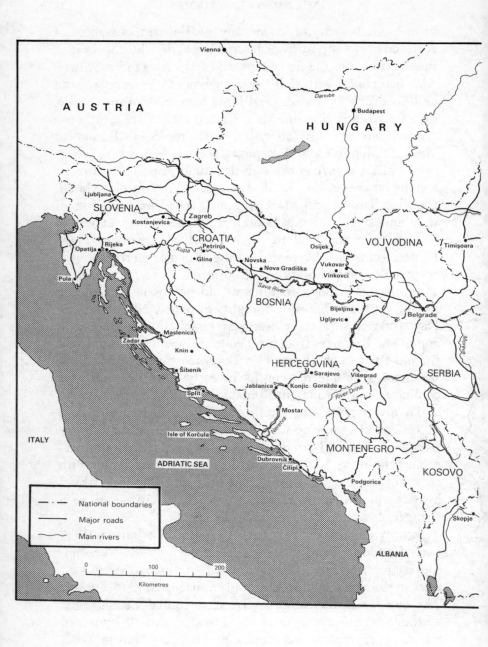

Introduction: 'Strange things happen here'

Timişoara, Romania, January 1990
Bijeljina, Serb-held Bosnia, January 1993

On a freezing January evening, a month after the overthrow of Nicolae Ceauşescu, I was almost co-opted to the Timişoara government. With three years' hindsight of the bizarre tendencies and traits of the Balkans, the occasion seems humdrum, even mundane. But at the time, a fortnight after my arrival in the region, it was a formative experience, initiating me to the quirky and illogical ethos which pervades south-eastern Europe, and instrumental in persuading me to stay.

My dabble with Balkan politics came as Timişoara swayed between various shades of misrule. In the four heady weeks since the revolution, the city had been led by two Fronts of National Salvation, a hellfire-and-brimstone man of the people and a military proconsul called General Popescu. The general had assumed power to avert a drift towards anarchy and his resignation had sparked an emergency session of the 'fifty-one', the remains of the revolutionary council. For a fledgling free-lance journalist it was a meeting to attend. Silviu, my guide and mentor, grudgingly agreed to forego his appointment at the local bridge club.

Outside the old Party headquarters, a squat Habsburg mansion where the councillors were due to meet, half a dozen trams were crackling like primitive fireworks, stalled while a drunken crowd milled on the lines. The revolution had instilled a taste for people-power among ordinary

Romanians. The passengers, obedient, disinterested, stayed in their seats watching a line of soldiers trying to beat back the demonstrators.

The sentries' orders were to let no one enter, but in their ill-fitting pre-war greatcoats they were more concerned with the cold than with security. Silviu's father knew the local police chief. We were soon inside, chatting with a tired-looking officer guarding the stairs.

'Our relief is two hours late,' he confided. 'And we haven't had a smoke all day . . .' Silviu offered a packet of Kent cigarettes. The officer gave a slight bow and waved us through.

Pursued by the demonstrators' cries of 'Democracy!', 'Liberty!', 'No more work!' and a frenzied banging at the door, we hurried up the ornate stairwell to find we had arrived at a crucial juncture. Amid clouds of smoke, thirty or forty councillors, soldiers, academics, workers, even the odd priest in full Orthodox robes, were discussing electoral procedures. They were apparently planning to vote.

'Why are they voting?' I whispered to Silviu.

'Shush. It's very important. They are trying to decide whether to make a list of those present.'

Four late arrivals bustled in, previous counts were nullified and the votes were recast. Twenty people were missing. Was the company quorate? The acting chairman, a Major Roman, the general's *aide de camp*, read out three lists. They conflicted. The thirty were to be eighteen. No, the fifty-one were to be retained . . .

For four decades of communism, the council chamber, with its garish inch-thick carpet and over-varnished table, had hosted endless Party sub-committees and planning groups, where little was achieved but the gratification of big-wigs' egoes and the writing of voluminous reports. The old practices were clearly enduring. The sixth or seventh speaker coughed and rose to his feet. The heating was on full . . . Silviu nudged me in the ribs and I shook myself awake. A masterful idea had been proposed – a secret ballot. I reached for my pen.

The purpose of this secret vote was clearly less important

than the fact that it had been agreed. The councillors solemnly shook hands. Rowdier spirits burst into a spate of singing and chanting.

'*Azi in Timişoara. Mîine in toata ţara*' (Today in Timişoara. Tomorrow in the whole country), they roared, echoing one of the old revolutionary chants. An old peasant who had slept through the speeches woke up and shook his fist. *Ţuica* (plum brandy), a clear and potent spirit, was brought round and cups of syrupy coffee; the policeman by the door asked my opinion of Mihai Eminescu, Ion Caragiale and other Romanian literary 'greats'; more *ţuica* arrived, the talk moved to historical heroes: Stefan cel Mare (Stephen the Great), Mihai Viteazul (Michael the Brave) – and then, as suddenly as it had appeared, the confidence evaporated and everyone was muttering about their 'right' to secrecy.

'It's our privilege to be unknown,' declared one delegate.

'Anonymity,' agreed a colleague.

This unswerving belief in the unaccountability of officials had a dubious flavour of the communist past. But with a tiny slice of history in the making, it didn't seem right to demur. I was frantically scribbling down Silviu's translation when a bright spark had a new idea.

'If I may make a few precisions,' he shouted. 'The British know all about democracy. We must have the mass media.' In these new and exciting times, 'mass media' was one of several catch-phrases deployed with abandon. Merely to talk of 'mass media' was to prove yourself *au fait* with democracy and pluralism. In this instance, by default, 'mass media' meant me, as the only other journalists in town, a French television crew, were blocked downstairs by a new detail of sentries.

The next meeting of the 'fifty-one' (or was it the 'fifty-two'?) was scheduled for the following morning. It was, I told Silviu hastily, time to leave. As we slipped out the door, another delegate stepped forward with another idea . . .

With the sub-zero temperature starting to offset the effects of cheap cognac, the demonstrators were drifting home and trams were clanking back into action. A diehard band of youths was holding hands and singing the old chants, with the conviviality of revellers leaving a pub after closing-time. In matching blue jackets, the French television crew were arguing with the obdurate new sentries. Waving them through, we went in search of a telephone line.

Such was a typically boisterous day in Romania in the aftermath of the collapse of communism, when East Europe was emerging from forty years in purgatory, when the Iron Curtain was no more and when the West was able to reacquaint itself with long-forgotten Balkan lands. This was, I suppose, my Balkan blooding. On leaving the 'fifty-one' to their deliberations, Silviu and I abandoned our attempts to procure a telephone line to London and instead retired to despatch a bottle of *ţuica*, chuckling over our experiences, talking excitedly about the future. While I had intended to stay in Romania only a few days, my encounter with the 'fifty-one' helped to change my mind. These were exciting times for the Balkan peoples who were waking from a centuries-old span of dictatorship and oppression, which had been only briefly broken between the world wars. Journalism in this nascent society was clearly not going to be dull.

I was reminded of the 'fifty-one' almost exactly three years later, on 9 January 1993, in a small east Bosnian town called Bijeljina, where a similar assortment of priests, soldiers, academics and grey-suited functionaries were holding an emergency session. All the old props and traits of atmosphere I remembered from Timişoara were there: the trays of plum brandy – albeit *slivovitz* and not *ţuica* – the clouds of cigarette smoke, the Orthodox regalia, the Ruritanian military uniforms, the endless speeches replete with history and bombast. The Byzantine blend of confusion and conspiracy was identical. There was even a dispute over the number of delegates present. In a last delicate touch of ring composition, I failed to file my story to London, almost for the first time since the evening in Timişoara.

However, there all resemblance between the two occasions ended. If the Timişoara Council represented for me all that was positive and hopeful about the Balkans, a sign of a society blinking its way into a new world, the Bijeljina gathering was the reverse. This was the self-proclaimed parliament of the Bosnian Serbs, at whose behest Europe had experienced its bloodiest fighting for forty-five years; in whose name had been committed an endless succession of rapes and murders. The delegates were gathering under the shadow of the threat of Western military intervention and calmly deciding to take on the world. The drinks which I consumed after the meeting with my companions, Zoran-jovanović from Belgrade and Matt Frei of the BBC, were accompanied not by chuckles but rather by dulled resignation. Serb warlords trying to justify their atrocities, ritual invocations of medieval battles, primitive tub-thumping and beating of the breast – this was the Balkans at its most intransigent, at its most barbaric, at its worst.

Maybe the delusion was all mine. Maybe I was wrong to be optimistic. In early 1990 there was no shortage of voices warning that in the demise of communism the old historical squabbles and psychoses would creep out of the woodwork. Maybe there is no light side to the Balkans. The trappings of civilisation there undoubtedly have more fragile foundations than in the rest of Europe. The origins of Balkan backwardness stretch beyond the Ottoman regime deep into the Dark Ages when the stream of invaders stampeding down the steppe made defence and survival the only viable concerns. Maybe the Balkan peninsula is doomed by its confused and troubled history to wallow in the mistakes of the past. But if so, it is a depressing view of humanity and not one I would willingly share.

A few days after my near election to the 'fifty-one' I asked Silviu if the delegates had really intended to co-opt me to their number. He laughed heartily: 'This is the Balkans, Alec. Strange things happen here.' In the early 1990s, as Bosnia burns, this is the sort of comment loved by Western politicians, desperate to portray the Balkans as a primitive place best left alone. It is an argument which stands against everything that was intended of this book.

My original hope was that the countless *Scoop*-like experiences of an accidental journalist finding and relaying the news would neatly mirror the Balkans' chaos and confusion and that weaving encounters with drunken Transylvanian priests, millionaire Carpathian shepherds and hesitant Bosnian housebreakers would balance the unremitting sequence of horrors which has emerged from the region since the short-lived euphoria over the collapse of communism. However, when I first thought about writing about the Balkans I envisaged I would be describing the optimistic rebirth of a society, not chronicling a death. As it seems did the great and good in the West, I wholly failed to appreciate the strength of the call of tribalism to the peoples clawing their way from communism.

On reflection, all I can conclude is that Silviu was right. From the Carpathians to the Peloponnese, from Romania and Yugoslavia down to Albania and Greece, the Balkan peninsula is an extraordinary part of Europe. Strange things do happen there – not that that forgives the statesmen for turning their backs.

Bucharest, April 1993

1

Balkan Beginnings

Timişoara, January 1990

'Old faces in new skins' – *Domnul Popović, host and friend*

ACCOMPANIED BY A friend on crutches and a garrulous Bolivian called Herman, I came to the Balkans in search of a job. Recently returned from cycling through Pakistan to China in a largely abortive bid to raise money and awareness about Tiananmen Square, I had missed the events of East Europe in late 1989. While the first chisels were hacking at the Berlin Wall, I was twelve thousand feet up the Karakorams, cursing the snow. When a Pathan ran from his radio to announce that Berlin was re-united, I rather fear I murmured politely and returned to my tea. The Velvet Revolution in Prague and the overthrow of Bulgaria's egregious Zhivkov all but bypassed the Hindu Kush. Somehow the conflicts in Afghanistan and Kashmir seemed more relevant.

Back in England in time for Christmas, I found interest in the Bulgarians had already switched to their northern neighbours. Romania's Christmas Revolution filled the holiday news screens as the extravagant finale to a dizzying show. Only tiny Albania still held out. East Europe was the buzz topic and Li Peng and Deng Xiaoping, the butchers of June, had been forgotten. It was like arriving in the closing stages of a complex film – confusing and unsatisfactory – and I skipped the execution of Ceauşescu to concentrate on starting a career.

London is a difficult place to find a job at the best of times, let alone between Christmas and the New Year. I enrolled on a cheap Oxford Street typing course and sent off letters to editors proposing articles on Pakistan. There was no response and three days of staring at a keyboard were powerful incentives for something new. When on New Year's Eve my girlfriend's sister Charlotte declared she and a friend were bound for Romania and looking for company, I was open to persuasion. Charlotte had a broken leg, Perdy had chronic asthma and my post-China debt was oppressive. But Charlotte's pledge of a free return ticket on a Bucharest-bound flight assuaged my financial worries – the Midland manager need never know. We would be back within a week with words to sell.

I borrowed a dictaphone and bought a camera – photo-journalism seemed another possible bet. An acquaintance part-timing as a researcher at Westminster spun a few lines about 'Britain entrusts' which, although handwritten, looked imposing on crested House of Commons paper and would, we thought, impress Romanian bureaucrats. I rang a friend of a friend on a glossy magazine, who coughed politely and put me on to an acquaintance at the *Telegraph*'s travel section.

'Not my line,' she said. 'Try the foreign desk.' I settled gratefully for a few words of cheer from the deputy foreign editor: 'Frankly, dear boy, we have it well covered . . . but I too was a free-lancer a long time ago; if you find something going, give us a call.' There were twelve hours to go. Pimlico Library had a book on the Romanian royal family. I left my typing course with a 'See you on Monday' and spent my final night forging credentials on photo-copied *Financial Times* note paper.

The journey strayed at the outset. Dozing in the early morning on the Piccadilly line, I woke to hear the distinctive tones of Amy and Ambrose, the key executives of a would-be employer. All week I had been courting their firm of corporate investigators, a gateway, I hoped, to investigative journalism. Two days previously, grey-suited and earnest, I had spent an hour in their office in Mayfair, trying to convince them of my commitment to the job. We were still a long way from Heathrow. My interview results were due any day.

'Er, uuhhm ... hello, Amy ... morning, Ambrose.' They focused slowly in their New York designer outfits. They were clearly non-plussed.

'Ah, yes ... Alec ... Hey, well, what a surprise! I mean, what are you ... I suppose that's obvious ... so are you off for long?' I rearranged my rucksack and juggled for a better grip on my walking boots. It was going to be hard to pretend I was meeting someone off a plane.

'I'm not really sure how long. That is, of course, I'll be back very soon ...' We talked politely about Eastern Europe all the way to Terminal Two. They even offered the name of a friend in Hungary. Not once did they ask why I was going to Bucharest. Not once did they mention my job application. (Four months later I retrieved a reply from Amy, written around the time of our impromptu meeting. It was full of the standard apologies: 'In the present climate ... very sorry ... impossible to ... we will of course get in touch if anything else ... have you thought of ...')

With a premonition of this rejection darkening my thoughts, a few hours later we touched down at Prague – seven hundred miles, two frontiers and a visa short of our destination. According to Czech Air, Bucharest was still classified as a war zone. It was a Saturday and there were no flights either way for two days. A deferential Czech official stamped our passports and smiled: 'Overland to Romania? You must understand in this situation nothing is certain ...'

The air crew headed for home and we for the station. Liberal doses of Johnnie Walker and shouts of '*Romania Libera*' enchanted the Czech frontier guards. The Hungarians, with hard-eyed Central European efficiency, were less pliable. They pounced at 3 a.m., determined to dispatch us into the snow for a visa. Flanked by two well-armed side-kicks, the chief fielded our emotion without a flicker – Yes, the visa office was five miles from the track. Yes, the snow was feet deep. No, the train couldn't wait ...

I missed much of the negotiating as Charlotte and Perdy ordered me to lie low while they marshalled our defence. When the officials shone torches into our compartment,

I lay face down in the top berth. From what I could gather, a combination of Charlotte's broken leg and blonde hair, Perdy's feigned tears and piercing green eyes, and a timely intervention from a fellow passenger called Hermán, saved our places on the train. A cheery Bolivian in a bright yellow shirt, Hermán never managed to explain how he was roaming East Europe with such impunity nor why he came to our aid. Maybe he was touched when I referred to Simón Bolívar, the only Bolivian figure whose name I knew. He spoke a range of East European languages and had a rapport with Stefan, the *chef du train*. It was Stefan who was produced as the ultimate arbiter on our behalf. Suddenly the Hungarians recalled they did have visa forms and that they could issue them on board. Pens were flourished. There were forgiving smiles all round.

Despite his success, the *chef du train* was in poor spirits. A Party member, he had, he declared with brief and sudden vigour, burned his card. Now he feared reckoning for the past was near.

'I had to join,' he reasoned. 'It was the only way to support my family. Otherwise they would have starved. What else was I to do?' Weak certainly, corrupt probably, Stefan was one of millions all over the communist bloc with a bad conscience and a long list of excuses. The last of the Johnnie Walker eased his nerves and cries of '*Libertate, fraternitate*,' echoed into the early morning.

We alighted at Arad to catch a local train, leaving Stefan to a hangover and, I suspect, a bout of prolonged self-recrimination. We parted company with Hermán at the next stop. It was Timişoara. Just three weeks before, thousands of demonstrators had defied Ceauşescu's security forces and taken to the streets. In five days of street-fighting, over seventy people were killed and, when the uprising spread to Bucharest, Ceauşescu was overthrown. The first accounts of the uprising told of sixty thousand dead on the streets of Timişoara. While later refuted, the reports confirmed the south-west Romanian city as the symbol of East Europe's heroic struggle for freedom, briefly lifting Timişoara from the grey haze which most West Europeans regard as the Balkans. Sir Sacheverell Sitwell opens his 1930s *Roumanian Journey* with an admission of ignorance. 'At the first mention of going to Roumania, a great many persons, as did myself, would take down the atlas and open the map ... for there can be no question that Roumania is one of the lesser known lands of Europe.' However, in January 1990 everyone had heard of Timişoara. It seemed the right place for us to start.

Connoisseurs of East European history were not surprised to hear that Timişoara was the banner waver in Romania's revolution. The city has a record of standing out. In a corridor between the Danube and the Carpathians, the surrounding region, known as the Banat, from the Persian word *ban* meaning fiefdom, is a natural battlefield for armies rolling in and out of Europe. It seems to breed independent spirits. In the second century AD the indigenous Dacians inflicted on an invading Roman army one of the Empire's most serious setbacks in the previous hundred years. Emperor Domitian even agreed to pay a tribute, a Dacian equivalent of Danegeld, to keep the Dacians at bay. After the Romans retreated south of the Danube in 271, the region which is modern Romania was overwhelmed by tribes sweeping down from the steppe. It was in this obscure period that the seeds of many of the territorial and ethnic disputes of the late twentieth century were planted.

However, although the Dacians, softened by a century of Romanisation, were killed or fled to the mountains, their defiant trail-blazing spirit appears to have endured around Timişoara. In the fifteenth century the castle of Temesvàr (like so many south-eastern European cities, Timişoara has known as many names as it has overlords) was the centre of Hungarian resistance against the Ottoman hordes. In the dying throes of the Austro-Hungarian Empire it was regarded as the innovative style-setter of the Balkans. Now the Austro-Hungarian legacy is showing signs of wear, with the lamps warped, the trams rusted and the once famed pastel paintwork starting to peel. But the civic pride hasn't died. Residents still love to huff and puff that theirs was the first city in Europe with electric street-lighting (1884), the first in the world with horse-drawn trams (1864). After a few plum brandies you tend to find you're drinking with the descendant of some 'world-famous' inventor or a well-known writer. It's a clever sort of place and Nicolae Ceauşescu never liked it.

Egged on by the presence of the world's TV crews, after the December Revolution locals set to work adorning the Timişoara myth. By the time of our arrival, the official story was that Ceauşescu had always had 'Birnam wood' nightmares about the city. 'He never stayed here; couldn't stand the place,' said the guards lounging around his Timişoara palace. Elena, I was told, had a foreboding that Timişoara would bring their end. Children booed and turned away when the pair came to call. Such fancy tales have a strong whiff of post-eventum reconstruction. There are plenty of photographs on record of Ceauşescu touring Timişoara – even if most were 'touched up' by his hagiographers. However, it requires no great imagination to believe that Ceauşescu, a peasant's son from Oltenia, the rural redneck heart of Romania, felt uneasy in a cosmopolitan centre like Timişoara. With its large Hungarian, German and Serbian minorities, Timişoara, near the Yugoslav border, must have been anathema to Ceauşescu, who was more at home in the high-rise urban horrorscapes of the north-east, where there was barely a shot fired throughout the revolution.

On arrival at Timişoara railway station, cold and hungry, we knew none of this and in swirling snow we had more pressing concerns than searching for traces of the past. It was night, thick, cloying without a chink of light. Stock lumbered past with heads peering furtively from windows as in footage of the cattle trucks of the last war. To reach the station proper we had to clamber over the tracks, expecting every moment that one of the trains would come clanking from the shadows. Figures loomed in the mist and slunk away. The unfamiliar smells of stale cooked fat hovered in the air, clinging to our clothes, seeping from the pores of fellow passengers. In the forecourt, as if in an Orwellian nightmare, officials were bellowing at stragglers. Amid the confusion floated a rumour, '*terroristi, sniperi . . .*'

I have since learned these are stock words in the Balkan argot. In a region which thrives on hyperbole and myth, anyone hostile is a 'terrorist', anyone with a gun is a 'sniper'. Your average Balkan man tends to be too keen on his local liquor, whether *raki* or *slivovitz*, *ţuica* or *cognac*, to make a good marksman. For the most part 'terrorist' and 'sniper' are slogan words which say more of the speaker's state of mind than the situation on the ground. Richard Wagner, an ethnic German writer who fled Ceauşescu's regime two years before the revolution, describes the prevalence of the word 'terrorist' in Timişoara in January 1990 as a means of collective escapism from guilt. 'People use it of Ceauşescu's secret police,' he wrote. 'It's an elementary linguistic rule to get over the intolerable fact that those in question lived in the neighbourhood until a matter of weeks ago, that the overwhelming majority were Romanians and that they opened fire on their own people.'

However, in the blacked-out streets of Timişoara there were suspect shadows at every turn. In the centre the only light came from the candles on the shrines of the fallen martyrs and the cigarette ends of patrolling soldiers. With their squashy Red Army lookalike hats, the sentries looked very alien and the Christmas card effect of the falling snow was offset by the bullet-scarred buildings and the absence of civilians. For all its bleak communist facade, the Hotel Banatul was intensely beguiling. With considerable relief we shouldered past a policeman into the lobby.

It took a good few minutes to attract the receptionist's attention. In the heady weeks after the revolution, the first details of the Ceauşescu clan's ritzy lifestyle were coming on air. Blurred and shaking, the images were as seductive as the glitziest Western soap opera and made a welcome change from the folk-dancing and bland panegyrics which graced TV sets in the previous era. So rapt was the receptionist, she seemed not to hear our request. With a heavily-stressed reluctance she swivelled our way.

'We are full.' She swivelled back. No one else, not the three attendant policemen, nor a gaggle of young conscripts, seemed interested in our arrival. Maybe it was the single electric-bar fire in the corner. Maybe it was the circulating plate of grey bread, fatty sausage and pickles.

There were rooms – of course – and there were complex forms to be filled, requiring the Christian names of grandparents, great-aunts and other minutiae beloved by communist bureaucrats. In a corridor upstairs we met Adam, a gloomy Polish journalist who was full of depressing stories about Romania's 1.7 million Hungarians and other ethnic minorities. I treated him as a fount of wisdom and was a little downcast when he launched a scathing attack on each and every subject we broached.

'You think Eastern Europe is saved? The problems are only just beginning. What about Lech Walesa – you think he is a hero, no? Well, what about democracy – he is democratic, huh? You in the West will never understand. Have you spoken to the Hungarians? No? And you want to write something.' He nodded. 'I will have to help you.'

Adam produced a book of Ceauşescu-approved art and started talking about the Orange Alternative, a Polish satire group of the mid-eighties. There was only one solution to his tales of woe. We dragged him off mid-tirade in search of food. At the Restaurant Timişoara all tables were '*reservat*' and a beetle-browed waiter shook his head to reinforce the point, but Adam knew the form and he sat us down at an empty table, edging to one side the reserved sign. In the absence of food we concentrated on our neighbours, two drunken Serbs, who were polishing off a dish of pork and pickles. Their barrel-chests and bushy moustaches seemed indistinguishable from the caricature Balkan features of the Romanian waiter and the two languages sounded identical in their unfamiliarity. But a prolonged burst of '*Serbski. Serbski*' accompanied by much breast-beating and thumping of the table left us in no doubt of their nationality.

Romania's Serb minority, whose ancestors fled north of the Danube from the Turks in the fourteenth century, are one of the smaller and less problematic minority issues in the Balkans. However, for two-and-a-half decades (1965–89) they had had to suffer the repressive policies of Ceauşescu, while south of the Danube fellow Serbs enjoyed

Yugoslavia's consumerist variant of communism. Our two boozy fellow-diners were ecstatically drunk. Time and again they toasted our arrival, rousing Adam from his depression and firing his Slav blood to join the revelry. Inevitably the British contingent were the kill-joys. After Adam the Pole's tortuous discourse on the ethnic questions of Transylvania and Ruthenia (to name a few), the hows and whys of the Serb community of Timişoara seemed too much to comprehend. Moreover we were a day-and-a-half on from the eateries of Heathrow, and the bawdy good humour of the Serbs, who had dined, was not readily appreciable by those of us who hadn't. Looking warily at roof tops for the phantom 'sniperi', we retired to the Hotel Banatul, pursued by shouts of 'Teemeeshwara. Teemeeshwara.' I fell asleep fully-dressed, wrapped in my overcoat and listening to Adam's fantastic conspiracy theories on the revolution.

In December 1989 television history was made when satellite dishes beamed across the world live images of the overthrow of Ceauşescu. Billed as the first television revolution, the story had all the ingredients of a Grimm's classic: oppressed people, heroism, an evil dictator, snow and a happy ending. Inside and outside Romania the images were intoxicating. For TV companies it was a technological triumph, subsequently surpassed only by the Gulf War. Unfortunately the Christmas fairy tale soured swiftly.

The official version of the revolution is tripartite and glorious. After forty-two years of communist dictatorship, the people of Timişoara rose in support of Laszlo Tökes, a persecuted priest from the ethnic Hungarian minority, and threw off their chains. In spiralling concomitant chaos, the National Salvation Front, which claimed to be a loose-knit grouping of dissidents and dissatisfied communists, took over in Bucharest under the leadership of Ion Iliescu, a former high-ranking Party official, who broke with Ceauşescu in the early eighties. At the same time the army joined the uprising. Finally there was a week of bitter street battles with pro-Ceauşescu 'terrorists', until the ultimate victory of the people, backed by the heroic Romanian soldiers.

Within the Byzantine confusion there are a few glimmers of poignant certainty. Whatever happened behind the scenes, there was real fighting and there were real heroes. In Timişoara on 16 and 17 December about seventy people were brutally gunned down by security forces. By the end of a week's fighting in cities all over the country, forty-two years of totalitarian rule were ended, up to a thousand people were dead and many more wounded. Blackened and bullet-scarred buildings testified to the intensity of the fire-fight. Three years later discoloured pools of wax still marked the shrines of the fallen heroes.

However, in the following weeks it became clear that the popular uprisings in Timişoara and Bucharest had merely led to the installation of former communists in the seat of power. This was neither surprising nor in itself reprehensible. Ceauşescu's ruthless security apparatus had crushed dissent and ensured there was no Civic Forum waiting in the wings. Of the three million Party members in Romania, many were talented and uncompromised – apart from their membership – and valuable participants in a new society. But what was unforgiveable was the old-style skulduggery which the Front leaders deployed to stay in control. To entrench their positions, they relied on the old Party propaganda machine, backed up by proletarian muscle against the more persistent political opponents. They also oversaw a cover-up of the abuses of the past, peddling the convenient line that everyone was a little tainted by communism, and they consistently obscured their passage to power. 'We are the emanations of the revolution,' was their stock answer to questions about the take-over. A classic case was the prime minister, Petre Roman, son of a top communist of the forties, who 'happened' to be walking past the Central Committee building at the right time.

Eight months after the fall of Ceauşescu, crucial new information emerged when two of the key figures in the Front, Professor Silviu Brucan and General Nicolae Militaru, gave details in a Romanian newspaper of an anti-Ceauşescu conspiracy that took place several years before the revolution. According to their joint declaration in the mid-eighties they and Iliescu had formed a cabal with army generals and secret police chiefs, plotting from within the Romanian Communist Party to oust Ceauşescu. This theory convincingly explains how an estimated twenty thousand Securitate officers melted away after Ceauşescu's fall. It also explains how Front leaders reached such a swift consensus in December 1989. The day after the interview appeared, Iliescu issued a riposte, but failed to produce a single concrete denial. A few months later he cultivated a rejoinder to queries about the revolution, asking interlocutors, 'Why don't you ask the United States who killed President Kennedy?' before moving swiftly on to another topic.

The obfuscation has spawned a myriad of conspiracy theories involving any combination of Freemasons, Zionists, Arab terrorists and the world's secret services. But amidst the more bizarre revolutionary myths there are a number of unresolved mysteries which add substance to the palace coup theory. Three years after the revolution there was still no official explanation of the 'terrorists' who fought on after Ceauşescu's downfall. None were captured. None were tried. The television headquarters, the key to Iliescu's popularity in the provinces, was almost untouched by the battle which supposedly raged for its control – while surrounding buildings, including the British Ambassador's residence, were devastated. When in late December 1989 Front leaders addressed crowds from the balcony of the Central Committee building, the shooting died down. Partly these facts attest to the confusion of the moment and the incompetence of the Romanian conscript army – at Otopeni Airport a detachment of cadets was mistakenly massacred by colleagues. But they also suggest a more sinister interpretation – that the Front directed the 'terrorists' to stir up chaos while they consolidated their grip on power.

By the time of my arrival in Timişoara these suspicions were already being aired in the West. As one by one dissidents associated with the Front renounced their membership, the Western press forfeited illusions about the new regime. Adam the Pole, who would have liked nothing better than to sit up all night consuming vodka and indicting the Front, proved a trenchant if impatient tutor in these ambiguities. After twenty-five years of communism in his own country, he had a healthy scepticism about the machinations of apparatchiks and was a witty retailer of conspiracy theories. However, domestically the Front was seen very differently. Iliescu, whose smiling features dominated the television screens, promising good times ahead, swiftly broke with the worst practices of Ceauşescu: rationing was abolished; the ban on abortions, which had been intended to raise Romania's population, was ended; the frontiers were opened; passports were available on request; and the Securitate was, officially at least, disbanded. Life in the eighties had been desperate. Now you could sing, you could shout, you could dance in the streets. Indeed there was a kind of anarchy in cities like Timişoara. But this was not the confrontational violence envisaged by modern organizations like Class War. It was anarchy in its purest form, as in the classical Greek *ana archia*, literally without officials, most of whom were a little shy of exerting their authority. It was for a while intoxicating.

'Excuse me, I'm setting up an international bridge tournament for all the world, here, in Timişoara ...' It was a terribly polite voice and I turned round to see a wispy-haired man in his twenties proffering a sheaf of hand-written papers. In his long overcoat, Janos 'Johnny' Marosan, veteran of the street-battles, looked like an overgrown schoolboy. 'I just need you to check our rules are the same as yours, that's all.' He stepped aside as a fellow student came forward.

'Maybe we'll be a free city, a sort of city-state like Venice, another Hong Kong.' This was Zoltan, who was to become a close friend over the ensuing months. 'Just teach us about democracy and we'll be fine.'

'We shall organise the first world-wide student congress here next week ... for peace and harmony between peoples,' interrupted a third. 'It will be a wonderful occasion, like the death of Ceauşescu. Now, what we really need is a guideline on setting up a trade union. What exactly can a trade union do? And where do we have ours, here, or in Bucharest?'

It was early evening on day two in Timişoara in the newly formed students league and the first of my two notebooks was already full. These were stirring days in Romania. It was a time for opening clubs and societies, groups and associations, and everyone was keen to talk about their plans, particularly in the university where the students strutted around like fighting cocks full of expansive visions. We reached Timişoara a full week after the shooting had stopped and most of the journalists had long since decamped to Bucharest. Charlotte followed the trail, hobbled into a riot, wrote the lead story of the *Scotsman* on two successive days and retired to the UK to finish a second degree; Perdy departed with an original 'exclusive' copy of Elena Ceauşescu's school reports; Adam the Pole returned to Warsaw still moaning that we would never understand the meaning of nationality; unsure whether a camera or a pencil was the best way to make a living, I opted to concentrate on Timişoara and make it my fiefdom. My first decision was to transfer from the Hotel Banatul to the headquarters of rumour and myth and the haunt of passing journalists, the Hotel Continental. It became my base for two weeks.

The designer of the Continental had a cruel sense of humour. There is nothing continental about its multi-storey-car-park facade, still less its gloomy interior, which, in the style of communist hotels from Tallinn to Tashkent, was adorned with an ectoplasmic tile decoration and plastic bulbous chandeliers. In the lobby, in a parody of a Western hotel, cheap clocks with peeling gilt professed (falsely) to show the time in Moscow, Peking and a range of other capitals. Thick velvet curtains defied entry to the most slender ray of light, masking the activities of the omnipresent black-marketeers, whose prime function seemed to be to mock Emil, the mishapen resident fool. Samuel Pepys would have recognized in this freak show echoes of seventeenth-century London's Bedlam. Everyone spoke in whispers. Soldiers ran up and down the stairs at strange times. When the phone in my room rang in the middle of the night; there was never anyone at the other end. Nothing overtly suspicious happened and yet I had the distinct impression that I was being watched. It was easy to become paranoid.

One morning I met in the foyer a young couple from Hertford who had taken a fortnight off work to drive a carload of teddy bears and clothes to Romania. Sally and Adrian were in the vanguard of a crusade of thousands of mini-buses trekking across Europe to Romania with clothes and food. Television pictures of abandoned babies in orphanages had stirred consciences all over Britain and the proceeds of thousands of fetes and bring-and-buy sales were targetting the new cause. Romania was one of the first 'deprivation zones' easily accessible overland. However, one night in the Continental had proved enough for these two pioneers. Their new plan was to dump the teddies in the nearest hospital and drive for the Hungarian border. They were terrified.

'It's unbelievable,' whispered Adrian, looking nervously at the receptionist. 'I'm sure the Securitate still function here.' Their hysteria bolstered my own flagging confidence. While Romanians were genuinely scared that the Securitate had survived intact, for foreigners, contact with the remnants of the old 'system' was something of a game. Telephones mysteriously cutting out mid-call provided my only brush with their activities. The fact that the old Securitate listening centre on the Continental's twelfth floor remained out of bounds seemed more comic than sinister. When a US TV network and William Mcpherson, a Pulitzer Prize winner from the *Washington Post*, decided to investigate, I gratefully tagged along. As a young British free-lancer, I was no competition. My only instructions were to keep to the back, out of the way of the camera.

In mid-December the Continental had been stormed by demonstrators and the corridor on the twelfth floor still bore the signs of skirmishing. A broken chair lay to one side. Holes (bullet-holes?) scarred the nearest door. It was dark, deserted and with the lift (which inexplicably stopped one floor down) cranking and grinding below, I had a sudden fit of nostalgia for my room several floors lower. Ted Koppel, the anchorman, saw a strip of light filtering from under a door. He stepped forward and gave a firm knock. Five seconds passed, another ten, and amazingly a face peered out. Thin, sallow and with spectacles, the 'weasel' immediately yanked his head back. The door banged against Ted's foot. The conversation between Ted and the now hidden occupant went as follows:

Ted, cheerily: 'I thought these listening posts had been dismantled. Can we come in?'

Muffled reply: 'There is nothing here.'

Ted even more ingenuously: 'Do you have something to hide?'

'Go away. This is a military objective.'

'Oh, so there is something . . .' After a few more pleasantries Ted agreed to remove his foot so the man could ring his superior.

Almost as he did so, on the double up came seven recruits, waving rifles, panting, clearly terrified. Their commander, a sergeant, took over as interlocutor.

'You must go. There is nothing here now. Everyone has gone home.'

'Everyone?' Like a ring-master toying with his audience, Ted paused for thought. Trained in a school of black-and-white certainties, the sergeant continued inexorably to his doom.

'There is no one here. The door is locked.'

'Then why are you here?' Ted waved airily at the soldiers, who hovering at one side appeared enthralled by the exchange.

'We guard the first floor.'

'Oh, the first floor.' Ted nodded as if to say that the need for seven soldiers to guard the first floor of a provincial hotel in peace time and then for them to materialize waving rifles on the twelfth was entirely natural – before delivering the *coup de grace*. 'But if there is no one here then what about our friend?' The sergeant strode forward knocked and entered. There was an angry exchange.

After further consultations, an officer arrived, unhurried, sharper, full of the candour displayed so effectively by the old establishment. Another half hour passed and the officer opened up, ushering us inside with a knowing smile. Padded walls and ceiling encased a narrow shelved outer room. An inner sanctum full of electrical gadgetry led off through a metal grille as if in a bank vault. The 'weasel', who wore a glistening tracksuit, lounged in a corner, scowling.

'This is the highest building in Timişoara,' explained the officer. 'It makes the best transmission point for the forces. Top secret, you must understand . . .'

While none of us believed his explanation, there didn't seem any point in challenging him. The difficulty of dismantling secret police apparatuses would vex former communist states for years. For Romania, where in the old days up to one person in four was rumoured to be an informer, the problem was particularly acute. 'We had more policemen than trees, you can't just chop them down,' Mircea Dinescu, Romania's sardonic national poet, told me later in the year. In March 1990 the Romanian authorities announced the formation of a new 'democratic' intelligence agency, the Romanian Service of Information (SRI). They omitted to explain that the new director, Virgil Magureanu, was a top former Securitate colonel, in Ceauşescu's time a professor in the Stefan Gheorghiu Academy, the communists' political training institute. In December 1990, on the anniversary of the revolution, Magureanu gave me an evasive interview conceding that telephone tapping continued. 'You should never forget that you need tens of years to qualify people at the high technical levels of an intelligence agency . . .' It's difficult to drop old habits.

Watching one of the most famous journalists in the United States at work was a memorable insight into the art of smooth-talking, not to say foot-in-the-door journalism. Ted Koppel was one of a number of correspondents passing through Timişoara who had valuable tips to impart. Most helpful of all was Chris Stephen, an experienced British free-lancer, who had arrived in Romania a few days before me, also on a whim, and also in search of a job. Chris travelled with a portable typewriter and a fluffy toy squirrel, with which he beguiled local officials, and his professionalism was daunting. He could sit down at a table and hammer out a script in a few minutes. When pressed for time he composed stories off the top of his head and dictated them down the telephone line without commiting a word to paper. He glanced at a tortured piece of my prose, nodded and gave me a first basic lesson in writing a news report.

'It's not an essay, you need the main point at the top like this . . . yes, that should do the trick. Try sending them this.' Chris took me under his wing and taught me several key tricks of the trade, including the crucial advice to free-lancers that you always file a piece first and only then ask the editorial desk if they want to commission it. 'That way you get paid whatever happens,' he explained. After two days Chris departed for Bucharest, where he became the *Guardian*'s correspondent. His whirlwind visit was as intimi-dating as it was instructive.

I soon realised I was as much in need of local help as professional advice. Food, drink and accommodation, not to mention telephone lines and information, all required con-tacts. I made for the headquarters of the Timişoara interpret-ers, a hotchpotch of students, entrepreneurs and police informers, who shot to stardom in the heyday of the revolu-tion. Still patiently waiting for the return of the cameras, they were unaware that interest in East Europe was already flagging, and they fell on visiting journalists like dignitaries. I think I said I worked for BBC Television and I was directed to look for Silviu. The deal was simple. The bigshots had gone. I had only a few hundred dollars. I would pay him as and when I had a piece published.

A Fats-lookalike, with a heated apartment, satellite dish and portable phone, Silviu was no ordinary Romanian. His family name, Sturdza, is that of one of Romania's most famous pre-communist political dynasties. Princes of the Sturdza clan dominated the political scene in the late nine-teenth century. In 1992 a surviving member of the dynasty was briefly tipped as prime minister. However, Silviu, I soon realized, was no relation of the famous clan. His family had more in common with the ruling strata of the communist decades than with their nineteenth-century patrician namesakes.

Director of the city's leather-goods factory, if ever there was '*un om de bine*' (Romanian communist-speak for a good party man, literally 'a man of good') it was Silviu's father. We met one Sunday lunch in the family's apartment where he sat almost silent, with his bull-neck protruding from a thick worsted suit, opening his mouth only to command another portion of roast meat or a glass of plum brandy. The Balkans is an unashamed bastion of male privilege and Silviu's mother only spoke to me in the seclusion of the kitchen. Even then she never replied to my question about her husband's job. But clearly his influence was undiluted by the Revolution. Silviu, with his flash Peugeot and jarring Brooklyn accent, knew everyone, and everyone paid him the closest attention.

Like the boyars, the landlords who dominated Romania in the nineteenth century, Silviu regally dispensed his patronage. Every evening while most of Timişoara's three hundred thousand residents retired to their blocks, a coterie would gather in Silviu's apartment to watch Sky Movie Channel and drink Johnnie Walker. In pride of place perched a green parrot, which insisted on squawking in my ear whenever I was dictating to London. I replaced the parrot as the court curiosity and would sit on Silviu's couch experimenting in Romanian. Of Latin origin with Slavic and Turkish infusions and then further Latinised by nineteenth-century Francophiles, Romanian sounds very like Portuguese. Fraught with syntax and structure, it is easy to speak badly, but harder to speak well. My early stabs at the unaccustomed long syllables, the iis of *pîine* or *cîine* (bread and dog), were humoured by my audience. But the attempts were unnecessary. Most of Silviu's friends shared his upbringing and spoke his cinema-gleaned Americanese. The women favoured mini-skirts and glittering blouses, tacky but striking when compared with the dowdy state styles. For the men, cheap Italian fashion was de rigueur. They laughed and joked, drank and planned for the future.

These were the nomenclatura, the rich kids, the nouveaux and parvenus of the communist world; and they were twice blest. Under Ceauşescu, by virtue of their parents' positions, they were destined for a cushy sinecure. After the revolution, through their connections and money they were bound for the West. In the old system the apparatchiks stood out by their number plates. Silviu's Peugeot was 1TM 200 – not bad in a system which peaked at 5 TM 9000. The lower the figure, the more important the owner, as Silviu proudly explained. By the summer of 1990 his group had emigrated West, using 'contacts' to gain employment. Most Romanians could only dream of gaining the hard currency for a trip abroad.

Into their lotus-eating existence complications did occasionally intrude. One evening, George, the most frequent visitor and usually the first to get drunk, arrived in tears. George had a podgy, weak face and pink, sweaty hands. He also had an important mother, the mayoress of a nearby town.

'She was a good mayor, Alec. She did her best for the people and now they want to try her. They won't let her home.' Not even the standard therapy of imported chocolate and thick liqueurs could assuage his fear. For forty-eight hours George's waking and sleeping moments were beset by visions of Romanian sans-culottes. But his mother was soon released to retire with a comfortable pension. Her arrest was an 'over-zealous mistake' according to an apologetic official. With a top former communist as president, Romania found it convenient to let bygones be bygones. A handful of senior Ceauşescu cronies stood trial. Functionaries like George's mother were able to retire to an old age of comfort and ease.

Silviu, whose principal guilt was his birth into an influential family, had little fear of retribution. His swanky, baby-faced confidence seemed genuinely popular with locals and he swaggered around like a young laird in a family estate, waving, chatting and tooting his horn to everyone he passed.

While conversant with the Western way of life, he found

Western thinking hard to understand. I remember he was particularly bemused when foreign-correspondent friends raised their eyebrows at his open admiration for Colonel Traian Sima, the former local Securitate chief. Sima was arrested in late December 1989 for his role in Ceauşescu's attempted cover-up of the Timişoara massacre. He personally masterminded the disposal of twenty-seven bodies from the shooting on 17 December. Before the Revolution he co-ordinated the oppression of Laszlo Tökes and ran Timişoara like a glorified mafia boss. Crowds found fifteen TV sets and Western video recorders in his villa, awaiting resale in return for favours rendered. Silviu had a selective memory and concentrated on Sima's 'business' activities, ignoring the darker side of the Securitate's work.

'You must remember he was a fair man,' he reasoned. 'If you gave him a leather jacket he would complete the deal – which was more than most in his position.' Even at the start of Sima's trial in March 1990, when horrific details emerged of the Securitate's attempts to flush bodies down sewers, Silviu remained unconvinced that Sima was worse than anyone else.

'I think maybe we are all a little guilty . . . is punishment really the answer?' This confusion about the nature of guilt and the need for justice may partly help to explain why it took the judiciary eighteen months to convict Sima and his twenty-two co-defendants. They were finally condemned in December 1991.

In Silviu's circle, Calin, a lined engineer old before his time, was probably the only one to understand the eviscerating horror of the communist system, maybe because he wasn't part of it and his family suffered the deprivations. Calin met Silviu through a mutual love of bridge, the semi-licit Romanian fixation which Ceauşescu almost banned in a fit of pique at Valentin, his bridge-playing son. On a walk in the central Roses Park, his despair suddenly poured out like a burst canker.

'Everything was permitted or not permitted depending on who or what you knew. Someone could always arrange things but it would cost you . . . and hanging over the deal is the fear of being demoted, of your wife losing her job of . . . We just never knew what would happen next . . .' He broke off to glance at two old men struggling to open a grimy bottle of *ţuica*.

'*Pe dracul!*' (Go to the devil) shouted the nearest suspiciously. Calin shrugged. 'Distrust, suspicion, that's how we live.'

Back at his apartment, his mother, a philology and classics professor, had prepared dinner. Like so many Romanian homes, theirs was a curio shop, packed with books, furniture and china, sunk in disrepair and disarray. She proffered a plate of chunky bacon rinds and over a bottle of Morelloe brandy launched excitedly into a Latin monologue, quoting now from Virgil, now Cicero. A copy of Catullus which for no good reason I had packed at the last minute in London, kindled new heights of excitement from my hostess. It was several hours later that Calin extricated us for a visit to his grandparents' house on the edge of the city. A tumbledown villa, it was in a poor way, with bricks attached at crazy angles and half-finished rafters protruding from the side. The joinery would have been penalised in a primary-school woodwork class.

'Maybe we can import British cement together,' said Calin. I think we both realised this was never to be.

With Silviu at my side, journalism seemed possible. For almost a week he put all his know-how and contacts at my disposal and anyone and everyone was approached for an interview, the mayor, the vice-mayor, the prefect, the head doctors, the food managers and most frequently of all the demonstrators who shouted each night outside the local government headquarters. When the officials changed, which they did every few days, we interviewed the replacements. Silviu even procured a couple of meetings with the temporary military proconsul of Timişoara, General Gheorghe Popescu, who had declared an inter-regnum a week after I arrived. A ruby-cheeked Alan Whicker lookalike, General Popescu was tightlipped on everything except his hero, the Dacian king Decebal. A plaque beside his office bears a snippet of the Roman historian Cassius Dio, who described Decebal as 'a master in war and master in deeds, knowing when to attack and when to withdraw . . . and how best to use a victory and defeat.' I wanted to ask Popescu if Dio's comment about the Dacians' skill in exploiting defeat and victory explained Romania's contortionist path in the two World Wars. I am glad I didn't. In both wars Romania flirted with both sides and emerged with the victors. It's easy to scoff. But it's not so easy being on the cutting edge of Europe.

The information soon filled half a dozen Romanian notebooks and Silviu was intensely proud of our efforts – particularly when he almost secured my election to the 'fifty-one', the local government. Unfortunately, as I explained, collating information and experience was only part of my task. I also needed to convince a newspaper to accept my writing. For this I required an international phone line – one of the most elusive prizes of all in the old Soviet bloc. Silviu seemed to realise that payment for his labours would not be forthcoming until at least one piece of my work was printed. This was the cue for his finest hour.

Timişoara, Romania's second city, had only four international connections. At the weekend the international operator was off duty – or so she said. During the week she was permanently engaged. On one occasion I waited five hours in the post office to be told flatly, 'No answer. Come back tomorrow.' On another occasion, after an agonising delay, I reached the *Daily Express* and I asked the switchboard to transfer me directly to the copy-takers. The copy-taker groaned and asked me to call back. 'It's an awful line, dear, and the dogs and horses results have just come in, we're rather busy.' Observing these frustrations, Silviu suggested we went shopping – not, he explained, for consumer therapy, but for '*cadouri*' (presents). When I asked why, he grinned and told me to wait and see.

First stop was the flagship of the shopping precinct, the Bega, a concrete and glass monstrosity, as despondent as its polluted namesake, the local river. Once through the entrance, the crowds streamed to the far end of the food hall where two queues stood shivering while a butcher dispensed slabs of meat. At the near end was a maze of deserted aisles where thousands of identical jars of pureed cabbage and pickled indescribables stared down like specimens in a pathology lab. The two queues merged. The butcher disappeared. At the entrance the shopping tide was still flowing. For some reason everyone else was clutching a blue metal urn. We left empty-handed and Silviu led the way to the duty-free store, which, dollars only, was out of bounds to most Romanians. Clutching an anonymous white bag with coffee, chocolate and the ubiquitous Kent cigarettes, currency before the revolution, he steered me back to the telephone centre. We entered by the back entrance – Silviu knew the guard.

Doamna Marcela, grande dame of the switchboard, ushered us in like time-honoured guests. As to the manor born, Silviu kissed her proffered hand while slipping the bag into her other. Secreting her 'little luxuries' under her coat, Marcela showed us to the international section, nerve centre of the city exchange where hundreds of young women in green uniforms were sitting in rows, pulling plugs in and out of sockets. Their bobbed hair and shy smiles could have been lifted from morale-boosting footage of the home front in the Blitz.

'Trunk calls on your left,' beamed Marcela, delicately manoeuvring her high heels over the broken floor tiles. 'My girls kept going all through the events,' she added proudly, using the popular euphemism, '*evenimentele*' (events) for the revolution, which Timişoarans were convinced had been rigged. In the 'international office' three older women, distinctive in blue uniforms and well-caked rouge, were chatting away, pausing only to light another cigarette, disdaining the mound of request slips in front of each desk. Five minutes and three international calls later it was time for fresh air.

In a classic account of East Europe in the 1960s, *Don't Send Me To Omsk* a celebrated foreign correspondent, Roy MacGregor-Hastie, describes how the charms of his

Securitate minder, whom he met on his first day in Bucharest, beguiled him into neglecting his journalistic duties. Most of his chapter on Romania describes visits to the Black Sea beaches and the Carpathians with his companion, who assured him that there was no news in Romania. There were times with Silviu and his network of corrupt contacts when I felt trapped in just such an intoxicating web of deception. In the sixties and seventies the West was blinded by Ceauşescu's reformist rhetoric and Romania became the darling of the Western chancelleries. The courtship culminated in 1978 with a reception for the two Ceauşescus at Buckingham Palace. As the days passed in Silviu's tutelage I began to wonder if I wasn't prey to a similar trick. On these occasions a young German teacher, Corina Popovici, provided my main avenue of escape and contact with the real Romanian world.

Corina was deservedly named after Ovid's fickle darling. Flighty and flaxen-haired, she came from a humble family – and yet refused to bow to the exigencies of the old system. During the revolution her linguistic skills brought her fame in the world's cameras. Only the doughty common sense of her parents, who eked out a standard dreary existence in a block on the edge of town, managed to restrain her impatience to challenge the power structures. Over cups of thick, black coffee, I would sit up late at the Popovicis' home discussing Bush and Reagan, Gorbachev and Thatcher, London and the outside world. A loyal patriot, Domnul (Mr) Popovici was, like many Romanians, convinced that his country had been sold by Bush to stay in Gorbachev's orbit. For the Popovici parents this was a heated and emotive issue; long before communism, Russia was Romania's enemy number one. When asked about domestic politics they would smile benignly and turn to other subjects. 'Old faces in new skins,' they muttered with the world-weary resignation that is at the same time Balkan man's great strength and weakness.

There were times with Corina when I felt very young and foolish. Self-taught and fluent in five languages, French, German, Italian, Spanish and Serbo-Croat, she had the fiery resilience of a Pankhurst and her grasp of West European literature and philosophy would have been the envy of her contemporaries in the West. However, her learning was tempered by her naivety. Her ideas were rooted in the 1950s. She knew nothing of late twentieth-century culture. Like so many of her East European peers, she had never been abroad. One of the first times I saw her she was in tears, running into the Continental restaurant, clutching a mottled green booklet, her first ever passport. Bill Mcpherson, the *Washington Post* writer who was 'thinking of staying', had a hire-car and generously offered to take us to Belgrade, eighty miles to the south-west. I had a vague idea of writing a piece about the meeting of cultures. For Corina it was a dream come true.

All the way to the border she babbled away in her hotchpotch of regional accents, British and American. She knew exactly what she wanted – a trip to McDonald's, a bunch of bananas – and remained studiously calm. However, on crossing the frontier her conversation slowed and in Belgrade she was reduced to awe-struck silence. After three weeks in Romania Bill and I found Belgrade's consumerism compelling. For Corina, who had spent all her life in Timişoara, Yugoslavia was another world.

'Have you seen their hair?' she said, gawping at a group of local punks on the Knez Mihailova main street. 'What's the matter with those guys? Hey, look at those shops. Did you ever see those toys? Everyone looks so smart.'

The bulbous Orthodox churches, the squat Slav build and the boisterous Balkan hospitality were familiar from Romania. But there all similarity ended. In early 1990 Yugoslavia was an oasis of prosperity in the former communist bloc, with the flames of nationalism kindled but not lit. The multi-party elections of April and May, when Slovenia and Croatia, the northern and most developed republics, first openly expressed their desires to leave the federation, were several months away. Backed by Western credits, the plans of the federal Yugoslav prime minister Ante Markovic to build a market economy were only just starting to fail.

Belgrade was a city of rock and roll and Levis, cash tills and credit cards. After a look of panic at the full shelves, Corina shopped with a frenzy, spending her hard-earned dollars with the abandon of a practised consumer. Bill and I followed suit. Seven hours after crossing the border, laden with fruit and chocolate, magazines and soap, we were back in the unlit streets of Timişoara.

In this period of my Balkan blooding, the middle two weeks of January, the Romanian 'story' was in Bucharest, where the Front was lurching from scandal to scandal and it was hard to muster any enthusiasm in the outside world for the latest from Timişoara. Every morning I would struggle up in the debris of the previous night's revelry, nudge a reluctant Silviu awake and walk round the corner to the Town Council. Every time Corneliu Vaida, one-time revolutionary now 'foreign protocol spokesman', would relay a hot new story. One morning the city's water supply had been poisoned, the next he had fresh figures about stolen corpses, the third a mysterious Swede called Eric was 'promising to repatriate thousands of Securitate agents who had fled to Stockholm.' Mostly uncheckable, these were almost always untrue. I soon realized that facts in the Balkans are a fluid commodity. Corneliu could never understand my frustration when I informed him that his previous day's 'leak from the government' proved false. Eager to please, he would promptly trump it with something even more extravagant. After a few days I treated my morning visits as a chance for an entertaining coffee. Inspired by visiting journalists to new heights of rhetoric, Corneliu informed or more often misinformed with a vengeance. There were some strange stories printed from Timişoara in this period.

Quirky things were unfolding in Timişoara. With residents refusing to accept official estimates of the numbers killed in the revolution, paranoia gripped the city. Anonymous hand-written leaflets circulated claiming that more bodies were disappearing from the cemeteries. By night unsigned posters were pinned in the central Opera Square with appeals for another revolution and Timişoara's autonomy. In a most unBalkan attempt to apply reason, a student, Ovidiu Sofronie, started a door-to-door search through the city to try to find the truth about the number of casualties. His plan broke down when house-holders accused the students of spying. One morning, truth surpassed my most fevered dreams. Shortly before dawn an old man arrived from north-east Romania to claim the body of his son, who was killed in the December street battles. After exhuming the corpse from the Heroes Cemetery, he replaced the soil and replanted the flowers. The half-buried stalks aroused the suspicions of a grave-digger. Within half an hour hundreds of locals were tearing at the earth in search of 'more stolen bodies'. Such was the power of Romanian paranoia. By the time I arrived with Silviu, who was putting on a credible imitation of an LA patrol car, seven yellowing corpses, sprinkled with money, were glistening on the frosted ground like newly-landed fish. The scene seemed to spring from the most brutal recess of Ceauşescu's Romania. But even in the isolated pressure cooker which was Timişoara I needed no reminding that this, while disturbing, was not front-line news for a London paper.

In two weeks my Timişoara news-trawl merited one anonymous paragraph in the *Daily Telegraph* and a line in a Sunday tabloid. My insecurity was heightened by my depreciating prestige, as after two weeks in town my aura as a resident Western journalist was starting to fade. General Popescu started to refuse my requests for interviews. Despairing of tips, the doormen at the Continental had become decidedly cold. My largesse with Marcela's ladies at the switchboard was losing its clout. Silviu started spending less time translating and more time out to lunch with his girlfriend. Even Corneliu the spokesman was a little puzzled. Never before had he had such a persistent visitor. Then in quick succession in the last weekend in January I had two strokes of luck.

The first came when I rang the *Daily Telegraph* with an idea and the deputy foreign editor, who back in London had encouraged me to call, picked up the phone. By chance a few minutes earlier he had read something which needed 'chasing up' in Timişoara. My 'idea' was jettisoned; his proved an interesting story. The following morning I had ten paragraphs in print. The piece quoted senior doctors who said that many of the bodies which sparked off the world's outrage in December about Timişoara were the corpses of tramps and not 'heroes of the revolution'. The scars on the bodies, which were reported to be the marks of Securitate torture, were the marks of autopsies. It was, the *Telegraph* said charitably, a 'little scoop'. Basking in the joy at being printed, I went off with Silviu to celebrate and we were en route to the smartest restaurant in town when I heard the second piece of good news: Laszlo Tökes, the dissident priest who sparked off the Timişoara uprising, was due to return home for the first time since the fighting to preach in his old church.

In the Middle Ages, a man of as uncompromising views as Tökes would have ended on the stake. Timişoara has an ugly record for dealing with nonconformists. In 1514, extorted by rapacious Magyar landlords and despairing at a series of bloody Turkish wars, local peasants launched an uprising under the command of a Szekler captain Gyorgy Dozsa. When the nobles regained control they exacted a monstrous revenge. Thrust on to a red-hot throne in the main square, half a mile from Tökes' church, Dozsa was crowned 'King of the Serfs' with a glowing circle of iron. According to local chroniclers his singed remains were then torn apart with pincers and force-fed to watching fellow rebels. The Romanian peasants were reluctant to support what was essentially a Hungarian serf rebellion. But when in mid-December 1989, almost five hundred years later, the whiff of rebellion was again in the air, Romanians were quick to join the Hungarians. The display of ethnic interaction was one of the most positive aspects of the revolution.

Like Dozsa, Tökes was willing to fight to the end. An ethnic Hungarian priest, in the iconoclastic tradition of his Calvinist predecessors, Tökes defied pressure from his superior Bishop Laszlo Pap, a Ceauşescu stooge, and preached against corruption and human-rights abuses. When in autumn 1989 Pap ordered his 'troublesome priest' to move to exile in the remote north Transylvanian village of Mineu, Tökes refused. In mid-December Securitate thugs isolated his house, a small crowd of congregants gathered in the street outside and through an attic window Tökes' rich melodious voice could be heard in the clear night, exhorting the watchers to prayer. The following night, 16 December, as the authorities came to take him away, a few hundred Timişoarans aired the first shouts of '*Jos Ceauşescu*' and '*Jos dictatura*' (Down with Ceauşescu. Down with the dictatorship). Nine days later Ceauşescu and his wife were facing a firing squad.

Several of Tökes' congregants gave their life for their pastor. When he leaned on the pulpit that late January morning and gazed down the church, I could almost understand why. In the arcana of Hungarian, the service was incomprehensible. It was also captivating. Tökes' deep tones, his commanding physique, his dark, penetrating eyes, mesmerised the congregation. In the tiny church, no bigger than a village schoolroom, hundreds of people were in tears, crying for the dead, crying for the past, crying with happiness at the return of their inspiration.

In his study afterwards Tökes loathfully turned from religion to politics. Within a few months he was being used as a mouthpiece for anti-Bucharest sentiment and by late 1992 he appeared to have become an unwitting pawn in the heated controversy between Romanian nationalists and their counterparts in Budapest. However, while his entanglement in politics slightly marred his image, his devotion to the 'good' was in my mind never in doubt. He was one of the only true heroes of the revolution. On that icy morning in January 1990 he contented himself with the dry observation that he had just seen in the crowd three of the Securitate who had originally been sent to arrest him ... 'CROWD WEEPS AS HOUNDED PRIEST RETURNS TO PREACH', ran a *Telegraph* headline the following day. In newspaper terms it was at last a real story.

In Bucharest, on the same day as Tökes' emotional

sermon, the opposition political parties held a rally outside the government headquarters. The following day thousands of pro-Front vigilantes attacked the opposition parties' headquarters and the leader of the Peasant Party had to be rescued in an armoured car. After a brief lull, Romania was suddenly back in the news and Timişoara was sucked in the flow. Local elections, drunken crowds, chaotic councils – for a few days anything and everything became of interest. The *Telegraph*'s Bucharest correspondent defected to another paper. I received a curt message from the foreign editor. 'Head for Bucharest.' The same evening I bid farewell to a tearful Silviu and caught the night-train.

2

The Government Spokesman

Bucharest – the Paris of the Balkans,

February 1990

'A change of rulers is the joy of fools' – *Medieval
Romanian Proverb*

IN THE LATE 1960s a left-wing British travel-writer took a
train to Bucharest and arrived in 'a bright spotless and
capacious station whose flower beds and geranium pots
seem to extend an unspoken welcome to the stranger.'
Maybe he was sedated by *ţuica*. To be fair, Romania in the
sixties was enjoying a lull between the political purges of
the fifties and the austerity policies of Ceauşescu in the
seventies. However, it's hard to imagine that Bucharest's
Gara de Nord has ever had much in common with its
Parisian namesake. Grinding in shortly before dawn was to
be thrust into the gloom of downtown Detroit or the
landscape of a nineteenth-century realist painter. Pylons
and factory towers were groping through the half-light.
Sulphurous fumes were pumping into the already smudged
sky. Bombay-style, hundreds of passengers jumped off early
and started running towards the terminus.

I had spent much of the night composing a piece about
Anda, Ceauşescu's pet Labrador, which I had seen in his
old Timişoara palace a few days before. It had been a
laborious process as the sheets of my notebook, a local
purchase, had insisted on tearing and smudging and I had
tried in vain to remember the surname of Silviu's girlfriend,
a trainee vet, whose opinion I had consulted and wanted to
quote. As the train slowed, I snatched the last moments in

bed, luxuriating in the grey but clean sheets. In post-communist Romania, anything, I was realising, was possible for a few extra dollars. (A year later I retraced the same journey, sleeping on the floor of the post van, as all the compartments were full. When offered dollars for a berth, the ticket collector was beside himself with remorse: 'I would love to take your money. But even in Romania I cannot sell something that doesn't exist.')

The jolting and screeching of brakes were familiar from a King's Cross-Edinburgh overnighter. With my eyes closed I could have been coasting into Waverley. Then a hand rapped against the window and a pair of ferret eyes set in a Mongolian face materialised through the mist. A thin nose was pressed against the glass. I could almost smell the staleness of his breath.

'You have dollars? You have cigarettes?' While black-market rates commanded a four-fold rise on the official price, changing money was a dangerous business. I had already learned the hard way after a dealer offered a very generous rate, took my dollars and left me clutching a wad of newspaper. My hands stayed in my pocket and 'Genghis Khan' vanished down the platform, in search of other prey. Indulging in a wave of nostalgia for the security of Silviu's domain and my Timişoara existence I descended on to the platform.

In the main station, scores of beggars and street children were sleeping on the ground. Gypsy families were emerging like beetles from corrugated-iron shelters. Stinking of cheap alcohol, the place was etched in the bleakest imagery of Dickens. More acquisitive figures with the spangly clothes and quick-step of the black-marketeer drew near asking to buy coffee, chocolate, cigarettes . . . Head bowed, I followed the crowd to the exit. It was an unprepossessing introduction to the Paris of the East.

There was a time when Bucharest was a peacock among the drab and uncultured capitals of South-East Europe. Like all the Balkan cities, with the exception of Athens, until the nineteenth century Bucharest was a nondescript place. From the Roman conquest of Dacia, the region which is now Romania was in thrall to foreign powers, with a break of just two years in the sixteenth century when a local prince, Michael the Brave, wrested together an independent kingdom. In this long period the territory of modern Romania was divided among a number of principalities and the idea of a Romanian state existed only in the fire-side yearnings of whimsical poets. However, in the nineteenth century came a breakthrough as the musings of radicals at the Sorbonne percolated to South-East Europe. Like castaways hailing a distant sail, Romanians clutched at the new inspiration. With the Ottoman Empire in terminal decline, Paris replaced the influence of the East. 'Romania would be for France a force and a glory,' gushed a Romanian nobleman in Paris. 'France would find there her soul ... we have never lost her from our sight we have always loved and hoped in her.'

On the streets of Bucharest the new bond induced a craving for Parisian culture and Romanian society plagiarised French habits and language – just as did the British nouveaux classes under Victoria. 'Whether she accepts or repudiates it,' wrote the French consul in Bucharest in 1849, 'France has on the banks of the Danube an inevitable clientele ... which tries every day to assimilate her language, her legislation, her literature and even her most futile fashions.' However, the link was no whim of fashion and soon blossomed into a trusted child-parent accord. In the 1860s France, keen to have a bastion in the Balkans, championed Romanians' desire to unite the principalities of Wallachia and Moldavia into one state. Around Christmas 1917 Paris again played the knight in shining armour when Romania was hard-pressed by the Germans and the royal court was in refuge in the north-east. It was at this nadir of Romanian fortunes that General Louis Berthelot arrived at the head of a French delegation. In a few months Berthelot, a barrel of a man who is reported to have needed a crane to mount his horse, transformed the mainly peasant Romanian army into a crack outfit. The Romanian army's valour shattered the British cliché that Balkan soldiers are clowns.

It's hardly surprising that after the war King Ferdinand modelled Bucharest's victory monument on the Arc de Triomphe.

Basking in the glory of emerging on the winning side, between the wars Bucharest flowered into one of the raciest capitals in Europe. In society circles it was regarded as the most exotic stopover from the Orient Express. Led by the example of King Carol II, who kept his mistress, the red-haired Elena Lupescu in a bower in the palace grounds, the top 'fifty families' partied in a considerably more liberated version of the London Season. Ivor Porter's account of Bucharest in the 1930s describes in mouth-watering detail both the cuisine and the *couturiers*. Art and music flourished – even if writing was caught up in the prevailing spirit of nationalism and anti-Semitism. Like the orchestra playing on the decks of the sinking *Titanic*, Bucharest's *joie de vivre* continued until 1940, long after the lights had gone out in the rest of Europe.

For Romanians this 'Frenchness' is pivotal to their national consciousness and to their belief that they are different from their neighbours. 'We are a Latin nation in a sea of Slavs' is a favourite Romanian slogan. However, in January 1990, after forty years of communism, few echoes of the *entente* remained. The 'fifty families' spent the first and second post-war decades in prisons or labour camps. Art sank into a trough of idolising drivel. The *confiseries* and milliners gave way to the empty-shelved multi-stores of communism. In the avenues which lead from the Gara de Nord, the overwhelming impression was of drab totalitarianism. The word '*patiserie*' caught my eye, crumbling and unlit above an identikit state shop. But the only sign of the old French rapport came from the dapper teams of *Médecins sans Frontières*, busily re-colonising the capital of their former confrère.

An acquaintance of Silviu's had given me the address of his estranged wife who lived the other side of the Cismigiu gardens. In the spring Cismigiu, rumoured originally to have belonged to a Turkish water inspector, is a riot of colours and a centre for lovers' trysts and tiffs – at which

Romanians are adepts. However, on my first night in Bucharest there was a violent storm. Water was coursing between the ice-ridges which covered the streets and the gardens were a quagmire. Surrounded by the dark and silent city, I tightened my coat and quickened my step. Arriving wet, cold and unannounced, I was invited to stay. Such is Romanian hospitality.

My instructions from the *Telegraph*'s foreign editor were to the point: 'Go to Bucharest and contact Bishop.' The hierarch in question was not a churchman but the *Telegraph*'s chief foreign correspondent, Patrick Bishop. I found him in the Hotel Bucharest, the only place in town with international phone lines, the adopted headquarters of the foreign press.

With its tree-trunk pink marble pillars (former Securitate listening posts) and smokescreen of oily-haired pimps, in time the Hotel Bucharest became familiar, almost friendly. But my arrival felt like a first day in a new school. The 'story' was on a roll and the big names in journalism were in situ. Every evening they held court in the press centre (the first-floor lobby) swapping anecdotes of wars past and predicting wars in the future, dispensing insights to newcomers, waiting for the elusive phone line. The vernacular of journalism, unknown and unnecessary during my stint in Timişoara, dominated the airwaves. The talk was of copy calls and deadlines, 'pressas' (press conferences) and space, stories and scoops. Balkan primadonnas could be heard over the clattering of the telex, voicing clipped analyses to 'unfeeling editors'. Pulling on a pipe, the *'envoyé special'* from *Libération* was arguing with the government press flunky. Three or four reporters were habitually scoffing at the latest emissions from Rompres, the renamed but not restaffed state news agency. Behind the insouciance lurked the unspoken menace of competition. When I walked in, rucksack in hand, the stentorian voice of the veteran *Times* correspondent was booming round the foyer as he thundered his story down the line to London.

'No, ducky, that's T as in Tommy ... bloody hell!'

(pause for breath) 'Hey, you! Can you shut up down there! Anyone would think it was Nicu's bordello; bloody foreigners . . . Where was I? Ah, yes, Securitate . . . point paragraph . . .' It was a boisterous, bewildering but fittingly Byzantine atmosphere.

In a four-day Arcadian lull, Patrick paid for my dinners and proffered advice. He also rewrote my pieces, steered them into the paper and negotiated a deal for me with the *Telegraph*. It all seemed very simple. I became their freelance correspondent or 'stringer'. The string was a monthly retainer of a hundred pounds, which was designed to keep my services from rival British papers. My terms reminded me of a Victorian rule threatened in jest in my childhood, that one should be 'seen but not heard'. I was expected to be on call at all times and never to answer back.

The day I arrived from Timişoara the threat of anarchy receded as the National Salvation Front bowed to street pressure and agreed to set up a multi-party interim parliament. The Provisional Council of National Unity, whose mandate was to debate an electoral law, was essentially a talking shop and bore no resemblance to democratic institutions in the West. However, its formation was a step away from chaos and the Romanian story slowed. With order returning to the streets, most of the big-shot correspondents withdrew. Patrick Bishop left for the Middle East with a parting 'Just don't believe what everyone tells you and you'll do fine.' Bucharest was mine. It seemed very large after Timişoara.

In the Balkans, information, the life-blood of journalism, is as elusive as the international phone line. In the days following Patrick's departure I found it impossible to pin down any facts, let alone find a story. All my competitors seemed to be scribbling away. Every night Chris Walker would march into the press centre with a sheaf of typed script, which he would proceed to bellow to the copytakers. The *Telegraph's* foreign desk kept broaching possible ideas for articles. However, four days' traipsing the streets of Bucharest produced nothing more than a few paragraphs about the sacking of a clique of bishops. An old-hand correspondent of the Algerian War, passing through in search of material for a novel, offered some timely advice.

'Touch base with the dips, dear boy. In my day they were always the first port of call. It'll be useful background material and, you never know, they may give you a steer.' Trying to look purposeful, glad to have a genuine reason to leave the press centre, I headed towards the British Embassy, mulling over memories of Evelyn Waugh's *Scoop*, where William Boot goes to the British Consulate in Ishmaelia, meets an old school-friend and gains a world exclusive. I had a vague idea that I would be met with a gin and tonic and given the strategic low-down on the machinations of the Front.

The Foreign Office has a chequered record in Romania – as indeed it has all over the Balkans. Between the wars Romania, with its large oil fields, was strategically vital and diplomats in Bucharest were briefed to counter the influence of the Germans. However, Whitehall was too caught up with domestic problems to adopt a decisive Balkan policy. It was a time of appeasement and oscillation – words with which I was to become all too familiar in the Yugoslav crisis in 1991. The Germans took control of the oil fields without a shot fired. After the war the diplomats returned to explain to the local politicians the terms of Yalta, which effectively ceded Romania to Soviet control. The reasoning was clear. The Red Army was in the ascendant and Romania, which between 1941 and 1944 had fought with the Germans, was not a priority case for the West's sympathy. But it was a shabby deal. The fact that most Romanians had borne no love for the pro-German regime and cared still less for the Russians was ignored. Older Romanians still bear a grudge against Churchill. Over many a late cognac, friends have adopted a mournful lecturing tone and started muttering, 'Ah, but what of Yalta?'

Under communism, the Bucharest embassy was essentially a listening post and was progressively downgraded. In the late eighties the British Ambassador Hugh Arbuthnott led the Western embassies' crusade to support

Romania's dissidents, hitting the headlines in 1989 when he was manhandled by the Securitate outside the house of Doina Cornea, Romania's most famous dissident. But this was an exception. In the first few months after the revolution, the embassy still seemed to be digesting the news of the change. One old hand confided only half-jokingly, 'It was so much quieter in the old days. You knew who was who and what was what.'

Three years after the revolution, with the Balkans again in the world spotlight, many of the Bucharest diplomats are close friends and among the better analysts of the political intrigues. However, on my first visit in February 1990, I was granted barely a minute with the 'Very busy. I'm terribly sorry. I have much too much to do' press attaché and ushered to the door. I didn't return for several months.

After my blank at the embassy, my next port of call was the government press office. It proved no more fruitful. The government spokesman, Cristian Unteanu (which appropriately enough means something like Mr Buttery, *unt* being Romanian for butter) had a long, pointed nose, a slippery hand and on the side of his face a massive mole – of which he appeared self-conscious. In the old order he was the chief of the 'Communist Youth' in a Bucharest secondary school and, until the overthrow of Ceauşescu, he worked for the state television. He loved to talk about his own journalistic past. 'Dear colleague, I understand exactly . . .' He appeared intensely lazy. He was intensely corrupt. In his suite in the Intercontinental Hotel, surrounded by dolled-up assistants, he looked and behaved like an overfed worm. Bribery was the only sure way to get information.

After two fruitless visits I entered his office with the relevant gratuity – a bottle of whisky – hidden in my bag. The problem was how or when to produce it. Anglo-Saxons are not by nature good bribers – or maybe we are just out of practice. The Romanian language is rich with greetings and so to buy time I launched into a series of salutations, before casually mentioning my hopes of meeting such and such a government minister. Cristian yawned, picked up the phone and started talking. Maria, his secretary, came in, tottering on high heels, with a sheaf of papers and a sugary smile. Cristian looked at his watch and put his feet on the desk. Should I go? No, not empty-handed again, and then, joy of joys, came the cue. Cristian rolled his eyes and smacked his lips, 'I could really do with a whisky.'

'Ah, well, er, hum . . . Mr Unteanu, by chance . . .'

I produced my half-bottle of Johnnie Walker and for a few minutes we talked of this or that while Maria fluttered her eyelashes and furnished two tumblers – with ice (my first in Romania). We toasted journalists and journalism. As if in passing he told me of two 'limited' press conferences later in the week. Feeling a little tainted, I vowed not to 'deliver' again. Resident correspondents later made an unofficial embargo on bribing Unteanu.

In the absence of 'official' sources, there was a third option, the most colourful source of information in the Balkans, the rumour industry. Southern Europe is more of an oral culture than the West. People hear things and people know things in an arcane process that has long since left our society. After the revolution the lobby of the Hotel Bucharest was like a giant fairground with an array of characters passing through to gawp, exploit, solicit and preach. My diary records consecutive evenings with two suspected Mossad agents, a Swedish psychologist and a Romanian emigrée returning to claim her estates. The lobby bar specialised in an Irish coffee with fake cream and a particularly persistent brand of money-changer. Of a biting February evening, the bar lacked sufficient shady corners for all the Balkan spin doctors.

The most garrulous and entertaining 'conspirator' was Nicolae Costel. Distinctive for his ghostly pallor and his slicked-back hair, he went everywhere in an elegant ankle-length overcoat. With his aura of faded dissipation he could have been modelled on Yakimov, the inveterate sponger of the *Balkan Trilogy*, Olivia Manning's autobiographical novel about the Balkans in the late thirties and forties. I half-expected to see Costel coasting around Bucharest in a Hispano-Suiza or Lagonda. His political loyalties were as fickle as his friendship – which depended on who was buying the next round. With a Thespian flourish he would put his arm round my shoulder and steer me round the aging hookers towards the nearest waiter. He had an astonishing propensity for whisky. He was also great for a quote on the latest conspiracy, or a veiled hint about some imminent crisis.

'My dear fellow, you must understand nothing is as it seems. This is the Balkans. Black is white, white is black. Everything is grey.' Such was his cherished opening line. With a theatrical toss of his head he would be off into the latest 'intrigue'.

The first time we met I took copious notes. Costel said he was the head of a newly formed political party; he seemed like an important man. Almost as importantly he spoke fluent English. Months later in London, when leafing through back-copies of British papers, I saw that Costel was quoted during the revolution by a range of respected foreign correspondents. 'In a lull in the fighting, Mr Nicolae Costel, Secretary of the newly formed Democratic Party said . . .' 'A rakish figure, with more than a touch of the old Romania, Mr Costel has recently set up a new political party. He looks set to play a prominent role in the new regime . . .' Costel would have loved this fame. If he'd known, he would probably have charged more for his time than the odd drink. His Democratic and Something Party was forever changing its name. It almost certainly never existed.

After a few weeks Costel disappeared and I forgot all about him until more than two years later in 1992, when I saw him mincing his way round a puddle in the city centre. Bucharest has two million inhabitants but it still seems more like a provincial town than a European capital. The centre is about the size of the precinct in Winchester. You are always bumping into old friends. It was if anything surprising I hadn't seen Costel more recently. Still in the same overcoat, he was as ever in need of money.

'I have left politics, my friend,' he said. 'I'm now in business.' His plan was to import televisions and he confidently promised me ('You couldn't just lend me a few dollars') an interview with the Bulgarian president. I am still waiting for the summons to Sofia.

Much of Bucharest's intrigue, purveyed by characters like Costel, was easily dissected into the possible, the improbable, and the completely absurd. But sometimes the distinction was less clear. These were early days after four decades of communism and the old establishment, which controlled most of the newspapers and operated like any Old Boy network, had a lot to hide and many perks to maintain. A series of scare stories blackening the opposition were served up to the reader. They could be very convincing.

One morning over cups of thick Turkish coffee, served with the waiter's customary ill-grace, a few of us were intrigued to read in *Adevarul* (the Truth) formerly the Party rag *Scînteia* (the Spark), excerpts from an 'interview' in a Spanish paper with Horia Sima, the last head of the Iron Guard, Romania's pre-war fascist movement which was crushed in 1941. Sima, who fled first to Nazi Germany and then Spain, was quoted as saying the Iron Guard was being regenerated and the 'interview' insinuated he would be helping the opposition. It was explosive stuff. Coinciding with shock horror reports of a 'desecrated' synagogue at Oradea, four hundred miles from Bucharest, it came as a frisson of anti-Semitic attacks swept through Europe. The interview seemed like a strong story to follow up.

Romania has a dark history of racial intolerance. For centuries Romanians have had to shout and kick to make themselves heard and this has led to discrimination and a strong streak of anti-Semitism. In the nineteenth century thousands of Jews started arriving in Romania, fleeing oppression in Russia. In times of hardship they became enemy number one. A peasants' revolt in 1907 targetted the Jewish administrators who managed the estates of absentee Romanian landlords. During the pro-German military dictatorship of Marshal Antonescu between 1940 and 1944, tens of thousands of Jews were deported and killed. The Iron Guard was responsible for some of the worst actions. In early 1941, chanting hymns and flanked by Orthodox priests, young guardists herded over a hundred Jews into a Bucharest abattoir and butchered them. News editors in the West in early 1990 were fixated by the idea of the potential resurrection of fascism. 'Watch it carefully, dear boy,' I was told. 'You are witnessing the rebirth of history. Got to keep an eye on these trends.'

My hazy knowledge of the past added credibility to the insinuations of the *Adevarul* 'interview'. I was aware that in 1938 the opposition parties had briefly formed an electoral agreement with the Iron Guard – albeit in a last ditch attempt to counter the dictatorial policies of King Carol II. A number of correspondents wrote at length on the subject, warning of the possible resurgence of anti-Semitism. There was one problem. The interview was a complete fake. The 'Spanish newspaper' didn't exist. A BBC correspondent tracked down a bewildered Sima, now a very old man in Spain, who said he hadn't spoken to the press for forty years. A testy *Adevarul* editor later refused a request for a copy of the interview. 'We're very busy right now; we don't have time to deal with such questions.' (A year later *Adevarul* started to shed its slavish pro-government stance and became one of the more reliable publications.) In search of the 'fascist rebirth' story, John Cole, a photographer friend, flew out from London and drove the four hundred winding miles to Oradea. He found the synagogue untouched. The whole affair was a deliberate attempt to discredit the opposition with the taint of fascism.

Chief Rabbi Moses Rosen, an old collaborator with Ceauşescu, likes to trumpet forebodings of doom by highlighting the extremist rantings in the right-wing press. Romania has a virulent section of press which loves to publish chauvinist filth. 'The Jews are plotting with the International Monetary Fund to turn Romanians into street-sweepers,' or 'Israel wants to enslave us all,' are classic lines in the extremist press. However, after the revolution anti-Semitism was low on the list of Romania's problems, if only because there were very few Jews left in the country. Most of the survivors of the holocaust left for Israel in the sixties and seventies when Ceauşescu 'sold' passports to Tel Aviv for hard currency. By December 1989 there were twenty thousand Jews left in Romania. In the autumn of 1990 Lord Jakobovits, Chief Rabbi of Britain and the Commonwealth,

came to Bucharest and cautioned against overdoing the
alarmism. 'We are concerned but we have to keep a sense of
proportion,' he said. 'Not every small incident means there
is a pogrom round the corner.' I heartily agreed. It was nice
to be able for once to forego the traditional Cassandra-role
of a journalist.

Learning of the *Adevarul* deception was a shock as this
was my first experience of such blatant abuse of the printed
word but of course for Romanians the vagaries of newsprint
were routine. These were heady days in the newspaper
world. For so long denied the right to self-expression and
force-fed a diet of Ceauşescu iconography, Romanians celebrated the revolution with an explosion into newsprint.
Almost a thousand publications opened in the first five
months after the revolution. Without exception they were
opinion-led. Facts and information came a distant second.
At last you could write what you wanted, about whom you
wanted – and people did. With no functioning law of libel,
unsubstantiated accusations poured off the front pages.
Frequently the opposition papers proved no more scrupulous with hard facts than the government press. It was
rather like working in a sauna. Everything was blurred.
Heroes were anti-heroes. Official statements were lies. Nicolae Costel's comment that everything in the Balkans was
grey, was often close to my mind.

One night I thought I had a clear-cut scoop. Major
Mihai Lupoi, the first army officer to join the revolution,
agreed to an interview. On 22 December, the day the
Ceauşescus fled from Bucharest, Lupoi's stocky khaki-clad
figure was beamed all over the world, as he called on the
army to join the revolution. '*Armata e cu noi*,' (the army is
with us) he shouted. Since then his career had declined
dramatically. After a few weeks as Minister of Tourism he
was sacked from the Front. He then narrowly escaped
injury when a truck veered on to the pavement in an
incident that sounded all too reminiscent of life under
Ceauşescu. On paper, if anyone was a hero in the revolution,
it was Lupoi. However, from the moment he swaggered in
to the interview with a bunch of heavies, it was clear

something was wrong. Opting for a comfortable chair in the centre of the Hotel Bucharest lobby – hardly the most discreet of places – he held court in the style more of a mafiosi than a furtive forgotten hero. I learned nothing but unsubstantiated allegations. Three months later he was accused of leading a mass anti-government riot and he flew to Switzerland for political asylum. The decline and fall of Captain Lupoi are a mirror-image of the withering of the ideals of the revolution.

The 'Lupoi scoop', the fake *Adevarul* 'interview' and many other stories failed to make the printed page of the *Daily Telegraph*. For a novice it wasn't easy to spot the news of the day. Like a fresher at university lectures, I fell for press conferences as a fount of important stories. My notebooks of the period are filled with the *'langue de bois'* ramblings of old communists – all but worthless. One morning a Spanish Foreign Ministry fact-finding team gave an elaborate parting *'conferinţa de presă'*. It was quite like the bountiful old days for foreign delegations. Coffee and cakes were distributed on one side. Deferential waiters hovered with trays of orange squash and water. After the flowery speeches, which talked of a 'shared Latin future', 'a climate of understanding' and 'inevitable progress', Romanian and Spanish journalists scribbled away. I followed suit and from my copious notes fashioned my dispatch.

'The Spanish Foreign Ministry yesterday declared its support for Romania's interim government and promised material and moral aid in the coming weeks. At a time of international disquiet over the role of the Front in the new multi-party coalition government due to assemble tomorrow, the Minister stressed that Spanish support would commence forthwith ...' And so it went on – hardly gripping reading. At the tenth or so paragraph the copy-taker who was receiving my dictation coughed politely. When I spoke to the desk for 'queries', there was a silence, followed by a chastening 'Call us before you file.'

On those days of duff stories and low morale it was a relief to retire to the saner world of 48 Strada Cobalcescu, where

I shared a bed and a mound of blankets with Anca, the estranged wife of Silviu's acquaintance, and Razvan, her new boyfriend.

The flat was a wonderful mixture of squalor and style, familiar to student accommodation all over the world. The high sculpted ceilings and yellowing plaster could have been from a draughty old Georgian residence in Edinburgh's New Town. The bath was a rusty tub in which I could barely kneel. Cockroaches had long ago won the battle for the kitchen. The exterior, with its banging shutters and cast-iron railings, reminded me of Montparnasse. Trams rattled along the cobbled street. Early diary entries record waking up to the sounds of stray cats and rain clattering on the lead gutter. Simenon would have recognised the cabbies who emerged cursing from the cellar taxi rank opposite, the old winos stumbling through the shadows and the painted ladies of the night heading home.

My four flat companions were all students. Anca, in her third year at the Faculty of Architecture, was seemingly a part-time nihilist. Razvan was an actor at the Jewish theatre, who dressed in black and lived off five hundred *lei* (a few pounds) a month. Anca had the pure creamy complexion of one untouched by the dietary abuses of the West. She also had her husband in Timişoara, a young child and a disintegrating affair with Razvan, which was probably not helped by my sharing their bed. Sabine and Barbel, two ethnic Germans from Transylvania, completed the household.

All four were bemused by the frenzy of daily journalism and found my need for regular communication with London rather comic. Their telephone was a magnificent apparatus, a black and gold wind-up, which could have come from the props department of a university rep. A party line, it only intermittently received incoming calls. One night I fell asleep while waiting for the Romanian operator to reach London. She did eventually, but about six hours late. When the phone rang the dawn trolley buses were already whirring into action outside. I was plucked from dreams of fawning Balkan waiters to hear the gruff tones of the *Telegraph*'s night porter. I'm not sure who was the more confused, particularly as the old man who shared the line was furious at being woken up.

'Foreign desk, please,' – half-drowned by a flood of angry Romanian.

'Er, there's no one in for at least an hour, mate.' I looked at my watch and realized the day was over. It was a new day, a different paper. My account of the chaotic opening of Romania's new multi-party parliament (one of the most important stories in the week which followed Patrick Bishop's departure) was one for the personal files. I fell back to sleep and a few minutes later was jerked awake again. It was the operator.

'*Aţi vorbit?* (You have spoken?). *Bine, la revedere.* (Fine, bye, bye).'

We lived very different hours. Like most Romanians, Anca, Razvan, Barbel and Sabina rose at first light, conditioned by the need for hot water (which flowed at dawn and dusk) an awareness of the best time for shopping (early morning) and the 8 a.m. start of lessons. I woke late and returned late, usually after a battle with the phones. Often days would pass without any contact. But on Saturday afternoons I would sit at the kitchen table, with its props of unwanted books, and try to teach myself to type on Barbel's old manual typewriter. With the ribbon worn and the keys arranged for Romanian letters, it was a tortuous process. I sometimes wondered if back in London, surrounded by high-technology, the editorial desk realized the humble beginnings of my pieces.

My commitment to the keyboard was poor and after an hour or so I broke off and we caught up on the previous week. Fuelled by food parcels from one of Sabine's relatives in Germany, these conversations launched into arguments on liberty, rights, rock music, democracy, sex, or anything else that appealed. One night Razvan produced a back copy of a Western glossy magazine with a detailed description of gay lifestyles and practices in San Francisco. It was too much for him to stomach.

'How can you expect people to read about this kind of thing? It's not natural. Look at this! You mean people really go around wearing this stuff?'

It was easy to feel smug and superior. But it was ironic and even chastening that in politics the students, the 'radicals' of Romania, espoused the exact reverse of their contemporaries in the West. Socialism was out. Capitalism was hip. They were 'right on', but in their own East European style. They were some of the most encouraging conversations of my early months. While the politicians appeared set on consigning Romania to Europe's back yard, the young were striving to show that their culture had not been lost under communism and that they were Europeans. One of the few reassuring aspects of covering Yugoslavia's descent into civil war was to see young Serbs and Croats resolutely rejecting nationalist rhetoric, retaining their education and refusing to immerse themselves in the past.

Forty-eight Strada Cobalcescu was not comfortable but it was a home, and by the middle of February an element of normality started to creep into my life. With my Romanian residence looking more permanent, the contents of my 'weekend' rucksack seemed increasingly inadequate. My wardrobe, the chunky walking boots, Mujahedeen cap and Pakistani shawl had been designed for a few days on an imagined snow-bound frontier and were outmoded in the plush conference halls of Bucharest. Paul Hill, one of the faceless but increasingly familiar voices in the London office, dispatched a package of clothes, pens and razor blades. 'Just don't tell anyone,' he said. 'We'll see if we can swing it through expenses.'

The consolidation of my domestic life was mirrored in my working arrangements. By the middle of February a colony of British stringers had set up base in Bucharest, Chris Stephen for the *Guardian*, Victoria Clark for the *Observer*, Catherine Adams for UPI, Marc Champion for the *Independent* and Tim Judah for *The Times*. In their mid to late twenties, they formed a nucleus of friends and colleagues. Sometimes friendships were strained by rival claims to a lucrative foreign 'string'. For some reason the *Toronto Globe and Mail* was a particularly contested outlet. But these disagreements seldom lasted long. The 'stringer

colony' was not exclusively British by design, but other
nationalities tend to rely on staff correspondents. We formed
a close-knit community.

Attached to our clique was a shadowy group of interpret-
ers, some drawn by money, some no doubt paid by the
authorities, some drawn by their desire to escape from the
humdrum normality of their existence. Mihai Radu was one
of the latter. A young, homely engineer from the industrial
town of Pitesti, Mihai was frustrated by the limitations of
his life and he transferred from engineering to journalism
with alacrity. Not once did he question the manic tooing
and froing which is the essence and absurdity of daily
journalism. Nor even did he baulk at asking politicians
sensitive questions. Best of all, he was an excellent *gospodar*
(house-holder), knowing which village was known for which
provisions, a crucial attribute in a corrupt and shambolic
economy like Romania's. Whenever we left Bucharest,
Mihai would suggest a detour at village x or y en route and
he would slip out of the car in defiance of my fraught tut-
tutting – to return laden with *brînza* (salty soft cheese),
caşcaval (a bland Edam equivalent), or better still bottles of
palincă (a stronger version of *ţuica*). Friends in the UK
have often asked me how I ever knew what was going on in
a strange country with an alien language. The answer was I
didn't – but Mihai, my eyes and ears as well as my closest
Romanian friend, did.

In the first two weeks of February the main Romanian
story was slow, as the pre-election negotiations were pro-
gressing cautiously. Mihai and I developed a routine of
checking the headquarters of the political parties, a stop off
with the Group for Social Dialogue (a forum of literary and
dissident figures) and then a jaunt up the central boulevard
to the two main flashpoints, the television station and the
government headquarters in Victory Square – or rather
Demonstration Square, as the stringers dubbed it. On these
trips we usually teamed up with another stringer. While
most mornings everyone pursued their own leads, in the
afternoon people congregated by the telephones at the
Hotel Bucharest and shared information gleaned about the

political situation. Too close co-operation with competitors makes for poor journalism. But withholding everything is counter-productive. If one day it was my good fortune to chance on a demonstration, the next day it was almost certainly someone else's. The handful of remaining staff correspondents stayed in the Intercontinental Hotel, beset by pimps and secret policemen, and were seldom able to relax. I found it all too easy to sink into the increasing familiarity of day-to-day life and forget the power-struggles going on behind the scenes – until they burst into the open.

In the third week of February anarchy returned to Romania. In the space of four days there was a military mutiny, the government headquarters was stormed and, for the second time in a month, thousands of club-wielding miners descended on Bucharest, baying for blood. My first big story. This was not my finest hour.

The first sign of trouble was when a few hundred soldiers assembled outside the government building in Victory Square, demanding better living conditions. Within forty-eight hours a thousand middle-ranking officers were also demonstrating, calling for the resignation of the defence minister, Nicolae Militaru, and twenty-five generals, who had been brought out of retirement during the revolution. By refusing to shoot on the demonstrators in December 1989, the army had played the key role in the overthrow of Ceauşescu and the installation of Iliescu. However, officers and also some generals were unhappy that Militaru, a Russophile who had been retired in the eighties by Ceauşescu, had been reinstated. The 'rebels' formed the Committee for Action to Democratise the Armed Forces (CADA) and rejected a proposal that the army might be used to resolve differences between the political parties. They also rejected a pay rise, the carrot with which Iliescu had already bought off discontent among the miners and transport workers.

It was a crisis moment for Romania. Iliescu needed a loyal army at his side. Bucharest was awash with rumours of a possible military coup. Three years on I still berate

myself for missing a magnificent opportunity to talk to the
CADA ringleaders. It was late afternoon and I was catching
the metro down from Victory Square, after spending all day
waiting in vain to try to talk to the mutineers, who were
meeting with the Front. The Romanian metro is seldom
crowded. I looked up from my seat and there, sitting on the
opposite seats, were three of the CADA leaders. Young
Marine officers, from the Black Sea port of Constanta, they
wore dark blue uniforms with gold epaulettes and were
clutching briefcases. (An officer later explained that regulations forbade them to be seen in uniform with a shopping
bag and so they carried a briefcase in case they chanced on
something to buy.) The trio were giggling like schoolchildren going home.

'*Nu vă supераţi*,' (Excuse me) I said in my fledgling
Romanian. 'Do you speak English?' One of them nodded.
'Aren't you the organisers of the mutiny – I mean demonstration?' Other passengers turned their heads. I lowered my
voice. The three grinned eagerly and nodded assent.

'So what's going to happen next?' I continued. 'Will you
agree to the government's offer? Or will you continue with
the protest?'

'It's confidential. A secret,' said one, tapping his lips.

'No one knows,' said the second.

'We are going home for tea,' said the third.

'But you must know something about what's going on?
How many resignations will you accept? What about President Iliescu? Are you happy with him?' This prompted
more shrugs and they switched the conversation to football.

'You should come and visit us in Constanta. We'll give
you a good time,' said the group leader as the train glided
into the University Square station, where I was due to get
off.

'But what about the coup? The rumours of the takeover?
What does the army want?' I was left on the platform
wondering where I went wrong. Mortified at my failure to
elicit information from such a timely encounter, I spent the
next twenty-four hours rehearsing the questions I thought I
should have asked. I retired early that night, berating

myself for my incompetence, and consequently missed a stand-off outside the television centre between a regiment of paratroopers and an infantry unit. The story was all over the pages of my British competitors the next morning. I still dream of the chance of a re-run.

Fighting for their survival, the Front leaders sacrificed General Militaru, forty-eight hours after my botched metro meeting, announcing his retirement 'on grounds of ill health'. It must have been a bitter twist for Militaru. An old Russia-hand, trained in Moscow, in the eighties he was involved in a series of plots against Ceauşescu and he was a key figure in the Front in the early days of the revolution. His replacement, General Victor Stanculescu, had an equally topsy-turvy career. Stanculescu, who came from a family of career soldiers, served as Ceauşescu's Deputy Minister of Defence until the revolution. After being des-patched to Timişoara to suppress the uprising, he feigned a disability. In the crucial hours of 22 December, when the dictator was trying to flee, Stanculescu emerged with his leg in plaster. By the time Ceauşescu was captured, the plaster cast was off. The swiftness of Ceauşescu's fall was matched only by the speed of the senior figures to change sides.

The sacking of Militaru satisfied the soldiers' immediate demands but it barely staunched the groundswell of discon-tent in Bucharest. In the University, students roamed the old baroque buildings, quoting the medieval Romanian proverb, 'A change of rulers is a joy of fools,' which was coined in the eighteenth century, when the principalities of Moldavia and Wallachia had over seventy rulers. Two days after Militaru fell, an anti-Front demonstration turned vio-lent and hundreds of demonstrators, a mixture of street kids, drifters and students, broke into the government headquarters, smashing the windows, rifling through the offices, hurling furniture into the street and threatening the same treatment on the deputy prime minister, Gelu Voican-Voiculescu. I missed the first moments of the assault as I had left the square half an hour earlier to write a despatch about another 'uneventful demonstration'. I was waiting for a telephone line in the Hotel Bucharest when Mihai came running in with the news. It was with a mixture of trepidation and reluctance that I abandoned my place in the queue – the nerves were for the story, the regret for the lost phone line.

The storming of the government headquarters, a monolithic casket of a building, was a huge blow to the prestige of the Front. Hundreds of people, mainly young men, were standing on the roof and the balcony, shouting the old revolutionary slogans along with 'The only solution is another revolution' and '*Jos Iliescu* (Down with Iliescu).' The most extraordinary sight was that of a cordon of soldiers standing to attention outside the building, looking resolutely ahead, while the pillaging flourished behind and above them.

'We have orders to guard the building,' said one.

'Well, why aren't you guarding it, then?' I remember shouting back at Mihai who passed on the question in more emollient tones. Back came the same reply.

'We have orders to guard the building.'

After the revolution the police still wore the same uniforms as before and felt vulnerable to public hostility. Ordinary policemen were too terrified of public retribution to apprehend motoring offenders, let alone intervene in a serious public disorder. ('Hey, you hassled us before the revolution. You shot us during it. And now you dare to stop us?' was the classic challenge of the astute motorist when pulled over for speeding.) In February 1990 the unspoken fear in many officials' minds was, what if there was another revolution and they emerged on the wrong side?

For five hours on that anarchic night of Sunday 18th the building was in the hands of the rioters. In the days and weeks that followed, the opposition parties claimed that the attack was stage-managed by *agents provocateurs* to discredit them. To support their case they pointed to a number of unexplained factors, most notably that the people who spearheaded the attack were tough-looking young men who displayed a remarkable athleticism in scaling the walls and who had played no role in the peaceful demonstration earlier in the afternoon. Their close-cropped hair and wiry frames brought to mind the black and white images of the street scum recruited for Europe's fascist movements in the thirties.

In the Balkans, the home of the conspiracy theory, Byzantine theorising has to be treated sceptically, pending very hard proof. In this instance, the apathy of the police does provide a plausible explanation for the demonstrators' ease of access to the building. After the previous week's display of discontent in the armed forces, Iliescu may have delayed calling on them to intervene until the last moment. However, what is certain is that the Front maximised the propaganda gain from the incident. State television pumped out a story of the 'slayers of Ceaușescu' under attack by right-wing extremists. The images, accompanied by a carefully slanted commentary, turned pro-Front feeling in the provinces from support to hero-worship.

When the army finally deployed around 10.30 p.m., the building came under the authorities' control within minutes. A hundred demonstrators, many looking drunk or half-witted, were captured. A young student grabbed my arm and pointed at two ambulances speeding away.

'They are drugging my friends, injecting them so they say false things.' It was a ridiculous claim. But the excitement of the moment was intoxicating. I have no record of the original piece I dictated to London, but I do remember that most of what I sent was not used. In hindsight I realize that this was for a very good reason.

Communists are not accustomed to protests and the Front was full of former high-ranking apparatchiks who were still coming to terms with the difference between autocracy and democracy. The day after the storming of Victory Square Iliescu reacted in the way he had learned as a child – with repression. In the early evening, between five and ten thousand club-wielding miners came to Bucharest to 'restore order'.

I came on the miners while I was completing a late-night drive through the fog-bound city. It was a terrible sight. With heads bowed and clubs at their side, they filled Bucharest's boulevards, sweeping aside oncoming cars.

From twenty yards only the gleam of headlamps betrayed their passage. Jack the Ripper couldn't have asked for a denser fog. It oozed around them, masking the outline of their hose pipes and chains, batons and pit-props. Mihai had a cool head and he jammed on the brakes. We slowed beside one of Ceauşescu's unfinished Legoland blocks near by and watched as they marched past. In their drab uniforms they looked like evil goblins, unleashed on an innocent world.

This was my first direct experience of the Fellinian darkness and manipulative brand of politics which over-shadow so much of the Balkans' history and which I was to encounter time and again in Yugoslavia. The coming of the miners in February 1990 was a return to the divide-and-rule tactics of the late forties when the communists took power. Romania's leaders claimed that the miners arrived spontaneously. It was patently a lie. The state railway laid on special transport for the miners to leave their homes in the Jiu Valley, two hundred miles away. In 1977 the miners of the Jiu Valley had organized one of the only serious protests against Ceauşescu. After the revolt was quelled, the ringleaders were imprisoned and Securitate agents infil-trated the mines to prevent a repeat. In February 1990 these same Securitate officers were still in place and able to marshal the miners like automatons. As the night wore on, state vans arrived bearing bread and yogurt. Iliescu orches-trated his coal-blackened supporters like the sheep in *Animal Farm*.

'*Luptăm, murim, vă apărăm*' (We fight, we die, we defend you), they roared when he appeared on the balcony. '*Muncim, nu gîndim.*' (We work, we don't think.) The chants came from Romania's darkest past.

With their waving sledge-hammers and bulging biceps, the miners were the stuff of copy-book Stalinist propaganda, a real-life incarnation of the 'proletarian posters' of the Russian Revolution. All the scene needed was a few peasants waving sickles *à la All Quiet Flows the Don*. In the Western newspaper headlines and commentaries that followed the coming of the miners, there were inevitable comparisons made with the Ceauşescu regime. This was an analogy that I too made on occasion, but it was misleading. Although Ceauşescu was a brutal dictator, he seldom resorted to proletarian muscle to prop up his rule, relying instead on the state security apparatus. The violence which marred Romania's early months after the revolution had its roots in a long tradition of political instability. In the seventeenth, eighteenth and nineteenth centuries Bucharest witnessed successive outbursts of civic strife. Between the world wars violence was the political currency. In the 1920s spores of Bolshevik sentiment drifting south from Russia sparked street battles between workers and the army. In the thirties a bloodier struggle flared between the authorities and the Iron Guard. Dedicated to the elimination of Jews, communists and parliamentary democracy, the Iron Guard couched its message with a quasi-romantic mysticism that appealed to the Romanian psyche. Its recruits, known as 'Greenshirts' or 'legionaries', assassinated some of Romania's ablest politicians, until in 1941 the authorities clamped down. After 1945 the communists pursued the same inglorious methods. *Agents provocateurs* fired on opposition demonstrations. The young King Michael who tried to re-establish a constitutional monarchy was forced to abdicate at gunpoint.

For the Romania which entered the 1990s, blinking and bewildered, this was a grim tradition. All over East Europe there was a power vacuum following the downfall of communism, as the old establishment – not just the politicians, but all the functionaries, the landlords, the police chiefs, the mayors, the factory bosses – fought to maintain their perks. In most countries the struggle was behind the scenes. However, in the ex-communist Balkan states, Romania and Bulgaria, the contest was harder and more open.

The display of proletarian muscle was a warning to the opposition. But in this, the second of four invasions by the miners, the city was quiet. After a speech of thanks, Iliescu ordered his stormtroopers home, promising to call them again if needed. By midnight his bloodhounds were streaming back to the railway station, passing over the cobbles in almost total silence, with their thick rubber boots muffling their tread. A cream-coloured Oltcit, Romania's tin-can version of a Citroën Visa, screeched past us into the throng. Too late the driver realized his mistake, panicked, span the wheel and was overwhelmed as if by a swarm of ants. Briefly it looked as if he would be lynched, and then the miners calmed down. The boss had spoken. Looking more like dirty children than vigilantes, they clustered around the back of the food-trucks, chattering about their experiences in the big city.

Bucharest was saved and an updated report was long overdue. The press centre had closed and my only chance for a line was Catherine Adams' apartment which was near Victory Square and which with foresight I had asked the *Telegraph* to call at midnight. With ten minutes to go, I was separated from the flat by the tide of homeward-bound miners. A minute passed, then another. There was no choice but to grin inanely and run through the stinking throng. Ignore the cat-calls, don't look round, stumble through the streets. Of course the lift isn't working nor the lights. Grope up the stairs. Fumble along the corridor. The phone is ringing. Insert the key. Shit! It doesn't work! Still the phone rings. Please keep dialling, London. The door resists – another ring of the phone. Back a few paces and a kick at the door. It splinters. I run through and pick up the phone.

'You all right, love? You sound rather breathless . . .' As I started to dictate, footsteps came crashing up the stairs. The door banged behind me and there was an anguished moan. It was Cath, waving her keys, staring at the broken door.

In the midst of this turbulence Patrick Leigh Fermor was due in Romania to write his post-revolutionary impressions for the *Telegraph* and I was ordered by the foreign desk to tend to his needs. Patrick's visit coincided with a long-planned weekend with my girlfriend, Sophie, who was flying to Bucharest to see if our relationship had survived its two-month long 'weekend' apart. With a wicked sense of timing the *Telegraph*'s foreign editor, who was oblivious to my personal plans, announced he was flying to Budapest. I was summoned for a meeting with the regional correspondents. Somehow these arrangements were juggled into place.

Profoundly depressed by the legacy of communism on the Romania he had known and loved in the thirties, Patrick returned from visits to his old friends full of regrets about happier times. But, with an unimpaired appetite for *ţuica* and late-night conversation, he made a fascinating travel companion, briefly raising the veil from an earlier and more glorious Balkan age. We flew together to Timişoara where regretfully we parted company.

Patrick and an accompanying photographer, Clare Arron, were bound for Maramureş in the far north. Sophie and I looked up my old Timişoara friend Silviu, who was still conducting a vigil for his friends from ITV ('They said they'd be back and they haven't called'), and asked him to drive us to Budapest.

The Romanian customs officials on the frontier were Silviu's friends so we bypassed the queue, but still arrived an hour late for my appointment.

The next morning I was back in Timişoara, wishing I had flown back to London with Sophie, dreaming of the Forum Hotel's goulash, reflecting on the foreign editor's encouragement and clutching a bag with his offerings – a book on how to be a stringer, a hunk of the Berlin Wall and a maxi-pack of condoms.

3

Patriots and Prejudices

Moldavia and Transylvania, March 1990

'And God gave the Romanians wit and intelligence and good looks, and then looking at his creation he reflected and decided he had been too generous – so he put them where they are now, in the playground of Europe.' – *Traditional Romanian saying*

SOMEONE SAID THAT something was going on somewhere in Moldavia. No one was quite sure what. Nor was it clear who had started the story. A whisper here, a hint there told of mass strikes, savage press censorship, a clampdown, a return to the old days. Of course it might have been a myth. But there had also been reports of unrest in Soviet Moldavia, the severed half of the old medieval kingdom. I pricked up my ears.

It was a stuffy Sunday afternoon in the Hotel Bucharest, a week after my return from Budapest. Barely a month into my stringership, I was paranoid about missing a major political development. Moldavia, in the north-east, seemed a long way from Bucharest. But the capital was quiet. Sunday was the traditional day of demonstrations and it had passed without incident. The only event of possible interest was a lecture given by British academics on democracy. When one of the delegates gave me a 'quiet word on the side' about the role of the Western press, suggesting we were not being hard enough on the National Salvation Front, I felt as if the dining clubs of London had shifted to Bucharest. I promptly telexed London – 'Parting for Moldavia.'

Dawn the next morning at Baneasa airport in north

Bucharest was a blur of bad-tempered officials, sweet coffee, pleas for a last-minute ticket and finally the unfamiliar whirring of propellers as a Tintinesque 1950s Antonov lumbered into the sky towards Iaşi (pronounced Yash), the old capital of Moldavia. George Staniţa, the sparky BBC Romanian Service correspondent, had a friend there. It seemed a good place to start. I woke an hour after take-off to find us skimming a few hundred feet above a plateau which stretched as far as the eye could see. It was the edge of the steppe, where Europe met the Soviet Union – the campaign territory for two millenia of wars and a breeding ground for another.

If the Banat was the bulldog of Romania's history, ever snapping at the heels of unwelcome overlords, then Moldavia was the lapdog, forced to cringe and whimper at its master's word. Blessed – or it might be fairer to say cursed – with fertile soil, a temperate climate, long open plains and no natural defences, Moldavia forms the junction box for Europe's invasion routes. For centuries it has been the plaything of great powers. Even when its hero, Stefan cel Mare (Stephen the Great), was beating back the Turks in the late fifteenth century, the threat of another Tatar invasion was such that he had to build the fortified monastery of Voroneţ one of Europe's architectural delights, in just three months. Ottoman rule gave Moldavia a couple of centuries' breathing space from the armies speeding down the steppe but, as the Turkish Empire started to decline in the seventeenth and eighteenth centuries, the Sublime Porte used Moldavia in a cynical game of pass-the-parcel, chopping off chunks to appease St Petersburg and Vienna. Bukovina (literally the beech forest) was hived off to the Habsburgs in 1775 and Bessarabia was claimed by the Tsars in 1812, leaving barely half of Moldavia intact.

At the Treaty of Versailles in 1919 Moldavia regained its lost territories, but only briefly. Ribbentrop and Molotov decided differently in 1940, shuffling the frontiers once more. According to the deal Stalin was to take only Bessarabia. He promptly broke ranks, 'read' an extra clause into the accord and grabbed Bukovina as well. After the war Stalin ensured the takeover would be all the harder to unravel by his trusted brand of ethnic engineering, sending in tens of thousands of ethnic Russian colonists and deporting like numbers of Moldavians to Siberia. Such a turbulent past should only be the stuff of burlesque comedy. For Moldavians sadly it is all too true and it's left them with a strong feel for the continuity of history and a world-weary sadness about the West. During the Cold War Western governments from time to time voiced outrage about the three Baltic States, the other victims of the Molotov-Ribbentrop pact. We always seemed to forget the partition of Moldavia.

I learned much of this rudimentary chronology while striding round Iaşi at breakneck speed with my 'Moldavian contact'. With bold, cheeky eyes, a droopy moustache and a magnificent laugh, George Pinzarў was one of the extraordinary band of cultural survivors of communism who had maintained hope in all the bad years, withstood the tendency to slide into mediocrity, and after the system's collapse emerged unscathed. He only stopped talking to laugh, and his infectious *joie de vivre* swiftly dispelled any lingering queasiness from the flight. Over two years later I was to be reminded of George in the southern Albanian town of Gjirokaster where a young French teacher was continuing to teach amid a climate of mounting xenophobia and anti-intellectualism. Two days before I met him, his door was burned down by xenophobic young Albanians. He shrugged: '*Qu est-ce qu'il faut faire? Il faut continuer. On peut pas ceder au vandalisme.*' He had never left Gjirokaster and yet his accent was pure Quai d'Orsay. It was a fleeting taste of Paris in the belly of the beast of communism.

George, an amateur film-maker, was not under threat of arson. But his jaunty step, quick tongue and mini-video camera were incongruous in the streets of Iaşi which had deteriorated from their cultural heyday in the late Middle Ages. Iaşi was the hometown of the founder of the Iron Guard, Corneliu Zelea Codreanu, whose malign brand of romanticism, anti-Semitism and nationalism impregnated the city between the wars. The charismatic Codreanu revealed his fanaticism in dramatic style in 1924, when he marched into a courtroom and shot dead the Prefect of Police and two officials. In the thirties and early forties Iaşi had the worst record in Romania for anti-Semitism and indulged in a wave of pogroms. Up to twelve thousand people were butchered in Iaşi – Ceauşescu put the figure at five hundred. As George whisked me through the centre it was almost as if the city was in purgatory for those horrors of half a century before.

George left me in the lobby of the Hotel Unirea with a cheery 'back in ten minutes' and I wandered in search of breakfast. The coffee bar was pitch dark, but the sign on the door said open. I had closed the door behind me and started moving to the counter when I realized that I was not alone. Dulled eyes were staring from every corner, not *at* me, but *through* me. The room was barely twenty foot square and yet there were at least a dozen men sprawled at various angles. A few seemed to be attempting to communicate. Most were comatose. The barman was upright but offered no obvious response to my request for coffee. There was neither menace nor hostility. But it was like walking into a cultural vacuum. I retreated to the breakfast room to find the same stinking smoke-filled and 'cognac only' story.

After forty-two years on the extremities of two diehard communist regimes, the Soviet and Romanian, Iaşi was a centre of reaction. Ceauşescu tried to eradicate Iaşi's traditional cultural ethos and he redesigned the centre with tower blocks, filling them with thousands of peasants. The result was an urban horror-scape inhabited by first-generation city-dwelling peasants still coming to terms with leaving the country and the obligations of their new environment. No one was smiling. Hardly anyone seemed to be talking in public. Drinking started at dawn and lasted all day. These thousands were the lumpen proletariat of marxist ideologues' dreams. They would be a potent force against reform and change for years. Their equivalents in Yugoslavia were already lapping up the nationalist rhetoric of the tinpot dictators in Serbia and Croatia.

George countered the anti-intellectual climate by living in a fantasy world in which he was a Winston Smith battling against the system – at least, I think it was a fantasy world. The revolution never happened in Iaşi, bar a few cosmetic reshuffles. George insisted that I adopt a series of disguises to avoid unwanted attention. I wasn't allowed to talk on the buses. I was hardly allowed to talk to his Russian girlfriend. When we went in search of a taxi I had to play the deaf-mute. What was intended as a bit-part became my role for the best part of an hour as successive taxi-drivers refused our business.

'It's late,' said one. 'It's almost lunch-time.'

'Why me? Take someone else,' said another.

'Not now,' said a third. Most just shook their heads. These were state taxi drivers in state-owned cars. They had fuel. Our destination was not too far and not too near. But why should they take us? They were paid whatever they did.

At the Post Office George enquired about the despatch of a telex to my office in London. He returned rolling his eyes.

'They say all telexes have to be approved by the mayor's office.' He chuckled and mimicked a caricature monotone bureaucrat's voice, 'You must come back in two days.' It was my turn to roll my eyes. After a couple of months in 'retirement' the communist mayor Dumitru Naguţ was campaigning to be reinstated. Most of his councillors had never stepped down.

Fortunately, for almost the first time in the two months since I had arrived in Romania, speed and facility of communications weren't a priority. A few words with George clarified that the reports which had enticed me from Bucharest had been heavily embroidered en route. The city's press censorship while egregious and intensifying was not a fast-moving crisis. Re-unification with Soviet Moldavia was not going to happen overnight. These were story ideas which could stand a leisurely pace. I had a twinge of conscience. This was the first time I had been out of touch with London for more than a few hours in a stretch and I had promised to contact them on arrival. But George had a clinching argument: 'It's very simple. Either you, and I suppose I, sit here and wait for several hours for a telex line that will never come and which even if it does come will certainly never send your message – or I go to work and you come with me, and as we go, you'll see Romania's most beautiful churches.' There was no contest. As the day wore on it felt distinctly liberating to be uncontactable. Two years later when working on the foreign desk with phones ringing from all corners of the globe, I realized that my concern that London was waiting to hear from me was misplaced. When you are in some remote place on the end of a crackly line, you forget that your interlocutor has probably just finished talking to Rio or Johannesburg. I was one of the *Telegraph*'s newest and youngest stringers – and not a high priority.

George's only appointment of the day was at the Iaşi Hospital. Like so many of Romania's medical institutions, it was chronically under-equipped and would have failed the most basic British health standard. One of Elena Ceauşescu's less inspirational ideas was to cut back spending on health care. Romania was, she considered, 'a healthy society' and so could and should direct its resources elsewhere. In the seventies she stopped state-funding for the training of nurses. The result was the deprivation in orphanages, asylums and hospitals, which when relayed on Western television after the revolution would scar the international reputation of Romania.

Iaşi hospital had to cope with its own private horror story. The rolling plains which surround Iaşi are a few hundred miles south-west of Chernobyl. When in 1985 the Chernobyl reactor exploded, Ceauşescu waited forty-eight hours before warning Romanians. For two days or more people continued to work and play in prime fall-out areas, drinking fresh milk and drawing local water. Iaşi hospital was designated to accommodate the result and became the regional centre for 'special' cases – a euphemism for the hundreds, possibly thousands of radiation-induced cancers afflicting north-east Romania.

The chief doctor relayed a few of these basic facts and figures while face down and struggling with a piece of wire to repair the echograph unit. He paused to ask a question.

'Have you ever heard of a radiology unit without an echograph?'

I mumbled something sympathetic, unsure whether I had ever heard of a radiology unit with an echograph – at least not with an echograph like his. Heath Robinson would have loved it.

'What we really need is a new hospital, tell your people that,' continued the doctor. 'Last week a British lorry came with food and we told them to come back with an echograph.' He lowered his voice. 'Of course, forget the official statistics, they don't matter. They're all cooked up.'

In the waiting room five or six patients in the regulation-issue tatty acrylic dressing-gowns were talking in a pall of smoke. An untended casualty was huddled in a corner. A hulking nurse wandered past yelling over her shoulder, munching at a hunk of bread, brushing past the patients as if they weren't there. Iaşi's saintly warrior hero, Stefan cel Mare, Romania's abbey-building equivalent of David of Scotland, and dubbed by Pope Pius VI 'the athlete of Christ', must have been turning in his tomb.

Some of my most searing early Romanian experiences were in medical institutions. In every Romanian hospital there are scores of well-trained, diligent and honest doctors. But there's also an underlying callousness which symbolises most sharply the brutalising legacy of the Ceauşescus and which was conveyed to the West by stark reports on the terrible state of the Romanian orphanages, where tens of thousands of children were abandoned each year. In my diary there is a blank page. It was for a day in Timişoara when, returning from my 'Budapest summit' I accompanied an American journalist to the city hospital to investigate how the Securitate stole the bodies of forty demonstrators during the revolution. I fell completely for the lies of the Head of the Institute of Legal Medicine, Professor Traian Crişan, a Securitate officer who assisted in the robbery. But the blank page is not a penance for my naivety. It is in memory of my horror at the state of the hospital morgue, which we found unlocked and unattended. The refrigeration wasn't working; corpses without identity tags were spread out like hunks of meat. Cases of unmarked blood samples on smear slides were gathering dust in a corner. The back door was swinging in the wind and the taint of rotting food from the yard mixed with the smell of death. That night, unable to write a word, not for the last time I wondered how communism managed to dehumanise society so thoroughly. Not for the last time the thought ceded to a second – how much blame devolves on communism and how much on society itself.

I have never liked hospitals and Iaşi was no exception. Sobered by the cancer ward, we sought solace in the grounds of the Palace of the Metropolitan (Archbishop). In the sixteenth and seventeenth centuries when the Moldavian boyars (noblemen) were devoted patrons of the arts, Iaşi was one of the cultural centres of the Balkans. The massive pillars and cupolas of the Metropolitan's church hinted at these more noble times – when Bucharest was still emerging from the Danubian swamp. Orthodox churches can be terribly cloying, with their heavy icons, dripping candle wax, smoke stains and powerful perfumes. In Bucharest many churches have an added claustrophobia as they are deep in shadow, encased by high-rise blocks, the result of Ceauşescu's attempts to camouflage all signs of piety. But against a clear blue sky the smooth white exterior of the Metropolitan's church exuded a freshness and serenity which I didn't associate with the Orthodox rite. It was as if it was endowed with the sanctity of the Aya Sofia and the clinical form of the Blue Mosque.

However, there was nothing in the architecture which I could see fitting in the foreign pages of the *Daily Telegraph*. Duty was nagging and I started to move on – and then checked myself and deliberately turned back; for a few minutes I would be a tourist, a traveller and not a journalist. Admiring the work of a team of restorers, I was revelling in the escape from two months of question and answer when the vision abruptly faded.

'It's a nice church. It's a beautiful church [the beautiful was bellowed as in Italian], but you should meet the bishop. Now that's what it's really all about.' George tapped his lips and pretended he had to be pressed for further details. 'His aides dined with all the Party bosses, informed to the Securitate.'

The list of charges hinted at the misrule of the Avignon Papacy or the notorious corruption of the Phanariots, the venal Greek pro-consuls who governed Wallachia and Moldavia for the Turks. The Metropolitate of Iaşi is second only to the Patriarch in the hierarchy of the Orthodox Church. My nascent journalist's antennae started waving once more.

I was still relying on my forged accreditation from January, whose paper was crumbling and print had faded. But, fortunately, in the provinces visiting Western journalists were rarities and no one dreamed of asking for identification. The see was vacant and, we were politely informed, the stand-in bishop, Pimen of Suceava, was at prayer. An appointment was fixed for the next morning. We retired for an afternoon of church-gazing and an evening of fruity Moldavian wine, while George told me of his plan to build Romania's largest collection of compact discs.

The interview started in good Borgia or Medici style. Although it was soon after breakfast, the hierarch handed us glasses of *ţuica* and left a full decanter on the tray. With his flowing white beard and ornate robes, surrounded by sumptious furnishings and ornaments, Bishop Pimen seemed every inch the Orthodox prelate of Western caricature. His opening words did little to change my impression.

'I entered the church through my love of a life of prayer. We were forced to join hands with the communists. Without saying things like "Ceauşescu was a flagman of peace" we would have been persecuted . . . Believers understood this was not from the heart.' Pausing for a sip of water he endowed his audience with a beatific smile. 'I was called to the offices of the church and asked to help sacking monks. The first three times I refused, the fourth I was threatened that, if I did not comply, the church would be closed.'

The phraseology seemed trite. The Romanian Orthodox Church had an appalling reputation for sycophancy under the communists. The Holy Synod incorporated the Ceauşescus into the Orthodox calendar of saints. The Patriarch Teoctist, a white-bearded saintly figure, sent a congratulatory telegram to Ceauşescu the day after the security forces opened fire in Timişoara. The priests were notorious for betraying confessions to the Securitate. The Bishop of Sibiu, Metropolitan Antonius, was a known Securitate agent who in the thirties was a member of the Iron Guard. While dutifully taking notes, I started to fit Pimen's words to the confines of the 'story', discarding much of the material as a standard apologia, sifting through the verbiage, looking for quotes. However, when his voice rose, I started paying more careful attention.

'It's easy to accuse,' sighed Pimen, 'but I was in a very delicate position. When you want to do good, the devil is fighting hard and the devil was represented by communism. What was extraordinary was the way the devil used communists. It was not a straight persecution of the Church, it was a trap . . . and it was possible to forget and serve the communists.'

Bishop Pimen's candid admission of failures by his Church was not the standard Orthodox line. It also re-opened for me the uncomfortable question of how I would have behaved under a totalitarian system. It's a difficult question for people from the West and one I normally try to avoid. It is, as Pimen said, easy to accuse. Later I was to learn that Pimen was one of the few Orthodox bishops who did not co-operate with the regime. In 1992 he openly courted controversy with his more subservient fellow bishops when he issued an invitation to Romania's exiled King Michael of Hohenzollern.

I retired in a more reflective mood. In twelve hours we had seen the symbol of the old Iaşi (the church) and the new (the hospital). Neither seemed in a very healthy state. Both merited further investigation. After twenty-four hours of following whims, the pressure to produce a piece for the paper was starting to grow. George led the way to the offices of the local newspapers.

The Iași newspaper controversy of March 1990 will not classify as one of the more dramatic reports to come out of Eastern Europe. A week before my arrival, the printing union refused to run an edition of the opposition paper *Opinia Studenteasca* because it carried a front-page criticism of Iliescu. In protest, local opposition papers called a strike. Like many things Balkan, the strike was more about rhetoric than reality – the journalists continued to produce their papers. But the conflict had a disturbing echo of the late forties, when the communist-controlled print unions refused to print opposition papers.

George smuggled me into the print works as an 'interested tourist' and we listened to the workers fulminating against the BBC and Radio Free Europe, 'the organs of capitalism'.

'Those liars in London, they are always trying to trick us. We have to be on our guard,' ranted one woman. 'We must keep working and not allow ourselves to be distracted. If these journalists of ours think they can go on writing their wickednesses they have another thought coming.' A stream of consciousness followed. George and I vied to express the heartiest support until the head engineer walked over. He must have suspected something.

'Gentlemen, allow me to show you the workings of the plant.' After a lecture on machinery he guided us to the door, but we already had the story. The dispute between the printers and journalists reached to the heart of an old schism in Romanian society. Romania has ever been rigidly delineated. At the turn of the century you were either a peasant or a land-owner, with the exception of a small urban class of bureaucrats. The Commissars removed the distinction of property, but in its place encouraged the classic Marxist divide between workers and intellectuals. The diatribe of the print-workers indicated these ideological divisions were set to endure.

The telex censor of the Mayor seemed unlikely to approve my story on the return of state censorship and so I caught the afternoon Antonov to Bucharest. In the early months of 1990 internal air-flights were still subsidised and cost under a dollar. For the British stringers the Antonovs became a much-loved taxi service. I composed a piece mid-air and three hours after leaving the print-works was in the warmth of the Hotel Bucharest, waiting for a telephone line. Newspapers like dispatches from exotic datelines. I rang George and suggested a trip to the Soviet border. At dawn the following morning I was back at Baneasa airport, once more arguing with officials, once more bound for Iaşi.

Second time round Iaşi seemed much more friendly. At the airline office there was a mini-delegation waiting. George had found a car to take us to the Soviet frontier even though he also had a wedding to film. The driver, who was meant to be on a mayorial mission to trace a missing British aid lorry, was standing to attention at his side. The local Peasant Party leader, Alexandru Butureanu, a grizzled survivor of the pre-war era, had heard the 'British press' were coming to town and had wandered over to stand me a drink.

It was 8 a.m. and I felt badly in need of sleep, or at least breakfast. The situation wasn't helped when Chris Stephen, the *Guardian* correspondent, who had flown with me from Bucharest, mistook Domnul Buţureanu for a vagrant.

'*Scusaţi, domnule!*' (Excuse me, mister!), he exclaimed, before reverting to English to shoo him away. Fortunately Butureanu spoke not a word of English and beamed in reply. He later took me aside and explained in fragmented French that '*Monsieur le Gwardienne*' was a very charming man.

Somehow we accommodated the variant plans. I seem to remember we had breakfast, then a drink with Buţureanu and then left on a fruitless search for the aid lorry. I must have slept for some of the journey. By midday we were bumping towards the Soviet border. My only nagging doubt is what happened about George's wedding.

Around the turn of the century Pavel Axelrod, one of Lenin's great comrades, declared that, taking into account Romania's national peasant character, 'not even the greatest optimist would dare entertain hopes that modern socialist ideals could take root in Romania.' Thirty years later, from a very different standpoint, Sir Sacheverell Sitwell closed his book expounding a similar view. His parting paragraphs expressed his hope and faith that the Romanian peasant would manage to survive intact the pains of industrialisation. Bumping down the road towards the frontier, overtaking clumpy carts with wooden wheels, slowing for gaggles (they do gaggle) of geese and passing oxen straining at the plough, I could appreciate the thinking of both commentators.

Idolisation of the peasant life has always seemed to me patronising. There is nothing romantic about depending for your wellbeing on the strength of your ploughshare or the vigour of your ox. The peasant existence in Moldavia is more about the despair of Steinbeck's *Grapes of Wrath* than the hayfields of Laurie Lee. But even so, in Romania the urban slums are so wretched and the rural landscape is so beautiful that I can find myself agreeing with Sitwell's reverie about the rural life. There was something timeless about our road to the Soviet border. For fifteen hundred odd years until the nineteenth century South-East Europe was a recruiting ground-cum-battlefield, and agricultural advances had to come second to defence or subservience. The result was the Balkan peasant, semi-literate, superstitious and sturdy, both a factor of stability and a brake on progress, the region's strength and yet also its weakness. In 1775, when Austria took over the Bukovina, they found no doctors, no bridges, no roads and only two or three recognized schools. At the turn of the century all the states of the Balkan peninsula were essentially peasant societies with an average per capita income of about a quarter of the industrialised economies of Western Europe. As we neared the Prut river it was easy to believe nothing had changed since the great Moldavian battles of the Middle Ages, fought by Mircea the Old, Bogdan the One-Eyed and other local heroes.

Our goal was Ungheni, a village straddling the Prut river, the frontier with the Soviet Union since 1940. Skirted with fruit trees, dependent on grapes and melons for a living, low, small and poor, Ungheni appeared little different from rural communities all over Romania. Under the soft mid-March sun there was a mellow feel in the air which spoke of lazy summer days and long siestas. But for Ungheni-ans, particularly of the older generations, their village could never be normal. When we arrived it had been divided for a few months short of half a century. The barrier, a barbed-wire fence on the far bank of the Prut, was nothing like as impressive as the Berlin Wall. You could even argue the divide made little difference, as ideologically the two halves of Ungheni were run on the same drab lines. But for the villagers, romance, over-the-fence gossip, sharing a *ţuica*, comparing turnip size, all were impossible.

Leaning against a pig-waggon, four or five elderly people were resting from herding their livestock. The tallest was barely five foot. In their peasant smocks and hats and with their brown gnarled faces they looked like the dwarfs in childrens' illustrated versions of Tolkien. All could remember the pre-war days and they gathered round the foreign visitors like conspirators, telling of their Heros and Leanders.

'My father was from that side and married a girl from this side.' Lazar Rotoru, a crinkle-cut septuagenarian, broke off to cackle something unintelligible and another took up the tale.

'Ah, but that was in the good old days when our girls married the boys over there and their girls married the boys over here. When the change came, at first we would swim across the water.'

The others butted in with a chorus of '*Libertate, libertate*'. They were full of dark rumours of how all the Romanian meat was transported by rail through their village to the Soviet Union. They pointed across the water to their sundered fellow villagers on the other bank. It seemed so tantalisingly close. A Russian soldier wandered into sight, pointed at my camera and shook his head.

Eighteen months passed before I reached the left bank of Ungheni. It was like completing a pilgrimage. It was a fortnight after the anti-Gorbachev coup attempt of autumn

1991 and there were the same dusty roads, the same Moldavian costumes, the same lethargic life-style, the same
shrunken peasants. One old man asked me into his garden,
barely fifty yards from where I had seen the Red Army
soldier. He spoke Romanian in a high-pitched twang and
sometimes lapsed into Russian. We toasted the future of
Moldavia.

'All this coming and going the politicians insist on doing,'
he said. 'Moldova. Romania. Russia. Who cares? I wish
they would just leave us to live and die in peace.'

It was a sentiment with which I heartily agreed. But two
years later it is a *cri de coeur* which echoes bitterly all over
the former Yugoslavia and storm-clouds continue to hover
over other parts of South-East Europe, including Moldavia.

Such gloomy prognostications were far from our thoughts
in March 1990 as we leaned against the pig-cart, inhaled
the rough smells and enjoyed the coarse jokes of the peasants. We left Ungheni much too late. A wedding invitation
from Lazar Rotoru took concerted agonising to decline.
George, an urban animal, seemed as enthralled by our
venture into 'Arcadia' as his British companions. A strong
vein of neo-peasant romanticism runs in many Romanians,
which to Ceauşescu's frustration he failed to eliminate. A
country house, a flagon of wine, these are the weekend
loves of the city-dweller; Romanian writers still tend to go
Tibullan about the joys of the pastoral life. Speeding for
the plane we skidded into a wooden bridge and for a few
moments the Dacia's front wheels span tantalisingly over a
river – our driver was, I'm convinced, still dreaming of a
pad in the country.

There are moments, not many, when you can't complain
about the old ways. Iaşi airport provided one of them.
Nowhere in the West would a flight let you board a few
minutes before take-off. The Moldavian air-hostess even
smiled a welcome.

'*Foarte bine* (very good) – just in time.'

Bucharest seemed like a metropolis after the north-east. It
felt good to be back. I retired home through the plane trees

and poplars of Cismigiu Park, tripping occasionally in the darkness, confident that the shadows held nothing sinister. An ex-police state will always be safer than an established liberal democracy – at least for a time. After the revolution there was a general amnesty and all the prison cells were emptied. Shortly afterwards the first crime figures for several decades indicated a massive increase in violent crime. This impression was enhanced by the television news which loved to focus on the gory murder and rape cases. But I suspected that the figures were exaggerated. In the early days after the revolution most criminals were as 'shy' as the police.

Back at Cobalcescu the cockroaches in the kitchen seemed more presumptuous and unbearable than before and my sleeping bag was suddenly looking a bit forlorn. It was the middle of March and Barbel and Sabine had left for the spring long holiday. The taps were croaking and refusing to offer water. The only food was a bowl of *mamaliga* (maize porridge) and dry bread. Maybe it was time to return to England, re-equip and reassess. 'Moldavia, been (twice) and done,' I wrote in my diary, with the smugness that accompanies a long day's running around and the successful securing of a phone line, blissfully unaware that in the Transylvanian town of Tîrgu Mureş, two hundred miles to the north-west, an ethnic Hungarian shop-owner had just repainted the sign above his pharmacy, using the Hungarian word *gyogyzertar* as well as the Romanian *farmacie*, and thereby inadvertently lit the fuse for one of Europe's most explosive ethnic flare-ups in several years.

Seasons can change overnight in the Balkans. During my two-day absence in Moldavia, spring had arrived. The diehard cakes of ice had disappeared from the potholes and linden-tree blossom was starting to soften the avenues. In the centre, the street corners were alive with the garish headscarves of gipsy flower-sellers, released from the purdah of winter clothing. Short dresses and shirt sleeves were in vogue. There were even the first baskets of fruit for sale – a joy after the winter's rigorous diet of pickles and meat. Of course the trams still groaned as if on their last run and the acres of urban wasteland left by Ceauşescu were no nearer completion. But the city looked cleaner and fresher, less down at heel. There was a briskness in the air. Even the pimps who clustered like harpies around the foyer of the Hotel Bucharest were willing to exchange more than a passing insult.

The change of weather was not conducive to journalism. I spent the afternoon in dilettante-style outside the main army barracks vaguely trying to pin down rumours of an armed forces summit. Nervous sentries kept suggesting I try the next gate along – anything to pass on the responsibility. Lacking purpose, enjoying the sun, I complied. The base commander was always 'on the point' of being free for an interview. The army hierarchs, I realized, were not as accessible as their ecclesiastical counterparts. When the Ministry of Defence announced the formation of a press bureau, they made the number confidential. The most I could glean was a thumbs-up from young officers filing back to their barracks. I toyed with a few phrases like 'A top secret meeting ended yesterday with army officers departing in a jubilant mood' and stopped, realizing that I knew absolutely nothing. I drifted back to the press centre to inform the *Telegraph* that it would be a day without a story, one of the first for several weeks.

It had obviously been a quiet day as the press centre was empty. Rather than rushing to place an order for the *Telegraph*, I called Sophie and made plans to meet in London at the weekend. Not even the three-hour wait for an air ticket at the headquarters of Tarom, Romanian state airlines, could break the spell. I was going to London and there were just two days to go. I bumped into an American missionary whom I had met in January and he suggested dinner at the Hotel Athenée Palace. I accepted with alacrity.

The doorman at the Athenée Palace could be the bandmaster from Trumpton, so glistening are his buttons, so scarlet his uniform and so bushy his moustache. The hotel's reputation is as flamboyant. In the thirties it was Bucharest's number one night-spot and a centre for Balkan intrigue.

Foreign correspondents based themselves there to cover
Romania's slide towards dictatorship. Olivia Manning gives
a lively account of the Romanian aristocracy flitting between
the rival German and British delegations at opposite ends of
the bar. In the fifties it was refitted as a Securitate monitoring post and became home to the corrupt and the powerful.
Red Horizons, the lurid memoirs of Ion Pacepa, Ceauşescu's
counter-intelligence chief who defected in 1978, offers a
welter of tales about the frolics of the nomenclatura in the
Athenée Palace. The most spicy centre on Nicu Ceauşescu,
the heir apparent of the dictator. In one anecdote, when the
lights are dimmed for the arrival of crepes suzettes, Nicu is
found in flagrante with a party official's wife. Even if
embroidered by the CIA, as has been widely reported, *Red
Horizons* gives a convincing flavour of communist rule.
Juvenal would have recognized the frailties of the luminaries
of Romania's Communist Party.

My host 'Bill' Earl Macdonough and his twelve missionar-
ies from Partners in Progress, Little Rock, Arkansas were
incongrous guests at such a notorious spot. They were
among a wave of proselytisers who invaded Romania after
the fall of Ceauşescu. Most treated Romanians as wayward
children to be lectured and chided and I grew to despise
them for their condescension. But I warmed to Bill, a
cheery open-hearted man with a genuine interest in Romania's past. They were celebrating their successful tour. I
was celebrating my imminent trip home: it was caviar,
chateaubriand and champagne all round.

By the time the ice-creams arrived, magnificent multi-
layered constructions topped with fake cream, the band was
striking up the lambada and the fat cats were taking to the
floor in their silvery suits and co-respondent shoes. In the
days that followed the revolution the lambada became the
unofficial anthem. Three years later I wince to hear its
distinctive catchy beat. As the tempo steps up I am transported into the midst of a nightmarish vision of portly
apparatchiks wiggling their hips, clapping their hands and
showering the band with grubby bank notes . . . I stayed
late and stumbled home, dreaming of London.

At breakfast the next morning I was still humming the lambada when I tuned into the BBC World Service. The lead item was from Romania. In the Transylvanian town of Tîrgu Mureş fighting had broken out between Romanians and ethnic Hungarians, vicious primeval fighting with scythes and pitchforks. Several people were reported dead. It was agonisingly clear why the press centre had been so deserted. While I had been enjoying the afternoon sun, my friends and rivals had seen an item on the state news agency Rompres, hurried to the domestic airport and caught the last flight to Tîrgu Mureş. It was lesson number umpteen and something: watch your colleagues' every move. Tîrgu Mureş was two hundred miles away and all phone lines to Bucharest were down. Mine was a sombre breakfast. I cancelled my ticket home.

Transylvania, the land tucked within the horseshoe of the Carpathians, is a name to conjure with. Mention it at a dinner party in London and the eyes and ears of those untuned to the complexities of East European geography will light up – well, sometimes. Bram Stoker, the nineteenth-century author of *Dracula*, did for Transylvania what Lord Byron did for Greece – albeit in a less literary or romantic fashion. His incarnation of a blood-sucking count flitting between the cemeteries of Hampstead and a castle in Central Europe plucked Transylvania into the public eye and subsequent black-cloaked elaborations have enthralled Western readers and cinema-goers for over a century. Stoker's novel was the nineteenth century's equivalent of a block buster. That his Dracula bears scant resemblance to his historical role-model, the fifteenth-century prince Vlad Ţepeş (pronounced Tsepesh, the Impaler) has been almost forgotten.

For Romanian historians this is a source of deep grievance. Not only was Ţepeş a Wallachian and not a Transylvanian, but he is something of a hero, featuring prominently in Romania's gallery of champions for his stalwart defiance of the Turks. Ţepeş (son of Vlad Dracul, meaning the Dragon) appears to have been a cross between Richard the Lionheart and Genghis Khan, probably more of the latter than the former. The name Dracula is generally believed to be a corruption of Draculea, meaning son of Dracul. His speciality was impaling recalcitrant subjects, whether too rich, poor or hungry, on sharpened stakes. But while barbarous even by the standards of the late Middle Ages, he did see off the Turks at a time when the states of West Europe were too busy fighting one another to tackle the Ottoman threat. Ţepeş lowest or finest hour (depending on which side you take) came in 1462 when he decapitated thousands of Turkish prisoners outside his capital Tîrgovişte and made a forest of their corpses. Balkan chroniclers record with glee that the scene of horror drove a Turkish invasion force under Sultan Mehmet II back to Constantinople in confusion.

Ceauşescu claimed that the West's portrayal of Dracula was an attempt to discredit Romania and his panegyrists rallied to the cause. Virgil Candea, a Romanian historian writing in the 1970s, describes Stoker as 'an obscure modern novelist' and Vlad as 'a valiant fighter for the freedom of his people, who, like so many of his contemporaries, punished his opponents by impaling them.' I feel disinclined to defend Vlad's reputation. But Transylvania is another matter. Forget the haunted castles and the howling wolves. Think instead of forested hills, not firs but hard-woods, oaks and beeches, laid out for mile after mile, presenting a landscape of a glory lost for centuries to contemporary England. Transylvania has five million Romanians and 1.7 million ethnic Hungarians. It's easy to understand why both peoples like to regard it as the cradle of their culture: the Transylvanian paysage has everything that the flatlands of Wallachia and the endless Hungarian plain lack. What is less straightforward and certainly less pleasurable to explain is how three months after fighting together against Ceauşescu the two peoples could start fighting each other in the worst ethnic violence in Romania since the Second World War and the most serious in Europe since the end of communism. The Tîrgu Mureş conflict of 19 and 20 March 1990 thrust the issue of minority rights to the attention of the West when we were still celebrating the fall of the Iron

Curtain. In time it would be seen as a signpost of the potential horrors dogging post-Soviet Europe and most especially Yugoslavia.

It took me over a month to understand the dynamics of the Tîrgu Mureş troubles. The *Telegraph* despatched the Belgrade correspondent, Michael Montgomery, to Transylvania and I was ordered to cover the story from Bucharest. It was not an easy task. If ever a Balkan city was awash with Byzantine conspiracies it was Bucharest during the 'Tîrgu Mureş days'. After a few hours' silence, as if to test the air, Rompres poured out a stream of suspiciously one-sided ticker-tape. Fired up by exaggerated state media reports of pogroms against Romanians, Bucharest became a pressure cooker in which no one knew what to think. Rumours and counter-rumours criss-crossed on the street, in bread queues, in lift-shafts, in stairwells. The Romanian government lost all semblance of control and issued a hysterical statement accusing Budapest of provoking the trouble. Romanian prime minister Petre Roman even claimed that the Iron Guard (the 1930s fascist movement) was involved. He didn't elaborate if he meant seventy-year-old veterans or a new generation. Conspiracies are entertaining enough on the quiet days when as a journalist you have the time and patience to grin politely. But they are hell in a crisis when time is tight and they flourish like mould on damp bread. In the Hotel Bucharest everyone from the porters to the telephone operators had their own bizarre theory. With one person it was the Freemasons, with another the Securitate, with a third the international Hungarian plot.

With phones to Tîrgu Mureş jammed, it was impossible to corroborate or disprove the Romanian media reports. My office in London which had access to the international news agencies, knew more about the situation than I did. But I realized this was not the right impression to give them and so I played a double game. On the telephone to London I pretended I was in full control and accepted tit-bits of information as if they were old news. 'Oh, right. Really. Well that's interesting you say that . . .' Meanwhile my interpreter, Mihai, and I were desperately searching for someone who knew what was happening. Discreetly omitting to tell London that the other British correspondents had scooped me, for the first time (and I hope the last) I even privately expressed a hope that my colleagues would be unable to transmit their dispatches. For once I was free from the standard journalistic wrench between the thrill of a good story and abhorrence at suffering – I was praying the situation would calm down. At night I scribbled depressed diary entries that the readers of the *Daily Telegraph* were being 'short-changed'. My despondency was increased by fruitless hours on the telephone, until, with a note of triumph, Mihai announced that he had traced the head of the Bucharest branch of the *Vatra Romaneasca* (Romanian Hearth), the main Romanian nationalist organization.

'Vatra' sounds like the evil mastermind of a Buck Rogers classic, which in contemporary Hungarian mythology is exactly what it is. The Vatra organizers liked to make out they were a cross between the Heritage Trust and Jimmy Shand and His Band and stressed they were founded as a Romanian patriotic and cultural organization. But if these 'homely' ideals were ever the intention, Vatra swiftly became a mouthpiece for Ceauşescuite xenophobia. Culture ceded to politics at every opportunity. I climbed the stairs of the Bucharest branch anticipating a hell-fire and brimstone demagogue, particularly as the Vatra president Radu Ceontea had just been on air saying Romanians were launching a 'spontaneous counter-revolt' and so were mildly surprised to be met by a calm and courteous man in his late middle age and a grey suit. Valentin Borda looked like a provincial British bank manager. He ushered me into his office, offered a coffee and came straight to the point.

'Do you know when the Magyars came to Transylvania? To be exact, yes, to be precise, in the tenth or eleventh century . . . They were conquering lands that were already Romanian . . . Now, of course we consider that both people can live peacefully . . . But look at history. You will see we have been there much longer . . . Do we now have to defend our culture against these relative newcomers? Is that fair?'

I broached the standard logical Western replies. I suggested that the situation had changed since 1940 (when Hungary under Hitler's protection took half of Transylvania) and that Hungary was more interested in furthering links with the EC than risking a territorial squabble. I pointed out that Hungary, with only fourteen million people, had no strategic interest in fighting with its larger neighbour. I gestured to the map to 'remind' Borda that the bulk of the Magyars lived in the counties of Harghita and Covasna, two hundred miles from Hungary, rendering a border change wholly impractical. It was all wasted breath.

'Ah, but wait a little,' retorted Borda. 'They talk of their rights, the right to speak, in their own tongue and so on. But that's not what they really want. Pure and simple they want one thing, to join with Hungary. Are we to sit back and let it happen? We don't want to fight. But if someone hits me I'll hit him back, is that not so? Imagine if the Muslims in Bradford tried to break away and link up with the Middle East. Would you like that in England?'

I came away with little to add to the day's despatch but a useful insight into the intensity and illogicality of Balkan thinking. For both Romanian and Hungarian nationalists, the centuries of peaceful co-habitation are irrelevant. All that matters is the historical question of who was there first. The Romanians insist they are the blue-blooded descendants of Romanised Dacians who retreated to the hills after the departure of Aurelian in 271. The Hungarian camp counter-trumpets that when the Magyars charged down the steppe they found Transylvania deserted. To an outsider there is an obvious compromise, namely that some Dacians did stay behind after the Romans left, but that they survived by mixing with incoming tribes. Most of my Romanian friends adopt this more moderate view which helps to account for the varied Romanian physiognomy. However, the lack of any firm historical evidence leaves the question open to the tampering and indulgence of both sides. In the Balkans where states have young borders, people have long memories and the past is often seen as more important than the present. After his walk through Transylvania in the

1930s, Patrick Leigh Fermor uttered a heart-felt prayer that some forester would stumble on a long-hidden case of papers which had survived the Mongol destruction and would settle the debate once and for all. But as he later concedes, such a find would do little good.

On quiet days in February fellow-stringers had hammered home to me the journalistic precept of getting both versions of a story. And so on successive mornings of the Tîrgu Mureş crisis I sat in the parliament building listening to Ladislau Lorintz, the ethnic Hungarian representative on Romania's minority rights commission. Like many old communist-trained officials, Lorintz appeared taken aback at first to be interviewed by someone less than half his age. For old hacks, trained in and treasuring the cult of grey hair, it was a shock to be questioned by their juniors. Time after time politicians would assume I was a trainee (which I suppose I was).

Lorintz suffered from the endemic Balkan problem of a selective memory. Referring to the 'civilizing role' of the Hungarians he avoided mention of the 1920s and 1930s when Hungary was ruled by a fascist dictator. He also omitted to point out that under Habsburg rule Transylvania was the least developed part of the Austro-Hungarian Empire and that the Hungarian barons had treated Romanians like serfs. The Hungarians have always been better at public relations than the Romanians and have consequently on the Transylvanian question attracted more support than they deserve. However, in hindsight, re-reading my old notebooks, I find my sessions with Lorintz did give a reasonable assessment of aspects of the problem. I only wish I had trusted him more at the time. In March 1990 I was so bombarded by rival propaganda that I assumed everyone was distorting the truth. And so I tended to reject everything I heard. This was a failure that I and many other journalists would repeat disastrously when covering the war in Yugoslavia in 1991, where in an obsession with balance we obscured the one-sided course of the fighting.

'We are dealing with two typical national tendencies here,' said Lorintz, after one particularly inept and ill-

informed question. 'After the revolution the Magyars
wanted to re-establish their lost rights, classes in their
mother tongue, and they pushed ahead maybe a little
recklessly, without waiting for a go-ahead from the Romanians ... Then there's another typical tendency, that of the
Romanians. They are much too jumpy. They just work
themselves into a frenzy, chanting the old Ceauşescu slogans
that the Hungarians want to take over Transylvania. You
see they are stirred up by people who want to hang on to
the privileges they held under Ceauşescu. Then of course
you have to look way back to the old Ottoman Habsburg
divide . . .'

With his final comment Lorintz was touching on one of
the major dynamics of the Transylvanian problem, the
cultural and religious split between the Catholic and the
Orthodox worlds, or as Hungarians would say between
West and East. It is a question which has achieved much
greater airing in the West since the eruption of the Serb/
Croat conflict in the former Yugoslavia. It is as important a
factor in Transylvania. The Romanian nationalist scribes
cover their pages with 'scandal' about the 'Vatican conspiracy'. Their opposite numbers in Budapest scribble as
demonically about Romania's 'barbarian Turkish legacy'.
Would that I had allowed Lorintz to talk on. As it was,
obsessed with finding out specifics about Tîgu Mureş, I
interrupted his flow and drew the interview to an end.

After forty-eight hours of fighting, woefully late, the authorities deployed tanks and troops on the streets, the situation
eased and my colleagues traipsed back to Bucharest. Later
the government tried to re-write history and claimed that
the troops were in place when the conflict began. Over a
welcome-back-to-Bucharest meal, Marc Champion and
Chris Stephen gave a very different account. On the first
night the mayor's office bussed down hundreds of Romanian
peasants, filled them with ţuica, handed out weapons and
pointed them to the headquarters of the Hungarian party.
Only on the second day, when the Hungarians started to
bus in their own peasants, did the authorities call in the

soldiers. It was a sorry story of manipulation and mismanagement.

Looking back three years later, I am firmly and a little bitterly convinced that the business of politics bears the largest responsibility for 'ethnic' flare-ups such as happened at Tîrgu Mureş. It is fashionable in the West to invoke history as the scapegoat and an excuse for post-communist conflicts. 'Ancestral fault-lines, antique feuds', intone the armchair analysts time and again. It's true the Balkans have a long record of instability and also of inter-communal violence. But history is neither a reason nor an explanation. It repeats itself only when leaders dabble in the mistakes of their predecessors and we should not allow this to be a given factor. Tîrgu Mureş was a copy-book ethnic squabble. Both sides had specific grievances. The Hungarians wanted to redress the injustices of communism and restore their old language rights. In their haste to take over schools, many Romanian teachers and pupils lost their classrooms mid-term. But this does not account for the six dead and hundreds wounded. For this you have to blame the politicians who, operating in an obviously sensitive environment, exploited the tensions for their own ends. Both Bucharest and Budapest made political capital from the incident. Later in 1990 and in 1991 Transylvania became a useful political issue, in sickening disregard for the ordinary people who live there and are the first to suffer the results of a rise in xenophobia.

Marc and Chris had agonised accounts of the difficulties of filing copy. With the phone lines down they relied on a telex machine, which for two days running managed to 'lose' their stories en route to the UK. Marc said wryly that by the time his stories reached London his foreign desk had lost interest. I was starting to feel a little more chipper when I met a Canadian photographer, Matt Glass. Matt had just returned from Tîrgu Mureş and his face was funereal with fatigue. He looked me up and down with a patronising disdain.

'I suppose you just have to know when to use an opportunity.'

4

Dabbling with Democracy

Bucharest, April to May 1990

'The poplar shall bring forth pears before socialism shall be overthrown in Romania' – *Nicolae Ceauşescu, December 1989*

As IF DAZED OR hung over, in the spring weather which followed the Tîrgu Mureş disturbances Romania quietened down. I slipped to England for a few days, caught up with the January rejection letter of my erstwhile would-be employer, and spent much of the time anxiously scanning the papers for news of Romania. On my return at the start of April with a bicycle, a portable computer, a press card and a mound of notebooks, I moved to the old Jewish quarter.

At my new lodgings the telephone cable was tangled up in the overhanging tree and was regularly disconnected by gusts of wind. I shared the kitchen with a particular persistent rat and the facade was, as one friend commented, 'more Beirut than Bucharest'. With mortar crumbling from between the bricks and only a few planks covering the windows, 28 Popa Soare was simple, even a little primitive. But it was also quiet, spacious, delightfully cool and my new landlady was blessed with many of Romania's good qualities and none of the bad.

On Saturday afternoons I would sit in the garden at the back and Doamna Patraşcu *would come running after me* with a rug, a plate of *sarmale* (stuffed cabbage leaves), sweet cakes and cherries, outraged that I was alone, amazed that I wanted to sit in the fresh air. Doamna Patraşcu looked like a little sparrow, a testimony to her seven years as a political prisoner in the 1950s, when she was half-starved and permitted to speak only in whispers. In winter she wore a jaunty pink beret, in summer faded flowery frocks, and she had a soft smile which told of her lifetime of suffering. I use the word landlady loosely as she refused to accept a *leu* in rent and insisted on calling me her '*baiat*' (boy). We communicated best in halting French mixed with a few words of Romanian and a few of English.

Doamna Patraşcu was too busy looking after her mother, who suffered from Alzheimers, to dwell on the past. I learned her story in dribs and drabs over the following months. The essence was tragically, brutally simple and a testimony to how the day-to-day horror of communist rule affected the lives of the ordinary and the innocent. It began one afternoon in 1958 when she stopped off at her aunt's, where she met a friend of the family who was passing through. She thought no more about the encounter until the police came to her door a few days later. The man at her aunt's table had been Josif Capota, an opposition politician who had been on the run for eleven years for refusing to falsify election results for the communists. The day after he met Doamna Patraşcu he was betrayed by a local thief trying to get off his sentence. Capota was sentenced to death and everyone he had met in his fugitive years, including Doamna Patraşcu and 270 people from her aunt's village, were thrown into prison. Doamna Patraşcu shared a cell with fifty people and they were punished by turns in solitary confinement; no one in her family knew her whereabouts. After her release in 1964, in penance for her 'crime', she was ordered to work in Cîmpulung, a small town four hours from Bucharest. All this happened before Ceauşescu came to power, a stark reminder that those who tried to blame Romania's troubles on Ceauşescu and to exonerate communism were radically rearranging the truth.

Doamna Patraşcu's husband, an Orthodox priest, had spent even longer in prison on an equally trifling charge and their eldest son, Mihai, who slept in the room next to mine, had, after four months of the new regime, made up his mind to emigrate. Refreshed after my break, I argued with Mihai that he was the hope for the future and should

stay to help his country. It was easy as a foreigner with a
Western passport to take the moral high ground. But it was
an argument I could never put with confidence when I
thought of his mother – seven years in prison and twenty-
five under observation, merely for setting eyes on the wrong
person.

Five minutes' bumpy cycling from the centre, Popa
Soare became my home and the *Daily Telegraph*'s base for
the elections, Romania's first exercise in democracy in fifty-
three years. The poll date was set for 20 May. Pumping up
my bike tyres on my first night back. I remember thinking
that seven weeks was not nearly long enough for me to
come to grips with the complexities of Romanian politics. It
was certainly not long enough for the Romanians to come
to grips with the unfamiliar obligations of democracy.

With the obvious exception of ancient Greece, democracy
in the Balkans has shaky foundations. On a July day in 1857
the Balkans held what was arguably their first election in
modern history. It set a poor precedent. The poll was in
Moldavia where twenty thousand-odd electors (hardly a full
franchise but a start) were voting to decide whether Moldavia (then under Ottoman suzerainty) should unite with
Wallachia. However, so brazenly did the Turks rig the
register, that barely 11 per cent of the electorate were able
to vote. One of the shabbiest aspects of the whole affair was
the role of the British government, which co-operated in
the fraud with an unseemly enthusiasm. The Palmerstonian
school of foreign policy, pragmatism over principle, was in
vogue. Gladstone's head of steam about the 'terrible Turk'
was a decade in the future.

The corruption of the 1857 poll seems to have permeated
the Balkans' subsequent dabblings with democracy. Britain
at the start of the nineteenth-century, with its pocket and
rotten boroughs, provides one of the most apt analogies for
Balkan voting procedures after 1918, when the situation in
Romania, Bulgaria and Yugoslavia bore little resemblance
to Western norms of democracy. The Balkan peninsula held
off from autocracy longer than Central Europe, which fell

prey to the lure of fascism. However, in the 1930s, affected by the world economic slump, Romania spiralled between varying shades of misrule and accompanied Bulgaria and Yugoslavia down the road towards royal dictatorship. The elections after the war were a rigged farce.

In the spring of 1990 the spectres of this 'democratic' past were lurking malevolently behind the scenes. Judy Dempsey, the forthright *Financial Times* correspondent for Eastern Europe and a Balkan veteran from the mid-eighties, had an acerbic line for Romania: 'All form and no content.' This was never more relevant than in the May 1990 elections. Although there were eighty-three parties registered, only one stood a chance.

With the kudos of replacing Ceauşescu, the National Salvation Front couldn't lose. Their policy of 'live and let live' won over most of the three million-odd ex-Party members. The Party media, coffers and muscle reinforced an impregnable position. While in programme the Front espoused a pragmatic liberalisation, in practice it resorted to the shenanigans of the past. State television was hopelessly partisan. In outlying districts the opposition faced intimidation and were often too scared to open an office. Part by design and part by tradition, Iliescu, the Front's presidential candidate, developed a personality cult eerily reminiscent of the support whipped up for Ceauşescu in his early days in power. While Ceauşescu had adopted ludicrous epithets for himself like 'the Genius of the Carpathians', at Front rallies in spring 1990 the crowds roared that when Iliescu smiled the sun came out.

Arrayed against the Front were two reborn pre-war parties, the National Liberal Party and the National Peasant Party. Led by silver-haired cabals with an average age of seventy, they emerged from their four-decade ban like elderly war horses for a last joust. Full of the ideals of the anti-communist crusade, they were woefully out of touch with the realities of the electorate. It didn't help that both their presidential candidates, Ion Raţiu for the Peasant Party and Radu Câmpeanu for the Liberals, were emigrés who after the revolution returned from exile in the West.

Both had impeccable anti-communist credentials. Câmpeanu was a political prisoner for six years in the 1950s. In 1978 when the Ceauşescus were at a state banquet at Claridges, Raţiu tied himself to the railings outside and had to be dragged away by the Metropolitan Police. However, both were white-haired old men whose years abroad pandered to the communist caricature of 'bogyman' capitalists coming to buy up the country. Front newspapers assiduously reminded readers that the two 'outsiders' had not shared the suffering under Ceauşescu – the fact that the Front leaders had been part of the old system was conveniently forgotten. Over late-night drinks with other stringers after my return, increasingly the only question was not 'Who?' but 'By how much?' and the most heated issue was whether the Front would deign to give the opposition a fair chance.

Seen with fresh eyes, Bucharest had shrugged off the winter's gloom and appeared to be taking to pluralism with a vengeance. In the centre every street corner was an impromptu talking shop. Politics was the buzz topic of conversation. To form a political party you only needed two hundred and fifty signatures and coalitions and counter-coalitions mushroomed. In Ceauşescu's designer boulevard, the Victory of Socialism, or as Romanians dubbed it, 'the Boulevard of the Victory of Socialism over the people', a tower block was set aside as offices for the new parties. All over the country, printing presses were churning out fliers for the new political formations. I still have a drawer of blurred leaflets bearing portentous titles with the catchwords 'Democratic', 'Liberal', 'Free', 'Independent'.

If you ignored the shouts of foul play emanating from the opposition headquarters, you could pretend a normal Western campaign was underway. The Central Electoral Bureau, which was masterminding the elections, was full of professors talking lofty fair-minded principles. The election law itself was a model of democratic procedure. Among the Front activists in Bucharest were bright young things, who, although the offspring of nomenclatura, appreciated that communism was finished and talked sensibly of the 'free market' and liberal reform. Their election posters and slick (well, quite slick) TV ads were the closest Romania came to US-style razzmatazz.

However, in the provinces the gospel of change was having a harder time. News of the revolution had hardly percolated through to the outlying districts of Romania where the grass-roots branches of the Front operated as they knew best. The manipulation was not copybook totalitarianism. The only man killed in the campaign, Vasile Velescu, a Peasant Party representative in the Moldavian village of Roşiori, was, it turned out, the victim of a personal feud, not a political disagreement, as was first reported. But while the Front leaders moaned that foreign correspondents were biased against them, they made little attempt to curb the 'zeal' of their heavies. Would-be opposition politicians in the country had to endure threats and stones at the windows. A number of Peasant Party branches were attacked. As a correspondent, the most extraordinary thing was that it wasn't remotely difficult to pin down the skulduggery, as I realized one spring morning when I looked at a map, picked a spot in the Carpathians a few hours' drive from Bucharest and decided to see how the campaign was going.

Contrary to the journalistic guidelines of competition and rivalry, foreign correspondents seldom travel alone. Sometimes this is for reasons of security. More often it's for camaraderie. In Romania it was the latter, and on this trip I was in particularly good company. My interpreter, Simona Răuţă, a student friend from the Carpathians, had a slender frame and delicate features which belied the standard bread-heavy Romanian diet; unlike many Romanian young women, she eschewed the garish make-up beloved in the Balkans. With us was a newly-arrived Swiss journalist, Arianne Genillard, who 'power-dressed' as if she had just stepped off Central Avenue. With Arianne in the first flush of captivation with Romania, and Simona chattering about her ambition of finishing medical studies in the West, it was a happy car and we were soon winding past the Royal Palace in Sinaia and into the Carpathians.

We opted for ambience as well as electoral atmosphere and on Simona's advice tried our luck in Poiana Mărului (The Apple's Meadow), a hamlet which in landscape although not amenities could have been Swiss. The mayor was resting from chopping logs and he ushered us in for a glass of *ţuica*. He was only too happy to talk about the local state of play.

'If I can tell you something sincere, from the bottom of my heart [with a grab of the arm] – strictly my own personal opinion, you understand – we have no problems of violence here. And you know why? There are no opposition parties. The Peasant Party was here before the war, but, you see, we didn't like it. Old people in the village advise us to keep away from them.'

With his bluff red face, just over the average peasant intelligence and love of communist clichés, Gheorghe Orzenica was an archetypal functionary of the old school. He had been re-elected after the revolution and with a hint of pride confided that the local farmers would vote according to his recommendation. Conditioned by his upbringing, he paraded the old propaganda.

'The Peasant Party will bankrupt us and sell our land.'

But he was a good-humoured man and, with a shrug of his shoulders and a 'You'd do better to stay here', willingly pointed us towards the nearest Peasant Party branch, in the weapons-producing town of Zarneşti. Our visit didn't last long.

The first man we asked for the Peasant Party's headquarters made as if to spit in our face. The next one laughed and pointed to an elderly man shuffling past on the other side of the road.

'Ask him,' he said. The man in question almost jumped in fear.

It was early evening and he spoke for barely a minute. I cannot recall the man's face, and he wouldn't give his name, but the skeleton of his story is scribbled in my notebook. He was sixty-three, had spent two years in a labour camp in the fifties on the communists' abortive project to build a Black Sea Canal, and his eyes shifted constantly behind us in case someone was watching.

'I wanted to set up a branch for the Peasant Party but they said it was not welcome here. There were stones at the windows and threatening phone calls. You see in a small place like this you can't take risks.' Simona was too sensitive to his unease to insist on any more questions. We whispered to her to ask who 'they' were and why he hadn't called the police. The man's voice rose as if at the absurdity of our question.

'Complain to the police? You would get a few surprises if you did a thing like that,' and he scuttled away down the road.

Ventures to the Zarneştis of Romania were profoundly depressing. The future for democracy in Romania seemed bleak. But my pessimism could never last long. While the Front was not democratic, it was far from Ceauşescuism and, on the campaign trail with the opposition, the Balkans' tendency to the bizarre and the burlesque kept impinging.

This was Romania's first democratic election since 1937 and there were times when it seemed little had changed in the intervening years. The Liberal and Peasant parties revived their old pre-war election symbols and their election-eering was all about dark conference rooms, chain-smoking and endless cups of coffee. To improve his image, Ion Raţiu of the Peasant Party brought in an adviser from a West End p.r. firm, a six-and-half foot ex-British army officer called Bertie Way. Bertie strode around Bucharest in a blazer and brogues like a character from P.G. Wodehouse. He only added to the theatre. One night he asked me for dinner and, over 'a spot of chow', talked about 'getting a head of steam up for the old boy . . . setting the band-waggon rolling, that sort of thing.' I enjoyed the meal, warmed to Bertie in his impossible task and privately assumed that someone in London was playing a mammoth practical joke.

For most of the campaign the politicians stayed in Bucharest. When the Liberal leader Radu Câmpeanu decided to take his band-waggon to Transylvania, most of the stringers made a firm date in their diary – not least because the first venue was the town of Sibiu, which was noted for its beauty. After missing a lift with some of the other correspondents, I caught the night train and arrived on Sibiu's outskirts before dawn. It was the start of a classic rollercoaster of a weekend covering the shifts and turns of Balkan politics.

Sibiu was a different world from the hubbub of the Gara de Nord. The apricots and blues of the old merchants' houses and trade towers look their best in the early-morning light. Walking through the old quarter as the sun came up made my jolting five-hour train ride worthwhile. The capital of the *Siebenburgen* (the seven medieval Saxon cities of Transylvania), Sibiu has a nine hundred year tradition as a cosmopolitan market centre and a liberal ethos which communism never managed to eliminate. The Saxons arrived in the twelfth century, invited by the Magyars to repopulate the wasteland left by the Mongols. Architecturally their legacy could fittingly be compared with Augustus' transformation of the city of Rome. When Augustus was near death, according to his biographer Suetonius, he boasted that he had found Rome in brick and left it in marble. The achievements of the medieval stonemasons of Sibiu were as striking, in a region previously known only for its flimsy structures, designed for hasty evacuation in the event of a raid.

Near the station many of the houses were shuttered and barred and I airily presumed that the townsfolk of Sibiu were leisurely risers. Later I thought differently. In 1978 Ceauşescu started to auction Romania's Germans to West Germany. Twelve thousand a year were allowed to leave at eight thousand marks a head. After the revolution the controlled exodus became a flood. When the Liberal election team came to town, Sibiu's German population was already down by two thirds on its pre-revolution figure and many of the surrounding villages were deserted. Between 1978 and 1992 Romania's German community dropped from three hundred and fifty thousand to less than a hundred and twenty thousand. For centuries the Saxons have had a moderating and civilizing influence on Transylvania. Even in the Second World War they tried to stay neutral and defied summons from Berlin to join the *Wehrmacht*. Now, like the Jews, they seem destined to die out of Romania's society – a tragedy for the peoples who remain.

Sibiu deserves hours of attention. But that morning my investigation had to go on hold. With a puff of red dust, half an hour after my arrival, the Liberal campaign team touched down on Sibiu airfield, narrowly avoiding pancaking on the rolling plain. The tour was underway.

In the reception hall, through the glass of the console, could be seen an Antonov, with its propellers slowing to a gentle whirr. Down came the gangplank. Beside me the welcome committee of four or five grey-suited delegates nervously brushed their lapels one last time. Câmpeanu, who was tipped as the most credible challenger to Iliescu, paused in the doorway, as if before an audience of thousands, and started the long walk across the airfield. In his long black coat, with his immaculately combed white hair and his imperious smile, he looked like a cross between a Sicilian godfather and a Byzantine noble.

After a minute of embraces, there was a revving of car engines and the motorcade of Dacias shot off – catching out a local photographer who fiddled with his lens once too often, missed his shot, and was left scrabbling with his equipment and desperate for a lift. I had met with the other correspondents, who had hitched a lift with Owen Bennett-Jones, the BBC stringer. Liviu, a local journalist friend, was sharing a ride. He grinned: 'Welcome to electioneering Balkan-style,' and we were off, down the long, straight road from the airport, with lights flashing and horns tooting, the kings of the road.

An excited police driver was in close attendance, jabbering into his walkie talkie. Somehow a tractor had bisected the convoy. Barely half a minute behind came the photographer, who had found – or maybe commandeered – a Trabant, which he was flogging along at a prodigious pace. With more tooting and more flashing lights, we swept into Sibiu, past people bent double with sacks of radishes and onions who were making for the stalls for market day. Like showmen with a prize exhibit, Câmpeanu's team screeched to a halt outside the Hotel Impăratul Romanilor (The Roman Emperor) and rushed inside.

'Talks, very important discussions. We are planning something massive,' blurted out Adrian, a self-important Liberal activist with an appropriately large briefcase. 'You wait,' he added later, emerging from the boardroom where Câmpeanu was ensconced with the party faithful. 'It will be worth it; we're going to shock you with a scandal, a big scandal . . .'

We had heard such talk before. Balkan 'scandals', while never dull, are seldom verified. As suspected, the meetings lasted all morning, beyond a midday round of *ţuica* and into the afternoon, while thousands of peasants came and went with their produce, trundling back to the countryside in tumbril-like carts, in blithe ignorance of the political occasion. A few peered at the handful of party posters stuck on shop-windows. For most it was their one and only contact with the opposition in the entire campaign.

Waiting in the Roman Emperor was no hardship as the hotel boasts one of Romania's premier restaurants, whose sliding roof and chintzy decor were, according to the waiters, designed by Nicu Ceauşescu. The chef was serving some of his customary delights, tranches of venison in a thick sauce and hot pancakes with jam. They made an agreeable change from the standard fare of Bucharest's state eateries – *friptura de porc* (fried pork cutlet served with chips and pickled cabbage). But by the early afternoon we were restless for a diversion. When Liviu, our local journalist friend, suggested a wander down to Nicu's old residence, a group of us gratefully opted for the distraction.

In the old days Sibiu was Nicu's town. He was Party Secretary there for the last few years of his father's rule and allegations of his exploits with the Sibiu womenfolk filled the British tabloids after the revolution. It was in his Sibiu villa on 21 December 1989 that he first heard of the uprising and where he spent his last night in liberty for nearly three years. On 22 December he was arrested on the outskirts of Bucharest, while motoring down to talk to the new government. When the Liberal Party band-waggon came to Sibiu, the Romanian judiciary was preparing their case against Nicu. It was rumoured to be nearly ready for trial.

For a foreign correspondent there are few things more satisfying than a good story in beautiful surroundings; the old quarter of Sibiu, often compared with Nuremberg, is rich with historical association. Liviu walked us past the church steps where in 1510 disgruntled townsfolk stabbed to death Vlad the Impaler's son. The gory tale was grimly appropriate for our mission. On 22 December 1989 Nicu Ceauşescu was stabbed in the stomach, moments after his arrest on the outskirts of Bucharest.

Nicu's old suburban villa was in a shaded street out beyond the city walls. A few people were enjoying the afternoon sun and they willingly opened up about their controversial former neighbour.

'Well,' said one after a reflective pause, 'he was rather quiet, really, kept himself to himself.'

'Of course, the taxis wouldn't come here,' interrupted another. 'But I do remember that, when a relative of mine died, Nicu's security men helped clear the street to let the coffin go past. You couldn't complain.' In the house opposite, Viorel Vlad, a chubby middle-aged bureaucrat, was about to take his daughter for a walk. He found our fascination with Nicu rather amusing.

'And his parties?' Liviu asked for us. 'We hear he had lists of the prettiest girls in town, that he roamed the factories looking for women. Do you know any of this?' Vlad chuckled.

'To be honest we only saw him a few times when he stopped his car to talk to passers by. As for rape – well, it's possible. But he didn't have many parties here. The only noise was when he used to play football in the yard.'

Lacking the gossip we needed for a 'pre-piece' on the trial, we retraced our steps in a more reflective mood. You can often tell when someone is lying, even in the Balkans where half-truth and deceit are frequently confused with honesty. While Nicu as 'the *enfant terrible* of Romania' made good copy, the more human picture of Nicu that emerged from the testimony of his neighbours was convincing. Nicu appears to have been more of a spoilt rich kid than a tyrant in the making. This impression was strengthened a month later when at the end of May his case came to court, in a parody of a trial. Without a shadow of proof, Nicu was accused of giving orders to shoot on anti-Ceauşescu demonstrators at the start of the revolution. He put up a spirited defence, frequently reducing the audience to laughter with throw-away references to his notorious drunken lifestyle. Successive witnesses exonerated him of blame. But he was found guilty all the same and originally sentenced to fifteen years in prison.

I could never make up my mind about Nicu. While he was no saint, his treatment by the judiciary was a farce and human rights workers suspected he was a scapegoat for the unpunished crimes of the communist era. Between 1990 and 1992 Nicu's sentence and charge were each changed twice. He ended in Jilava prison south of Bucharest for 'illegal possession of fire-arms'. It was a bizarre twist of fate as his father Nicolae had served time in Jilava in the as a young communist. The wilderness which surrounds Jilava is as different from the rolling hills of Sibiu as Romania can provide.

Overlooking the cobbles of Sibiu's Great Square, Câmpeanu was limbering up for a rally, the big moment of the day. The 'rally' is a key part of the Balkan election ritual and in the month before Romania's polling day there was one every few days. For British correspondents they merited few column inches in a newspaper. Our only task was to assess the size of the crowd, which I rapidly learned is a controversial business. For journalists the bigger the crowd the better is the story, and so when the adrenalin flows it is easy to let the figure rise . . . One of the most rigorous crowd-assessors was the Agence France Presse bureau chief, Bernard Lestrade, who wielded a ruler and pencil, sub-dividing people into boxes. He advised me to put crowds into manageable units like tennis courts, a process which I attempted only once. After twenty minutes' feverish measuring, I lost count of how many tennis courts I had estimated would fit in the crowd-space. I returned to guesswork.

In Sibiu there was no such problem. Fifteen hundred, maybe two thousand, Sibians were gathered under the balcony of the German cultural centre, chattering away on their Saturday afternoon out. Câmpeanu could have been a burgomaster in the Middle Ages, addressing his townsfolk, bolstering their morale against a Turkish onslaught. For centuries Sibiu was a key fortress on the front line of East and West. In 1241 Sibiu was taken by the Tatars; rebuilt with towers, it never fell again.

'Romanians!' declared Câmpeanu to polite applause. 'Now is the time we have to face the future and break with the past. It is not enough to . . .' As he warmed to his theme, a murmur rose from the back of the crowd. Then the murmurs became heckling. Half an hour later he was back in his suite while rival factions shouted good-tempered insults at each other across a line of policemen in the street.

'*Jos Iliescu* (down with Iliescu), the Front equals the Communist Party,' shouted his supporters.

'You old fool. Go back to France,' shouted the Front supporters. Inside the suite no one knew what to do. Câmpeanu was sitting dispiritedly on a sofa. Every now and then he would wander on to the balcony to look at the crowd. He looked a little lost. With the conviviality of pub-revellers after closing time, the crowd drifted home and the campaign managers retired for a post-mortem.

'It was a plot to destabilise the whole day,' muttered Adrian, the party worker. 'Did you see the thousands of people listening to Mr Câmpeanu? It's a shame. It's more than a shame, it's a crime. Would that be allowed in England? In a real democracy? Look, we are besieged.'

The reality was that the electorate was not ready to hear the message of the opposition. Talk of radical change was terrifying to a people used to an orderly and simple life. As for the opposition, they were besieged almost as much by their own obsession with the past as by the boot-boy tactics of the Front. Some of the stringers opted to stay in Sibiu to accompany Câmpeanu on the next stage of his tour. I had had enough of the Liberal caravan and caught a lift back to Bucharest. One of the funniest moments of the day happened moments after our departure, when Cath Adams rang Chris Stephen who had decided to stay in Sibiu. Pretending she was the BBC in London, Cath asked for a live report on the day's events.

'The Romanian election campaign ran into trouble . . . er, no,' stuttered Chris in a dry-run.

'Can't wait,' shouted Cath. 'We're going live now . . .' and as Chris launched into a report she started laughing. Chris ripped the telephone from its socket. Counter-hoaxes would punctuate and enliven the months that followed.

I slept late the following morning, as the only item on the day's 'electoral agenda' was a Peasant Party rally scheduled for the afternoon. When I was finally woken around midday, Doamna Patraşcu was hovering downstairs with breakfast: a mound of bread, a cup of coffee and a plate brimming with *slanina* (bacon fat) – pure, glistening fat, without the faintest streak of lean.

'*Buna dimineaţa. Poftiţi. Poftiţi.*' (Good morning. Here you are. Here you are.) So often an English translation doesn't do justice to the genteel formality of Romanian – nor in this instance to the warmth of Doamna Patraşcu's expression. It took all my discipline to express the same warmth as I retreated with the tray into my room.

Breakfast at Popa Soare was an intimidating routine. On some occasions I secreted the *slanina* in a carrier bag and took it with me on my journey into town – not so that Sunday. I recall that morning with particular clarity, as it was the start of a demonstration which would pose Romania with its most serious political challenge since the revolution. It was also, according to my diary, one of my most angst-ridden days since coming to Romania.

Sun 22.4.90 (time, early hours of Mon)

I feel somewhat dazed. The day started so smoothly – despite the *slanina* dilemma. Mihai called after monitoring

the news all yesterday. 'Hey, boss, I think we'd better go to
the rally. You never know what will happen.' Wave to
Doamna P. & off to Peasant Party rally in Aviators' Square.
Loads of flashy yellow balloons and carrier bags – Bertie
Way's work, at a guess. Scorching hot and pen explodes
over my jacket. Speakers drone on & on & on. I try to
work out how many tennis courts fit in Aviators' Square
and how many people fit in a tennis court. Falling asleep at
back of crowd. Mihai hears of stabbing. Ha! – political
violence at last. Race to P. Party HQ to find the victim.
'Try the hospital,' we're told. We try ALL hospitals.
Jacket inkier and sweatier. No sign of casualty. Back to P.
Party HQ. Real gem of a doorman says victim not at
hospital but at home. 'Hospital, did I say? Oh, sorry.
Maybe he's gone home.' 'Home?' said another. 'No idea.
Somewhere in Sector 2, I think – or is it Sector 3?'
Aaaargh – general thoughts about who would be a journalist
in the Balkans . . . Back to rally – it's over. New demo
marching to centre. Fight with hotel switchie for line to
London. Refile (REPEAT PHONE HORRORS). Where are the
marchers? Find them in Univ Square. Anarchy looms as
they take over square. On come riot police. Must refile –
run around to phone bureaux, beg, plead, beseech, swear
and still no line . . . Two hours late, communication with
London at last. Now absolutely knackered and only food
around is remains of *slanina* – was Sibiu only yesterday?
Must sleep.

There are days when the Balkans seem decades out of step
with the rest of Europe – Sunday 22 April was such a day.
The frustrations began in the closing stages of the Peasant
Party rally, when Mihai and I were trying to investigate the
story of a stabbed Party worker, a certain Ilie Dumitrescu.
It was a good chance to penetrate the smokescreen of
rumours, by documenting a specific instance of violence.
But the urgency of deadlines does not impress in the
Balkans. For weeks the stalwarts at the Peasant Party
headquarters had been recycling dramatic stories of violence
and unfortunately for me could no longer see the difference
between rumours and the real thing. This was the first
time I had been impeded from reaching a story by the very
people the piece was intended to benefit. It was not the last.

The day deteriorated further. Communications in the summer of 1990 remained as diabolical as before and I can still recall the sweat pouring down my back and the blood suffusing my face as I pleaded with one hotel after another for a line to England. Even after three years' experience of Balkan communications, I haven't learned the art of passively watching deadlines tick past while waiting for a telephone line. Drained but triumphant, I walked out of the Hotel Continental (no connection with its namesake in Timişoara) and straight into a squad of riot police. I had expended energy, nerves, good will and contacts on transmitting a short, dull report about 'yet more opposition rallies in Sibiu and Bucharest', and my piece was already outdated.

In the main boulevard the remnants of the Peasant Party rally had joined with another opposition demonstration and taken up residence in University Square. Half a dozen young boys were lying down on the road. Several women in funeral garb laid wreaths at the shrines to the martyrs of the revolution. Others knelt and started singing hymns and shouting '*Nu plecam*' (We won't leave), and '*Jos Iliescu*' (Down with Iliescu). The riot police were hovering in a side-street, seemingly uncertain what to do. I ran back to the Continental and started pleading for another line. It took two hours.

Such was a weekend covering Romania's election. I had spent the Friday night on a train to Sibiu and much of the Saturday night coming back by car. I had attended two rallies, met Nicu Ceauşescu's neighbours, alienated a key telephone operator, filled a notebook and consumed a portion of *slanina* as well as several glasses of *ţuica*. I had also witnessed – not that I knew it at the time – the beginning of Romania's most significant political protest since the revolution. The blockade of University Square was to end in June with a brutal government crackdown and the alienation of Romania by the outside world for two years. It was fortunate for my morale that a fortnight passed before a copy of Monday morning's paper reached Bucharest and I learned that my weekend's endeavours had merited five short paragraphs.

*

Fenomenonul Piaţei Universitaţi (the phenomenon of University Square) was a return to the confrontational politics of January and February and, in the four weeks remaining before the election, it became the focus of the media coverage. The protestors' principal demand was a ten-year ban from office for former Communist Party activists. While the impetus for the protest came from the students and opposition groups, old dissidents and academics lent credibility to their cause. Emil Constantinescu, the Rector of the University – who in 1992 became the opposition leader – authorised students to use the balcony overlooking the square. A strong Orthodox vein added intensity to the action. Night after night, the demonstrators, who swelled to ten thousand in the early evenings, knelt to pray and sing hymns. Marian Munteanu, the students' leader and unofficial head of the demonstration, grew his beard and hair in an apparently self-conscious imitation of Christ. A dozen or more announced they were starting a hunger strike.

There was something delightfully comic about the protest. The barricades were made of flowerpots and streetsigns. With tents springing up on the lawn outside the Intercontinental, which overlooked the square, and banners hanging from overlooking windows, the atmosphere was often reminiscent of a rock festival. It was as if the message of Woodstock and flower-power had finally moved east; for young people it was an unrivalled opportunity to display the national talent at composing rhymes. Day after day, jokers would make up new epigrams mocking Iliescu and Roman. At night most people retired to bed, leaving a hard core of students and drifters. The hunger-strikers were very Balkan. After a few days on duty most went home for a feed-up and ceded their places to friends.

However, the demonstration reflected a deep – albeit minority – undercurrent of bitterness in Romanian society. In *The Balkan Trilogy* Olivia Manning describes the palpable threat of violence hanging over Bucharest in 1940, as the Iron Guardists roamed the streets. There was a similar feeling at the end of April 1990. By occupying the square, the students had laid down the gauntlet and were challenging the authorities to react. Addressing the interim parliament, Iliescu condemned the protestors as '*golani*' (hooligans). It was a tactless choice of words. Ceauşescu had said the same of the demonstrators in the first days of Timişoara in December 1989.

A month of single-sentence diary entries are testimony to the hectic schedule of covering University Square. On the third day of the blockade, the police launched a dawn raid and briefly cleared the protestors before they were forced to leave by a fresh group of demonstrators. While a long-running demonstration loses news value after a few days, the fear of another police raid was always hanging over us; it was hard to leave the square for more than an hour or so, lest something happened.

As ever in the Balkans, rumours were the main source of information and they flitted across the café tables like fleas. Interpreting them was like tackling a giant crossword – for which I was paranoid that everyone else knew more clues. While on occasion the 'staffers' would divulge some tit-bit of information, often these pickings from the 'high table' only increased my confusion, as when Bernard Lestrade, the AFP bureau chief of pencil and ruler fame, tipped me off about an army declaration.

'*C'est très important*,' he said, frowning and tapping the side of his face. 'Just make sure you don't tell my competition.' I sat down with Tim Judah of *The Times* to wrangle over the enigmatic statement. 'Was it false? Who does it represent? Why is it important? How do we check it out?' Bernard, who had long black hair and a piratical moustache, was sitting a few feet away, tapping furiously at his little computer. Infuriating pride stopped me from asking why exactly he thought the statement mattered.

I tended to spend my mornings interviewing politicians, and afternoons monitoring the demonstration. Much of this reporting was wasted time and energy. A few extra hours in bed would have been more beneficial than another notebook of politicians' rhetoric. But, if nothing else, it was an apprenticeship in interview technique. I have a prized recording of a session with the former apparatchik Silviu

Brucan, which sounds like a cross between a radio play and a Socratic dialogue. Brucan was one of six top communists who in April 1989 signed an open letter criticizing Ceauşescu, and during the revolution he was the *eminence grise* of the Front. He toyed with me like an errant pupil, dismissing my questions, firing back his own, pausing to break into his distinctive cackling laugh.

Brucan had two main points he wished to make. The first was that it was unfair to accuse the Front of sticking to the past, the second was that the University Square demonstrators were undemocratic. That these conclusions did not follow his premises did not seem to matter. Overwhelmed in a torrent of rhetoric, I was reminded of my university entrance interview when I sat on a squashy low sofa faced by four academics.

'Sir. You say there is no democracy [I hadn't]. How can you say this? [with a rhetorical harrumph]. I turn to the facts [pause]. The fact that there is free press. The fact there are more than seventy political parties. We are giving them a fair chance . . . It's a move to democracy; it's a basic fact that there are so many parties. They have newspapers and access to television – and you say we continue the same policies. How can you say that? [His voice rises.] You ignore the facts [ten-second break for laughter]. And what about the demonstrators? Is blockading the country's main street a democratic course of action? On the contrary, it leads to anarchy . . .

'You are a journalist. Don't you see, to make up your mind you must start from the facts? Do you think Ceauşescu was in favour of the free market and a free press? And you say we have not broken with the past? Sir, you are the manipulated one. You are trying to find arguments to support your bias. Do you expect a complete and radical break in five months? Is that possible? Democracy will take twenty years.'

I wanted to dislike, even despise, Brucan, who in the fifties ran the propaganda section of the Communist Party, when thousands of opposition leaders were being purged and tens of thousands more like Doamna Patraşcu were thrown in prison. But like ideologues of any creed, he was curiously fascinating and his parting comment that democracy cannot happen overnight was one of the few astute remarks that I heard a Romanian politician utter in the entire campaign.

Through incompetence I didn't write up the interview. Brucan never forgave me. When a month or so later I called him again, he snorted and the phone went dead.

In this whirlwind period everything was subordinated to the daily task of covering the square and I spent even less time in my new home in Popa Soare than I had in Cobalcescu. Granny Patraşcu, who had taken a turn for the worse, was convinced that I was deliberately abandoning her.

'Alec, I don't mean to pry,' a Romanian friend said delicately one day, 'but do you have a difficult relationship with someone's grandmother? There's this old woman who answers the phone when you're not there. She says you're a monster and never pay her any attention.' The accusation was not unfounded. Days passed in a crazy blur of waiting for telephones and running around University Square. On Saturdays, my one free day in the week, I gratefully luxuriated in the warm hospitality of Doamna Ruxanda Goga, a survivor of one of the 'fifty families' of the thirties.

A niece of Octavian Goga, Romania's premier poet of 1938, Doamna Goga had spent the previous four decades living in a garret flat off the Calea Floreasca, where period furniture, prints and hangings cluttered every corner like an antique shop. In the fifties her family had been given three days to leave their estates. Every Saturday she had members of her extended family to lunch and I became an irregular addition. Different nephews and grandnieces were always passing through, speaking in French as often as the vernacular. Lunch, preceded by a vodka, started at two-thirty and lasted until the early evening. The food was excellent and a reminder of Bucharest's pre-war reputation as a culinary paradise. It was also a hint that communism hadn't destroyed the Romanian palate, as I sometimes supposed. The lively atmosphere and conversation were more reminiscent of a sprawling Breton country house than a Balkan side street.

Never one to dramatise the past, Doamna Goga would, when prompted, give vignettes of her youth in the thirties, when Bucharest was *the* city in the Balkans and life was Trollopian in style. Visiting cards, nicknames and private carriages were the order of the day; everyone knew everyone; industrialisation was barely underway and many of the market towns, that in the seventies and eighties Ceauşescu disfigured with tower blocks, were 'delightful little places where so and so lived . . .' With the memory of a party here, an estate there, drab towns like Craiova or Buzau came to life. With a few deft words, the confines of the apartment disappeared and we were trotting along the capital's boulevards in a *trasura* (carriage), with a Skoptje coachman in his flowing plumes and dark cloak.

Sir Sacheverell Sitwell retells with awe the account of a nineteenth-century British visitor to Bucharest who sees the reigning prince being carried under his shoulders, Baghdad-style by two servants. I found Doamna Goga's casual asides about the Skoptzi, a fanatical Orthodox sect who castrated themselves to strengthen their belief that Christ never died, no less extraordinary. Of Russian origin, the Skoptzi, who ran Bucharest's taxi service before the Second World War, claimed that Christ wandered the earth in the image of Peter III of Russia. That thousands of them were still living in Romania in the thirties epitomises how the Second World War and communism changed the face of Eastern Europe for ever.

The Saturday lunch coterie was ardently monarchist and in early spring the conversation focused on the exiled King Michael, who in mid-April was at the last minute denied access to his old kingdom. But as 20 May drew near, the lunches turned to speculation on the campaign, about which Doamna Goga had clear and trenchant views. The Front she despised as opportunists. Her arguments were given all the more force by her acquaintance with the parents of some of the Front key figures.

'My dear, I saw his mother the other day,' she said of the

deputy prime minister, Gelu Voican-Voiculescu, who in February had been almost thrown out of the government headquarters by rioters. 'She was terribly ashamed by what he was up to.'

But Doamna Goga's fire was by no means reserved for the Front. She also had stern words for the opposition, whom she accused of incompetence and lethargy.

'Before an election my father used to retire to his constituency for seven weeks to discuss matters with the electorate. Politicians don't do that today. They just sit and talk and look where it gets them.' There followed an uproar as a pro-Peasant Party side of the table reacted.

These lunches never failed to inspire me about Romania. Floreasca and Popa Soare were separated by a ten-minute ride through the back streets. Bumping home over the potholes, fortified by these glimpses into the past, I felt more optimistic for the future.

However, the conversations also underlined one of the fundamental weaknesses of Romanian society. Romania did not lack voices of reason and moderation. There were plenty of liberal thinkers, who, while despising the Front, understood the difficulties of transition to democracy and appreciated the inadequacies of the opposition. But there was no one ready to take the torch to the people, as did the pro-Solidarity Catholic intellectuals in Poland, or Charter 77 in Czechoslovakia.

A share of the blame goes to the former regime which, as Romanians are quick to remind you, was 'the most terrible of Eastern Europe'. A system in which you queued two hours for bread on a Thursday because there was none on Friday and bakers were closed at the weekend, sapped the spirits of the most rebellious. The daily grind left intellectuals too humiliated to take the lead that was so desperately needed. The Securitate mopped up any vestigial dissidents. In 1977 the novelist Paul Goma declared his support for Charter 77 and sent an open letter to Ceauşescu suggesting he did the same. He was promptly arrested and beaten. Further, communism tainted the business of politics. After forty years of the Party's corruption, the very word 'politics' was stigmatised and dirty. In January 1990 the Group for Social Dialogue, a gathering of literary and dissident figures, tipped itself as a liberal forum. But the members shrank from direct involvement in the political process. Many student friends who had participated in the revolution threw up their hands in horror if I suggested they should consider a role in public life.

However, Ceauşescu and communism are not the whole explanation for the apathy of Romania's 'chattering classes'. You have to go back to the old Carpathian divide, the Byzantine/Catholic split. The Orthodox tradition is about biding your time and subservience – not independence of thought or action. People are not accustomed to sticking out their necks. In the writers and thinkers served the prevailing nationalism and anti-Semitism. In the seventies and eighties most writers worshipped readily at the altar of Ceauşescu and regarded a tugging of the forelock as a small price to pay to have a work published. The Serbian intellectual movement was guilty of a similar sycophancy in Serbia's poisoned culture of the early 1990s.

As the Romanian election juddered to its conclusion in an atmosphere of recrimination and jealousy, many Romanians were craving for a voice untainted by the past, someone who was branded neither with the chaos of the thirties nor the corruption of communism. I asked Mircea Dinescu, the angry young man of Romanian poetry, why the writers didn't take more of a lead. He almost erupted.

'I think writers did quite enough in politics in the past,' he said. 'All over Eastern Europe there is a fashion for writers to become politicians. Personally, I reckon Plato was right when he wanted to ban poets on the grounds that they misled citizens.'

In the week before polling day the big-shot correspondents returned to Bucharest. Suddenly the press centre was humming and the story was on a roll. CNN took an entire floor in the Intercontinental and captivated the University Square demonstrators with their satellite dishes and hundreds of aluminium suitcases of equipment. In the wake of the journalists came hundreds of election observers, keen to explain the rights and wrongs of democracy, embarking on a lucrative career in the brave new world. The government spokesman, Cristian Unteanu, was forced to stir from his office, and he scuttled around after the requests of the network chiefs. For stringers it was the chance to air local knowledge, dine on expense accounts and briefly feel part of the big world picture.

With Patrick Bishop back in town, the *Telegraph*'s operation became mainstream. Patrick politely suggested I made use of the Intercontinental dry-cleaners for my jacket, which had long since lost its summer colour. He also took control of the political coverage and I was free to write about more diverse subjects, which I had been wanting to do for several weeks, in particular Romania's forgotten minority, the gipsies.

Trapped in a spiral of poverty and crime, Romania's gipsies were a virtual underclass. Officially there were three hundred thousand in Romania, but the figure was widely believed to be nearer two million, almost 10 per cent of the population. After the revolution, the Front tried to win them over by returning their gold ornaments, which had been confiscated under Ceauşescu. But relations between gipsies and Romanians remained extremely poor; gipsies were subject to abuse, discrimination and worse. In 1990 three gipsy settlements were burned to the ground and their communities were driven into the fields. Romanians, who categorised all gipsies as robbers and cheats, blithely refused to accept there was a problem.

After a visit to a gipsy ghetto in Transylvania which was sunk in decay and despair, I went in search of the King of the Gipsies for an official view, tracing him to a gloomy hotel room in downtown Bucharest, where he was conducting the last stages of his campaign for a seat in parliament. In the royal suite, his daughter, Luminiţa, asked for cigarettes and a camera film. A young buck was snoring softly on the bed. The king lumbered in a few minutes later.

Ion Cioaba, the official representative for the gipsies at the United Nations, had an imposing bulk, which threatened to burst from his grey suit. He also claimed he had been misrepresented by journalists many times before and with the greatest reluctance muttered a few platitudes about the election, refusing to contemplate the chances of defeat. I wasn't so sure. Romania's gipsies were divided into at least ten different tribes and loyalty to Cioaba seemed to extend only to his home town, Sibiu. I was trying to make this point when Cioaba lost patience.

'They will vote for me!' he said, turning away to mutter something in Romany. The audience was over. I was shown to the door.

On the eve of polling day there was a ban on alcohol and a violent storm. As the booths opened the next morning, shaking with nerves, the senior official at Bucharest's Boulevard Dacia station peeled back the tape covering the voting urn and shone his torch inside.

'Look, there is no one inside – and no false bottom.' The relief on his face when the observers concurred with his conclusion was patent. The smooth beginning set the tone for the day. After all the build-up, all the stories of intimidation and skulduggery, the population flocked to the polling booths and recorded their democratic voice in an orderly and dignified fashion – 85 per cent for Iliescu and 66 per cent for the Front. The second-biggest share of the vote went to the ethnic Hungarian party, who polled 8 per cent. For the opposition it was a disaster. The Liberal and Peasant parties trailed home with six and two per cent respectively.

It was a difficult result for the West. It was in essence a democratic election – and yet the 'bad guys' won. While the election was flawed, the basic story was that instances of fraud had not significantly influenced the result. The final figures reflected the views of the Romanian people, most of whom were desperately worried about rapid reform. This reaction was repeated elsewhere in the Balkans, accentuating the divide between South-East and Central Europe. In Bulgaria in June 1990 the Bulgarian Socialist Party (the revamped communists) were swept into office. In Serbia in December 1990 the former communist leader, Slobodan

Milošević, and the Serbian Socialist Party gained a landslide victory. The Balkan peasant is reluctant to change.

'Was it democracy?' we asked the observers in Bucharest.

'Yes . . . no . . . well, maybe,' they replied. Possibly the fairest response was given by an Austrian observer, Andreas Kohl, chairman of the European Democratic Union delegation, who, while conceding that the poll would have been considered null in Austria, refrained from outright condemnation. I suspect many of the observers were just coming to grips with the realization that trying to apply absolutes to elections in fledgling democracies was impossible and maybe even irrelevant. More scathing was Jim Hoagland of the *Washington Post* who wrote that the one-sided results 'do little to dispel the feeling that the country has undergone a prison riot, not a revolution. The toughest and smartest inmates killed the cruel warden and have taken over.' His comment is reminiscent of a 1938 piece in the *Daily Despatch*, quoted by Ivor Porter, which says that 'democracy as practised in Romania bore little resemblance to democracy at home.'

The day of the elections, an Israeli gunman killed eleven Palestinians in the Gaza Strip and Patrick and other Middle East hands left within forty-eight hours; the satellite dishes were pulled down; Bertie Way packed his bags; Cristian Unteanu celebrated; and the University Square contingent looked scruffier and less consequential by the hour. Mihai Patraşcu obtained a visa for Belgium and left the next day. The king of the gipsies, ignominiously rejected by his people, retired to Sibiu, where he stayed in relative seclusion for two years until a rival, a gipsy emperor, arrived to threaten his position.

In the Intercontinental I noticed that the fresh oranges, which had appeared for breakfast two weeks before the election, were off the menu – they would not reappear for over a year. For the first time in the four-and-a-half months since my arrival in Timişoara, I considered leaving the Balkans. A week after polling day I flew to London for an interview with a rival Fleet Street broadsheet. As I walked through the door at home the phone was ringing. It was the *Daily Telegraph* and it was not a welcome home.

'There's been an earthquake in East Europe, shock waves from Sofia to Moscow, no casualty figures yet, epicentre Focşani in the Carpathians, Romania. Your patch I think . . .'

The Carpathians is a well-known seismic fault-line. In 1940 and again in 1977 earthquakes killed over a thousand people in Romania. Within half an hour I was back at Heathrow queuing for a flight to the Bulgarian capital, Sofia, the nearest I could get to Bucharest. There was just time for an apology to the putative interviewer and for an even more grovelling message to Sophie to say that I would not be in Edinburgh that night for dinner. Michael Montgomery, the *Telegraph*'s Belgrade correspondent who had covered the fighting in Tîrgu Mureş, was in Sofia preparing for Bulgaria's elections. We drove together through the night and arrived at dawn.

In half-light the south side of Bucharest is not a pretty sight. It suffered the worst destruction in Ceauşescu's crazed plan to rebuild his capital in his own modern style. Several acres are a demolished wasteland of half-built tower blocks. However, the bulk of the buildings seemed suspiciously intact. The Intercontinental, Bucharest's token skyscraper, which in February Patrick Leigh Fermor had dubbed 'a monstrous mouth organ', still glowered over University Square. I rang Marc Champion to find where the worst damage was. He groaned – not only in the pain of being woken at five.

'Al, I don't know how to tell you, but there's no story . . . Well, there was an earthquake. But that was yesterday, and, anyway, it was a small one and we didn't really feel it . . . What? They've sent two of you?'

Bucharest was unscathed. In all, six people died – most by jumping from their windows in panic.

After hitching a lift to the epicentre, I missed the afternoon plane back to England and it took me another twenty-four hours to reach London. I arrived for the interview two days late, unshaven, in my favourite Romanian jacket, a purple number from a state boutique, and a tie bought five minutes earlier at the airport. The editor was wearing a charcoal-grey pinstriped suit. He looked me up and down quizzically. I pre-empted the rejection slip and flew back to Bucharest.

5

The Darker Side of the Balkans – a Preview

Bucharest to the Carpathians, June to July 1990

'Let not the holy god make us want blood instead of land' – *George Coşbuc, nineteenth-century Romanian peasant poet*

'More can happen in an hour than in a whole year' – *Romanian proverb*

IT IS HARD TO read the runes in the Balkans. For journalists, luck and timing are everything. Twenty-four hours after I flew back to Bucharest, Romanian security forces moved into University Square and arrested the anti-government protestors. The raid signalled the start of three days of anarchy which would alter the short-term course of Romania's history and would leave it a pariah in Europe. For Romanians and Romania-watchers the news of the clampdown was of a significance second only to hearing of the uprising in December 1989. I was woken at dawn and the phone barely penetrated my hangover.

To a percipient few the 13 June raid was expected. In the wake of their election triumph, the Front had been making increasingly hardline statements about the blockade of University Square, a humiliating embarrassment. When foreign delegations visited the capital they had to make a detour round the centre. On 12 June the authorities deployed helicopters, armoured cars and hundreds of troops against a few hundred demonstrators straggling up and down the main boulevard. The government's patience was clearly waning. Acting on a hunch and a rumour, Adrian

Popescu, a photographer working for Reuters News Agency, spent the night of the 12th/13th hidden in the back of a car in University Square and emerged at dawn with world scoop pictures – while most of the foreign correspondents were sleeping off sore heads.

The night before, the old company of stringers had recongregated for the first time in weeks. Some had returned from the Bulgarian elections – won, as in Romania, by opportunistic communists, the Bulgarian Socialist Party – others were back from England or the mountains. It was a happy gathering, first in the terrace restaurant at the Athenée Palace where the band was playing Maria Tanase, Romania's Edith Piaf of the thirties, and then back at the *Observer*'s apartment where we took a rest from the Balkans and played Patsy Cline and Bob Dylan. *Ţuica*-makers pride their brew on its clarity. We must have had a bad batch.

I arrived in University Square to find black Dacias patrolling the fringes, plain-clothes policemen picking up stragglers, and traces of blood by a subway entrance. A young Romanian journalist was being hustled into a van. A group of us wandered closer and a security man barged into our path. He had the shoebox face of an old Party member and a stereotypical ill-fitting suit. He pointed to the Intercontinental: 'Get back over there. This is none of your business.' We dutifully retreated, and the journalist was driven away. We still agonise over our cowardice.

It was a scene from the bad old days. All the old Securitate characters had come out of hiding and were strutting around without a trace of embarrassment. It was as if for six months we had been in a Looking Glass world and the mirror had suddenly been reversed.

The operation was marked by a remorseless efficiency rarely found in the Balkans. By 7 a.m. municipal street-cleaners were hosing down the streets. By 7.30 cranes were removing the anti-Iliescu banners which hung from the University buildings. By 8 a.m. gipsy women were digging up the lawn which had been the hunger-strikers' camp-site. By 9 a.m. they were planting rose bushes on the freshly-tilled earth. The staff of the Intercontinental, which overlooks the square, were watching the events from the foyer. It was a re-run of 22 December 1989 when Ceauşescu's forces recaptured and hosed down University Square – probably with the same lantern-jawed personnel. The 'Intercon' was my *poste restante* and I knew many of the staff. Coco, one of the least suspect of the receptionists, shook his head in despair. 'Just watch,' he said. 'There'll be trouble.'

It's one of the ironies of an efficient totalitarian state that it doesn't breed an effective police force. So rigorous was Ceauşescu's machine of fear that his riot troops gained minimal experience of crowd control. Until the last twenty-four hours of his rule, his capital was a model of decorum. When on the morning of 13 June a few hundred students and drifters gathered to jeer, the police were paralysed by indecision. When the taunts turned to stone-throwing they launched a few dispirited baton charges and then downed their shields and ran. I ran, too, slipped in the rain and sprawled in no-man's land in the middle of the square.

This was my first experience covering street violence. I learned fast. It's a peculiar art with only one rule – always retain an avenue of escape. Face down, I cursed myself for wearing hard-soled shoes and, more heinously, for trusting in the police line. A balanced despatch penned on time from behind the scenes will always be worth more than an eyewitness account, however dramatic, a day late. My most probable immediate fate was either the inside of a police cell – in my shabby jacket, aged twenty-four, I looked like a student – or the hospital – I was in the line of fire for the stone-throwing demonstrators. I wanted to shout that for months my pen had been lambasting the government. Then a police charge distracted the protestors and the projectiles changed tack. I almost cheered.

The course of the next twelve hours has developed into a Romanian myth of a complexity second only to the revolution. Events moved so fast that it was impossible to keep track of the whole picture. My fact-finding operation was scuppered by the defection of Bogdan, my interpreter, to the demonstrators. It came at a critical moment. The police had just fled for the final time; police buses were burning;

Marian Munteanu, the unofficial leader of the demonstration, was addressing the triumphant crowd in University Square. Three years later he drifted to the right, helping to found an organization seen locally as reminiscent of the prewar Iron Guard. But in June 1990 he was a much-needed figurehead for an opposition sorely lacking in leaders. In the drama of the moment my rudimentary Romanian was unable to cope with his speech. Turning to Bogdan for a rendition, I found him jumping up and down, waving his fist and chanting the anti-Iliescu slogans.

'What's he saying?' I bawled, half-deafened by the shouts of '*Jos Iliescu*' and 'Iliescu equals Ceauşescu.'

'To the police station!' screamed Bogdan. 'To the police station!'

'What? Did Munteanu say this?'

'Don't worry what he said. We must all go to the station. We must free the prisoners from the morning.' Bogdan had totally forgotten his commitment to journalism and was off running and singing.

My next 'source' proved as incoherent. Careering round a corner came Jason Turner, a young photographer – in stringers' gossip, 'the local spook'. Tall, blonde and blue-eyed, Jason was the first of a trickle of West Europeans to head east after the fall of the Berlin Wall. He soon sold his camera and was 'marketing TVs', or was he setting up a business consultancy? We were convinced he was 'the MI6 man in Bucharest' and teased him mercilessly. His chaotic performance on 13 June suggested he was after all 'just passing through'.

'Hey, Alec, man! They are shooting. There are bodies . . .'

'Where, Jason? How many?'

'At least five or ten. All over the place . . .'

Five days later I obtained the transcript of a radio ham's recording of a low-frequency police conversation which suggested that the authorities deliberately provoked the violence, both to discredit the opposition and to pave the way for a clampdown. In one section an officer number 53 says his men have set fire to the buses. 'Do you see any possibility of informing the president?' he tells officer 52. 'We are starting to burn all of the buses. This was the agreement.' In another excerpt, officer 52 mentions a superior called Magureanu – the same name as the head of the reformed secret police, Dr Virgil Magureanu. 'I don't know how we can resolve this,' runs the passage. 'Mr Magureanu retreated and we don't know where he is. This was his business . . . The prime minister's orders were to keep control until the miners arrived.'

The government subsequently denounced the tape as a forgery. I met the man who claimed to have made the recording, saw his equipment and listened to what he called the 'original'. All that can be said is that, if the tape is forged, the man, who was unwilling to be named, made it professionally. Further, the theory does fit two pieces of circumstantial evidence. The police deserted the city in the middle of the afternoon. As in the February attack on the government headquarters, the most active rioters were drifters and unemployed, fodder for the highest payer.

Within the murk a few facts were clear. By late afternoon protestors were attacking the police headquarters. One group then commandeered vehicles to take them to the state television; another laid siege to the Interior Ministry building and an old Securitate office. In all there were never more than three or four thousand demonstrators of whom a few hundred were actively participating in the violence. At least three people were shot dead after gunmen inside the Interior Ministry opened fire. The security forces made no attempt to restrain the mob until 2 a.m., when army units deployed and shepherded the rioters away from the burning buildings.

The foreign correspondents had moved to the Intercontinental for a good vantage point; from the sixteenth floor I watched the dispersal of the last fifty or so rioters, many of whom were barefoot street children. By 3.30 a.m the city was quiet.

There is a much-satirised journalistic tradition of foreign correspondents penning vivid 'colour' pieces from the luxury of their hotel bedrooms and the depths of their imagination. In *Scoop*, Sir Jocelyn Hitchcock hides in his room in Jacksonburg's Hotel Liberty, sends a dramatic despatch, claiming to be hundreds of miles away at the 'rebel headquarters', waits until his rivals have left in hot pursuit and then, 'with the story cleaned-up', retires to Lucerne. I stayed in the Intercontinental for most of 14 June. But the attraction was not its comfort, and the day's story was more Byzantine than the most exotic fiction.

Bill Mcpherson, the *Washington Post* columnist from my Timişoara days, was sleeping on my sofa, as his hotel had been engulfed by the rioting. He woke me after less than an hour of sleep. From the street below there came a faint humming as from tiny insects. Then, through the early morning mist gleamed a few torches. Five, ten, fifteen, they became twenty, a hundred, five hundred, a thousand. The lights flickered from a swirling grey mass in front of which three mannequin figures were skipping and twirling their arms as if in some primitive mating ritual. Reminded of the antics of the witch Gagool in Rider Haggard, I rubbed my eyes. Then one of these dancing high-priests lifted an arm on high. The hum turned to a roar and Bill swore in horror as the arm came down and a passing woman on her way to work crumpled beneath a flurry of blows.

The miners of the Jiu Valley had returned to Bucharest. They filled the main General Magheru boulevard, sweeping aside early risers, leaving barely a ripple in their advance. It was a scene mixing feverish childhood nightmares of the Khyber Pass with the stylised horrors of Spielberg. They came at a run in almost total silence waving pit-props and chains; their rubber pit-boots muffled their tread. The grey overalls and coal-dust added to the Stygian impression. Like giant killer ants, one would scuttle off, find a victim, and five or ten more would come scurrying over, until their prey was hidden by flailing clubs. Phalanxes trotted off to the headquarters of opposition parties and to the University buildings, which they looted and ransacked.

The Faustian blackness intensified at first hand. In the lobby a delegation of Japanese businessmen were checking their watches, tut-tutting as if late for a rendez-vous, while five feet away an ox of a man was stuck in the revolving doors, gazing through the glass at the normality so close and yet so far, as three miners pummelled him from behind, smashing his legs and arms with crowbars and hose-pipes until finally he gave up the struggle and was hauled away.

For the second dawn running, University Square was a battlefield. But although Iliescu had launched a diatribe against the Western press, anti-journalist sentiment was confined to photographers and cameramen, with their obvious tools of the trade. As long as pens and notebooks remained hidden, writers could walk among the carnage. It was as if we were wraiths in a Romanians-only freak show.

One miner approached brandishing a copy of the US constitution, the ultimate in proof. Another was clutching a cheque for a few dollars.

'Look,' they shouted indignantly. 'They are paid by the West. See what we have to protect our country from.' I was looking – but over their shoulders at a man on all fours squealing like a pig as he was brought to the ground by a posse of miners.

A few minutes later a young woman in a bright red T-shirt emerged from a side-street. Maybe the red was a little too eye-catching. Maybe her handbag spoke of an 'intellectual' background. Maybe her unsteady step was a little suspicious. A gang assaulted her, ripping off her T-shirt, pummelling her back with tools intended for a coal-face until the bruises turned to blood and the blood to gore. Screaming, clutching her bare breasts, the woman was dragged out of sight.

The incident was over in half a minute. One of the assailants took a respite, leaning on his club and Victoria Clark, who spoke the best Romanian of the British stringers, asked him why he was savaging his fellow-Romanians. Not the slightest nonplussed, the miner nodded sagely.

'She's a prostitute. We found her like that . . . Tear her shirt off? No we didn't. She did. She's a whore, paid by foreign money.'

Forfeiting any dwindling credibility as a would-be

democrat, Iliescu gloried in the carnage. He welcomed the miners with a rousing speech from the balcony of the government headquarters and then pointed them to University Square – even though the army had ended the rioting and restored control. Later, in a grotesque distortion of the truth, he thanked them for their 'attitude of high civic awareness' and urged them 'to keep in check the degenerate, déclassé and fanatical elements'. His phraseology was vintage Ceauşescu. Inevitably he blamed the foreign journalists. The nearest he came to apologising was via his prime minister, Petre Roman, who, the following day in a press conference awash with lies, admitted 'there were some unpleasant moments when certain citizens were molested without reason'. By implication others were molested with reason.

Humanity's facade of civilization is more fragile in the Balkans than in Western Europe. On 14 June 1990 Romania's society reverted to the law of the jungle. By the early afternoon Bucharesters were lining the streets in their thousands, exhorting the miners to redouble their beatings 'against the dirty students'. Some Front supporters even joined in the beating, wielding chair-legs or hosepipes, egging on fresh atrocities. The rapid descent of society into primal violence was again a stark preview of Yugoslavia in 1991 and 1992, where, almost overnight, neighbour turned on neighbour, friend on friend. To compound the surreal horror, the police deployed behind the miners, arresting their bloodied victims and driving them to the former Securitate training school at Baneesa for further beating. Marian Munteanu, the student leader, was battered unconscious in the Architecture Faculty and then arrested from a hospital bed, where he lay swathed in bandages.

The day's events completed my crash-course in covering street violence. My final two lessons came simultaneously and via the blows of a cudgel: always forewarn colleagues of your movements and never trust in the power of a press card. Around midday, when the force of the attacks was abating, I hitched a lift to Victory Square, where a demonstration of pro-Iliescu workers was reported to be gathering.

I was making a circumspect walk around the outskirts of the crowd with Bill Mcpherson when we saw two American tourists taking photos. It was too late to warn them of their mistake and they were seized by the mob. Waving our press-passes and shouting imperiously, we pushed through the crowd and followed their captors. It was a mistake. An army officer took one look at us, wrenched away our ID cards and my notebook and swore angrily. A shout went up. Maybe we were foreign provocateurs, or spies, or fascists. Like hounds sniffing prey a trio of vigilantes paced around us. With two sharp blows to the ribs, Bill was on the ground. More miners closed in. Again the club rose. Moving in slow motion it reached the zenith and started to descend when a young Front activist stepped forward waving his hands.

'Go home,' he told us, parting the miners and assuaging the officer. 'This is not for you. Go home.'

Shaking, we walked away, not daring to look behind, resisting the urge to run as open-topped trucks laden with Iliescu's proletarian stormtroopers trundled past. It was a twenty-minute walk to the haven of the Intercon. It seemed like an hour. When we returned to the hotel we found no one had realized we were missing. Cristian Unteanu, the government spokesman later drove Bill and me to the government headquarters where our IDs – but not my notebook – were returned. Groans and muffled screams could be heard through a locked door.

Bogdan, my interpreter, safely returned from his session on the streets, was more interested in watching the latest World Cup football match than translating Iliescu's speech. I dictated my report against the televised roar of a Madrid crowd, which easily drowned the howls from University Square.

'In Bucharest, are you Alec?' joked the copy-taker. 'I thought it was a bit hairy down there. Sounds more like a Saturday afternoon at the local . . . Slow down, slow down . . . Hang on a minute . . . Are you sure you want that word? I'm not sure it's English, sounds a bit Romanianised to me. How about this one instead . . . ?'

*

The June events were, in newsman's parlance, a great story. For two days Romania dominated the headlines and provoked for resident correspondents the classic journalist's dichotomy of interest, between hunger for a front-page spread and anguish at the suffering of an adopted home. In the months that followed we argued interminably over the origins of the savagery. The most vexing question was whether to blame the swamp or the monster, Romania and the Balkans or Ceauşescu and communism. On balance we concluded you had to blame both.

In the light of the carnage in Yugoslavia in 1991 onwards, two particularly interesting conclusions emerged from those late-night reflections on the Balkans. The first is that norms of behaviour in the Balkans are totally different from those in the West. The Romanian authorities were genuinely startled at the extent of the world's opprobrium against the miners' rampage. Iliescu miscalculated – just as in 1992 the Bosnian Serbs misjudged the world's reaction when they opened their detention camps to the media, expecting them to be granted a clean bill of health. This in part reflects the naivety of Balkan politicians, but also the existence in South-East Europe of very un-European criteria of judgement. Iliescu did not anticipate plaudits, but he believed he could avoid too much censure. With the exception of Ion Raţiu, the returned émigré millionaire, who had contested the presidential election, the opposition parties proved scarcely more *au fait* with Western thinking. A few days after the miners' rampage they were calmly debating in parliament with the Front deputies as if the devastation of their headquarters and the maiming of their supporters was just one of those things that happen.

The second and more alarming conclusion was about the mind of the Balkan proletariat. It is a psyche that has no place for logic and for which falsehood is reality. When the miner retired from assaulting the red-T-shirted woman and said he found her 'with her shirt off as a prostitute', he was lying. Seconds earlier we had watched as the woman was picked at random. But the miner was not lying to dupe us – the distortion of the truth was too obvious. Nor was he trying to dupe himself. He believed the lie. So many times had he been told by the state propaganda machine that the female opposition supporters in Bucharest were prostitutes and needed 'cleansing', that he believed it – even though the truth was patently otherwise. This is no excuse for the thugs and their thuggery. The miners' leaders knew exactly what they were doing. But with the ordinary club-wielders it was different. They were living in a make-believe world created by a powerful propaganda working on very simple brains. The result is a mind-blankness and the potential for terrible cruelty. The same attitudes were on display time and again in the war in Yugoslavia. Outside Sarajevo in 1992 Serb gunners looked me in the eye and swore they were firing only in self-defence, while twenty yards away their colleagues casually lobbed shells into the Bosnian capital, laid out like a toytown below. When the miners returned to Bucharest for another rampage in September 1991, this time against the government, they explained they had been manipulated in June 1990. 'And what makes you think you are not being manipulated now?' I asked one group. 'Oh, we know we are not,' they chorused.

None of this in the slightest attenuates Iliescu's guilt in June 1990. In a broadcast on state television he called the miners to town. His agents guided and fed them. He publicly thanked them. It was a sickening display of totalitarian power-politics. Apologists explain away the violence as an aberration and chide journalists that Romania in June 1990 was a young democracy. 'What about the West? Are we much better?' one Western official asked me a few weeks later. 'We have riots. Look at the poll-tax riot in Trafalgar Square.' The same style of apologist in 1991 watched the obliteration of the Croatian town of Vukovar by Serb artillery and pointed out that in the Second World War Croats killed a lot of Serbs.

In 1990 Romania was a young would-be democracy. But the sanctioning of club-rule is the hallmark of a tyrant, not a would-be democrat. It was later proved that many of the miners' leaders were former Securitate officers. Most Romanians liked Iliescu, but for Romania he was a disaster. His single-minded pursuit of power sacrificed the final well of support in the West for post-Ceauşescu Romania. The EC suspended an aid package. Corporate investors focused on Central Europe. The US imposed a purgatory which lasted until June 1992, when the misdeeds of Serbia necessitated a strategic rethink and upped the potential importance of neighbouring Romania. Iliescu followed a long tradition of Balkan authoritarian rulers. He was among the first of the new crop sprouting in post-communist Europe. By 1992 Iliescu, the ultimate opportunist, appeared to be donning the garb of a democrat and was behaving in a more enlightened fashion, backing cautious reform and muzzling hardliners. But while the West welcomed this new incarnation, the more astute foreign diplomats were under no illusion that, if there was a mood change in Moscow, Iliescu too might swing away from the West. His career and methods in 1990 bear interesting comparisons with the early moves of the Serbian president Slobodan Milošević, another ex-communist, whose tub-thumping politics were loved by the ordinary Serb, but brought Serbia to ruin.

There is a cruel nineteenth-century French tag about Romania, that it consists of '*Des hommes sans honneur, des femmes sans pudeur, des titres sans valeur, des fleurs sans odeur.*' In the buoyant days of spring I had found this distasteful. For a month after the miners' rampage I wasn't so sure. Bucharest became a sullen, brooding city. Piqued at the West's hostility, bureaucrats resorted to an intrusive bossiness, reminiscent of the old days. Procuring international phone lines became more difficult. When I was dictating to the copy-takers, connections would mysteriously break at politically sensitive parts of the story. I even received letters justifying the miners' actions, such as the following, which was signed by 'an outraged intellectual'.

'Would the citizens of your country have allowed the main square of your capital city to become a nest of prostitution, of black market dealings (which we had been previously free of), of permanent inciting to violence, all these in the name of democracy . . .?

'The miners came to Bucharest. They helped in establishing order. They made abuses, it is true, and it is regrettable. But, before blaming them, ask the miners and workers of your country what they would have done in such a situation. And also ask the Romanian miners what they found in the places they devastated – guns, ammunition, drugs, money, faxing machines – the gifts given us by the opposition and the "pure-hearted" demonstrators.'

The juxtaposition of 'faxing machines' with 'guns, ammunition, drugs, money' as symbols of evil, shows the extent of this 'intellectual''s enlightenment. The letter exactly reflects the official line. Romanian state TV was one of the few networks in the world which didn't broadcast footage of the miners. Instead it concentrated on images of weapons allegedly taken from the hunger strikers and it broadcast interviews with alleged students, who obligingly confessed their role in 'the fascist conspiracy'. People hear what they want to hear and most Romanians thought the students and opposition had got what they deserved.

Within the gloom there were lighter moments, among them the fall of the egregious government spokesman Cristian Unteanu. It was recounted in luxuriant detail by the BBC's Owen Bennett-Jones, who went to Unteanu's suite – scene of my initiation into the world of bribery – to find a stranger at his desk, going through the drawers. The conversation was worthy of Eugen Ionescu, Romania's great playwright of the absurd. It went something like this:

Owen.   'I'm looking for Mr Unteanu, the government spokesman.'

Stranger.   'He's not the government spokesman, I am.'

O.   'He's not the spokesman? What do you mean? He's been calling himself the government spokesman for the last six months.'

S.   'If I say I'm the prime minister, do you believe me? No? Well, then, he may call himself what he likes, but he's never been the spokesman.'

O.   'This is ridiculous. Unteanu has been quoted in newspapers all over the world.'

S.   'Did you ever send us the papers?'

O. 'Well, of course not. That's your Embassy's job in London . . .'

At this juncture Mr Unteanu himself emerged from the next room, waving his arms and shouting.

Unteanu. 'Of course I am quoted in the papers. Mr Roman appointed me. I am the spokesman . . .'

S. 'No you're not.'

U. 'Yes I am.'

Mr Unteanu lost the argument. It was an important day for Romania's public relations. For six months visiting correspondents had met Unteanu and had all their preconceptions confirmed that Romania was Europe's very own banana republic. Mircea Podina, the replacement, was quiet, courteous and efficient. If he drank whisky he never let us know. Gollum-like, Unteanu retired to the bowels of the government building in Victory Square.

But most of the people leaving Bucharest's stage in the wake of the miners were less easily replaced. Thousands of young Romanians, the life-blood of the revolution, headed west. Bogdan, my wayward part-time interpreter, somehow reached London and kept sending messages from a Brixton bed-sit asking for an affidavit that he was a Securitate target. His thesis was that I had witnessed an attempt on his life. My memory of the incident was that he stepped off the pavement on to Calea Victoriei (Victory Avenue) without looking and a car brushed his leg. A Home Office bureaucrat was more charitable and Bogdan was granted political asylum.

Lunatic and scatty-brained, Bogdan was lucky. By the middle of 1990 the West was already regretting the blandishments made in the dark days of communism. Capitalism's 'Golden Curtain' proved almost as restrictive as its Iron predecessor and many students returned to Romania visaless and bitter. Rejected by their own society and barred from the West, some resorted to more traditional East European methods of escape. One of my closest friends from Bucharest University, Diana Ghionescu, married a visiting Dane. Diana, an English student with massive oval glasses, had read practically the entire literary corpus of the Western

World. Aghast at my relative ignorance she spent several evenings trying to remedy the gaps in my education with renditions of Proust and Joyce. Stefan, her chosen ticket out, was into weight-lifting and was not, I suspected, of her dream milieu. In 1991 I received a series of unhappy letters from Copenhagen, pining for the boulevards of Bucharest.

A week after the '*mineriada*', right-wing movements held a memorial service for Marshal Antonescu, Romania's Second World War fascist dictator, the first since his execution in 1946. With old generals jangling their medals and talk of the need for a strong man, it was profoundly depressing. 'The Balkans erode me,' commented Hermán Tersch, the *El Pais* correspondent for Eastern Europe. I agreed. My trusty 'Dawes diplomat' bicycle, which had been chained to the front of the Intercontinental throughout the miners assault, had a puncture. Its failure seemed symbolic of the state of Bucharest. When Sophie arrived after her finals we sought solace in the mountains.

For centuries the Carpathians have offered pilgrims shade, cool water and the ancient Romanian refreshment of a dollop of bitter-cherry jam. Legend links their valleys with the refuge of the children of the Pied Piper of Hamlyn. Travelling in the remoter parts was like stepping into a lost world. On our fourth night away from Bucharest, Sandu, a newly-made student friend from Sibiu, made a casual remark about a shepherd coming to town with a sack of money.

'You'll never guess. He came to the bank a month ago with a whole hempen sack full of *lei*. There he was in his smock and muddy boots and yet a full-blown millionaire. Bam! Down he thumped his money on the counter and waited for the clerk. It was a silly thing, really . . . You want to go there? . . . Tomorrow? . . . Why not.'

The approach route to the village of Poiana Sibiului told of centuries of isolation. The cartwheel had precedence over the combustion engine. The locals wore traditional peasant costume – cream-coloured smocks and Charlie Chaplinesque '*clop*' hats. Sandu filled in some sketchy details about

Poiana's wealth. The gist seemed to be that Poiana, like all Romania's mountainous areas, avoided the drive for collectivization in the 1950s, and that the shepherds, left to their flocks, bought off the authorities and prospered. He was mid-lecture on a rather complicated technical point about taxes, and I was dozing off, when we rounded the final hill and were plunged into the most feverish of Hollywood fantasias.

Roman columns, Gothic arches, mosaics, fiddly pavilions, scarlets, turquoises, stuccoed chalets, crazy-pavings – anything goes in Poiana and in any combination. The exotic architecture was balanced by a few more conventional status symbols, satellite dishes hanging from crenellated balconies and Aro jeeps – at 350,000 *lei*, about ten times the average annual salary – parked at the gates.

Uneducated but extremely rich, the peasants of Poiana are the *kulaks* of Romania and their society was a closed and private world. They swiftly appraised their new arrivals and within minutes we were ensconced with the priest. He seemed to think we were tax collectors and fended off questions with a practised guile.

'My friends, you of course appreciate that we shepherds have received no favours.' We nodded earnestly. 'Well, everyone has their contracts to fulfil, and we've always worked hard and paid our dues.' He produced a packet of Kent cigarettes from a fold in his habit. 'It's just . . . our products are the best . . .'

Friar Tuckian in girth and affinity to liquor, Father Vasile Buja had a magnificent beard, a booming laugh and a crucifix which bounced up and down on his chest. On a shelf behind him a row of empty Coke cans and deodorants was laid out like the family silver. The pride of the show was a Sony Trinitron TV. In a deference to piety, on the main wall hung a 'Last Supper'. Through a film of dark paint, the twelve could just be seen gazing down on the riot of purple and pink which was Father Buja's luxury carpet.

'A shepherd's existence is very unsure. You have to go into the fields day after day. And if you get caught in a storm you can lose half your flock, just like that.'

Father Buja's reticence was reminiscent of petty party bureaucrats. But this was not the whine of communist small-mindedness. This was a wilier voice from the feudal past. Father Buja was minding the interests of his parish. In rural communities in East Europe the priest is often the only man with higher education. The Orthodox rite has never been strong on pastoral work but it has traditionally fostered peasant superstition. Even in the late twentieth century, the Acatist, a prayer which commoners pay priests to commit heavenwards, is a staple part of the Romanian catechism. The Acatist is a direct throwback to the medieval pardon – a good way for priests to make money on the side. If Father Buja's Chaucerian bulk was any clue, his villagers were keen devotees of the custom.

There's a time in any interview when pertinent questions should cede to charm. Steering the conversation away from wealth, we broached the 'legendary' fame of Poiana's lamb. Father Buja was a man transformed. Within moments the *ţuica* bottle was on the table. He decreed a feast for the following day.

At this point my notebook and diary go blank for twenty-four hours. I remember bumping up a forest track in a jeep while Father Buja dispensed swigs of *ţuica*, all the while singing merrily out the window. I dimly see a mountain grove and a bench where a forester was preparing hunks of lamb on an open fire. But the only clear memory is that of the priest, flat on his back within minutes of our arrival.

The priest was out cold for the next four hours, as first the sugary home-made wine arrived and then the sheep's cheese. Even when the lamb was ready, thick tranches dripping juices, he could not be stirred. He merely rolled over and grunted before returning to his dreams.

The strength of the wine and the recumbence of the priest emboldened the locals to frankness. One young *baci*, husband of the heiress to a thousand sheep 'mega-flock', confided that life had been best in the last years of the previous regime, 'when everyone needed our food'.

'We shepherds are like cats. We always fall on our feet. Every now and then we even regret the passing of the old days.' He laughed. 'The shepherds and the Securitate, these are the true children of Ceauşescu.' Sandu hummed a Transylvanian folk tune. All the while the rich baritone of the priest's snores resounded from the long grass.

In this Carpathian idyll, the harum-scarum life of a Balkan correspondent seemed another world. We spent two timeless days with the shepherds of Poiana. On the evening of the third we were back in Sibiu where I was handed a telex by a sombre-faced hotel receptionist.

> 374567 teleg
> 36947 hiremr
> urgent qqxxease for alec russ ell usesxx in your hotel
> urgent can he retn bucharest soonest tonight if pss
> story on riots and general Stanculescu
> please ring.
>
> tlx t
> 190 (..? ssxe duratal.00 4 +

I glanced idly at the wording, almost threw it aside, read it again and − I'm reliably informed − started in alarm. Chris Stephen of the *Guardian* was sauntering across the hotel lobby. I ran over to consult.

'Phew, sounds bad,' ventured Chris. 'What are you going to do?'

'Er, well the train is out − much too slow. What about a plane? Yes, a plane. Excuse me *doamna*! Do you know what time the planes leave for Bucharest? . . . Only one . . . In the afternoon . . . Oh . . .' It was the nightmare come true − the wrong side of Romania on a breaking story.

'Well, I can't be there tonight. It'll have to wait. I suppose we could find some petrol and drive down through the night . . .' and then I saw Chris was chuckling and I reread the message and realised that not even Romanian telex machines could garble a cable to such an extent. The telex was a Chris forgery. At least he spared me the embarrassment of ringing London with a fake story. On another occasion a few days after our return to Bucharest,

Cath Adams was less fortunate. She was connected to *The Times* as a rumour about an ecological disaster flitted around the press centre. Busily pleading with the operator for a line, she didn't hear that the 'Cluj crisis' was a hoax. Nor did we appreciate that she was through to her foreign editor.

'Hello, is that the foreign desk? Yes, it's Cath here in Bucharest. There's a great story breaking – a massive explosion in Transylvania ... Well, we don't know much yet, details are still coming in ... Sure. I could be there in a few hours ... Casualties? Well, I should certainly think so ...'

At this point we started waving frantically and mouthing, 'No story. It's a joke.' Cath's eyes flashed in alarm. She thought fast.

'But, there again, when I say good story, it's not that big. In fact I don't think it's that important at all ... Yes, well, I know I said ... but, with these places, it's better to be cautious. You never can tell. In fact I think I had better stay in Bucharest just to be on the safe side ...' We could only conjecture the reaction of the foreign editor who in the space of a minute had heard one of his keenest correspondents talk herself into and out of a story.

In 1893 Queen Marie, on her first visit to Romania, confided to her diary: 'It's difficult to get up in the mornings here.' In the lazy days following our return from Sibiu this was a sentiment with which I could readily agree. In high summer, temperatures in the Balkans are of a Delhi-intensity; like Raj nawabs, the privileged leave for the hills and the less fortunate retire to afternoons of siestas, sweet coffee and gossip. Sunk in torpor, in July 1990 the entire Balkan peninsula dropped from the news. An insurrection reported to be imminent in Albania failed to materialise. Bulgaria's opposition took stock of its election defeat by the neo-communist Socialist Party and prepared for the autumn. In Yugoslavia, although prophets of doom were warning of trouble to come, the contentions shimmered like distant mirages. The Balkan summer of 1990, the first after the fall of communism and the last before the Yugoslav war, would, in the years to come, be remembered with dreamy eyes, as the summer of 1914 was recalled by the survivors of the Great War.

In Bucharest these were days when humdrum activities like changing money or fixing an interview took on a new meaning, when sweat glistened at the slightest exertion, when parked cars sank into the low-grade tar and when self-respecting functionaries migrated by the thousand to the Black Sea port of Constantşa. For Ovid, who spent his last years exiled in Constantşa, or Tomis, as he knew it, the Black Sea was an incarnation of hell. He wrote his final work there, the *Tristia*, an unrelieved lament about the lack of culture and the barbarians. That Tomis would become a rich man's playground, with the decadent lifestyle depicted in the lyrics of his *Ars Amatoria*, was, I'm sure, beyond his wildest dreams.

The more prestigious state restaurants opened up terrace bars whose tattered parasols and rusty champagne buckets hinted at better times. At the back of 28 Popa Soare, Doamna Patraşcu had a wild strawberry bush and several cherry trees and she placed bowls of these fruit, mixed with apricots and peaches, beside the telephone, aware this was the scene of my greatest frustrations. But the best solace of all against the pressures of the heat was to ape the chattering classes and retire from the city. So Sophie and I bought a car and made for the smart side of the Balkans – Yugoslavia.

It was about this time that the foreign desk of a London newspaper telexed their correspondent, a close friend of mine, 'to cross into Albania'. The said correspondent had to compose a delicate reply, explaining the journey would take some time as Yugoslavia blocked the way. There was a pause before, with a whirr of telex paper, back came a exasperated: 'Hold. Am consulting map. Stop.'

6

How the Other Half Live

Bucharest to Belgrade, July to December 1990

'God save me from Serbian heroism and Croatian culture.' – *Miroslav Krleža, Croatian playwright and novelist*

TRAVELLING IN THE Balkans seldom runs to plan. Five hours out of Bucharest we rounded a corner and came to a halt. We were over a mile from the Danube and a line of East European bangers stretched into the distance. Children were playing with a wheel-hoop in the shadows while their mothers tended meatballs over open fires. Blankets were draped over windscreens to counter the heat. Backseats were piled high with sheep's cheese, bread-crumbed pork, pickles and the other essentials of Romanian picnics. The scene had a disturbing air of permanence. It looked like a cross between Greenham Common and an August Bank Holiday on the M3.

'Yugoslavia?' chuckled one passer-by. 'Phew . . . Three days – maybe a little more.'

Bisecting Central Europe like an Imperial decree, the Danube has been disrupting travel for centuries. In the Dark Ages it proved the first effective check for the barbarians thundering south. It even halted the Slavs, one of the greatest movements of people Europe has seen. The forefathers of the Yugoslav peoples, the Slavs were after land not plunder. Their flat-bottomed boats, fashioned for the Polish marshes, were no use in the turbulent gorges of the Kazan and the Iron Gates. On the right bank the Romans fiercely defended more navigable stretches. Twice in the sixth century, Narses and Belisarius, the champions of the last days of the Roman Empire, drove Slav advance parties back across the Danube. Only when Justinian died in 567 did the Roman defences crumble; the torch of civilisation moved to Byzantium and the Slav tribes were able to cross *en masse*, nearing the end of their long migration.

Since then science and 'progress' have tackled the worst obstacle. The Iron Gates are no more. At the end of the last century Serb engineers hacked at the cliffs and dredged a safe-channel. In the 1950s Romania and Yugoslavia began Europe's largest hydro-electric project, turning the bane of the Slavs into a giant millpond. The name 'Iron Gates' remains, appropriated for the dam. But it's a hollow title. The gorge which traumatised sailors through the ages has disappeared, as has the isle of Ada Kaleh. In the first half of this century Ada Kaleh was a defiant remnant of Ottoman culture, forgotten by the peace talkers in 1878, an anachronism complete with bazaars and mosque. It's now submerged beneath hundreds of feet of water and is remembered only in myth, as the origin of the first olive tree, supposedly discovered there by Jason *en route* to Colchis. For Danube romantics, mourning Ada Kaleh has become a rite of passage. But a mile to the south we had a more pressing concern. The long hot summer of 1990 had spawned a new barrier – bureaucracy.

Laziness is one of the worst legacies of communism. Under Ceauşescu, when foreign travel was banned, the Danube customs officials dealt with a handful of cars a week. After the revolution they saw no reason to raise their rate. Sophie did a foray to the frontier. She returned with a long face. There were four customs officials. Three were smoking. The other was telling a joke. With two cars an hour passing through, it was a minimum four-day wait.

We were harbouring dark thoughts about the state of the Romanian nation when the queue-leader arrived.

'You want to go to the front? Whatever for? Are you in a rush or something?' He seemed genuinely puzzled by our impatience. We muttered something about 'crucial interviews' and he beckoned us past. Smiling and waving, the drivers in front pushed their cars to the side.

At the time we were so relieved to escape that we didn't stop to consider the motives of our fellow-travellers. On reflection their self-effacement was extraordinary. Queuing in Romania often induces a wild primitivism. After twenty minutes waiting in line for bread, the mildest-mannered people can break into screaming – particularly if someone dares to jump the queue. My only conclusion is that the wait at the frontier was seen as part of the holiday. In the summer of 1990, for your average Romanian, Yugoslavia beckoned like the promised land. For many this was the first chance of a holiday abroad in forty years.

It was a minor triumph. But as we rolled up to the frontier we were aware the key test was still to come. Daubed with stamps and seals worthy of the Peshawar postal clerks – I know their practices to my cost – our car documents filled two A4 envelopes. They looked magnificent. They were meaningless.

Car-buying in Romania is a ritual designed by the most fevered communist mind and the previous weekend I had cheated the system. Officially you signed a list, returned home and waited five years. I went to a wasteland on the edge of Bucharest known as the 'Sunday Market', handed over a wad of dollars and bought an Oltcit. A turquoise saloon complete with crank handle, dangling electric wires and bicycle-like tyres, it was a dream-machine and I drove around Bucharest quite the envy of the foreign press corps (or at least I liked to think so). There was one problem. On paper the Oltcit belonged to Mihai, my interpreter, as foreigners were banned from buying local cars. According to law 527, sub-section 11a, paragraph 3 (or something like that), Mihai and Mihai alone was allowed to drive the Oltcit out of the country.

Kafka would have appreciated our attempts to legalise the purchase. Dispensing baksheesh like a veteran, I ran around the law courts, completing forms in triplicate, begging with appropriate – and inappropriate – clerks and descending to levels of subservience and grovelling I never knew existed. The results, which looked like the more fanciful pages of a Stanley Gibbons catalogue, were stuffed in the glove-compartment. Unfortunately they were fake, as we well knew. Winding down the windows we flashed our cheeriest smiles.

'Papers.' With his sullen pop-eyed face and 'why-should-I-help-you' tone of voice, the chief customs officer was the sort of bossy ex-communist official you long to insult. His sagging belly told of years of preferment, years of the best cut of meat, years of bribes and corruption, a life of time-serving. He was all that was rotten about the old system. I voiced an unctious reply and he stomped off to his office. He didn't take long.

'You must return to Bucharest,' he said. (Was that a hint of triumph in his voice?) 'You can't leave Romania.' He waved his book of regulations at us and turned back to his colleagues.

'*Domnule*, one moment.' Sophie's peremptory tone stopped him short. 'Your book. It's out of date. *Kaput, Terminat*. Haven't you heard about the revolution? There is democracy now. *Democratţia*. New rules.'

The rule book, as thick as a telephone directory, was indeed dated in 1976. The man retreated a few steps. I lent my voice to the rout, trying to sound more important than my T-shirt and shorts might suggest.

Şeful [chief]. Yesterday I spoke with the prime minister (a complete lie). 'This afternoon we are seeing the Serbian government in Belgrade' (another lie). 'Ring this number . . . here. See what Mr Roman says about our having to wait.'

It was a gamble, but a small one. On a scorching Sunday afternoon I knew no self-respecting functionary would be at his desk. Anyway, the chances of his getting a connection to the capital were slight.

He grunted and disappeared with our papers, only returning after an interval befitting his self-importance. He lowered his head through the car window.

'But what do I do with the register? What about the column for departing cars? You do promise to bring it back?'

We were off. It felt good to be leaving Romania.

*

In the summer of 1990 the Yugoslav frontier marked one of the greatest demarcations of Balkan lifestyles since the coming of the Slavs, over a thousand years before. In the ninth and tenth centuries, as the steppe conveyor belt slowed, anarchy ceded to annexation and tribal chieftains marked out territory. Although the lines on the map ebbed and flowed, there is no sign that one society was more developed than the other. The scant evidence that exists suggests that the regional power, Byzantium, kept a tight monopoly on technological advances. The tenth-century Bulgarian empire, which included modern Serbia, Macedonia, Bosnia and parts of Croatia, had no coinage and relied on taxes in kind to pay its army.

This period, rose-tinted in the works of Balkan chroniclers, ceded to the centuries under the Habsburg and Ottoman empires. To a West European contemporary, the two ethoses defied comparison. The Habsburgs were the cultural heart of Europe, while the Ottomans were backward and barbarous. The Austrians ran a civil service renowned for efficiency and honesty. Under the Ottomans justice was summary, corruption was rife and cities were disease-ridden – between 1812 and 1814 Belgrade and Bucharest lost a quarter of their populations to bubonic plague, 150 years after the last serious epidemic in Britain.

However, most historians agree that for a peasant (until the twentieth century 90 per cent of the Balkans' population) life was as hard under the Habsburgs as under the Turks. The administrative reforms of the eighteenth-century 'liberalising' Emperor Joseph II bypassed the rural proletariat. Uprisings in Transylvania and Croatia were suppressed by the Hungarians with a savagery equalling the most barbaric Ottoman practices. Horia and Cloşca, the two leaders of a peasant revolt in Transylvania in 1784, were broken on the wheel and then their limbs were impaled on pikes as an example for would-be revolters.

In the first half of the twentieth century the Balkan states kept to a pattern. After the 1914–18 War they embarked on industrialisation and in the thirties all fell prey to the world recession. By 1932 world grain prices were down by almost a half from 1929, savaging agricultural profits, the basis of Balkan economies. The ravages of the Second World War compounded the hardship. Victors and vanquished were devastated economically. While Yugoslavia had suffered the worst physical destruction, Romania and Bulgaria, as one-time allies of the Germans, lost millions of pounds to the depredations of the Red Army. Under the lead weight of communism, the entire Balkan peninsula looked set to endure a similar slog towards recovery.

Then came the schism. In 1965, with the backing of huge Western credits, Yugoslavia's head of state, Marshal Tito, the Second World War communist leader, abandoned doctrinaire communism for quasi-market economics. Imports were liberalised and many price subsidies were abolished. Two years later the Yugoslav parliament legalised joint ventures with Western companies. By the 1970s up to a million Yugoslavs were working in the West as *gastarbeiters* and tourists were pouring into the Adriatic coast, spawning Benettons, McDonald's and other icons of twentieth-century Western culture. The *gastarbeiters'* income helped to lift Yugoslav living standards way above the rest of East Europe. For the first time in centuries the right bank of the Danube was unquestionably the better.

The people of former Yugoslavia regard the 1965 change as irrelevant. They see the reforms as 'bread and circuses', distracting attention from the more critical issue of political freedom, and in a way they are right. In 1967, under pressure from aggrieved party bosses, Tito back-tracked. The new system of 'self-management socialism', the brain-child of his chief-ideologue Edvard Kardelj, was a parody of communist incompetence. According to some estimates, the principle, to break up industry into thousands of self-managing units, left Yugoslavia with more wealth-distributors than wealth-creators. The outbreak of fighting in 1991 showed that a call to arms was more powerful than ties of affluence.

'But what about the freezers and the Pepsi?' counter the peoples of the ex-Soviet bloc. Yugoslavism may have been flawed but it had a consumerist face. It was the difference between the United Kingdom in the late forties and the mid sixties – between rationing and plenty, between a kilo of meat a week and unlimited prosciutto, between heavy bread and croissants, between nylon and cashmere, between mangles and washing-machines . . . We crossed the Danube in high spirits.

Slowing underneath a huge 'Welcome to Yugoslavia' sign, I felt I could empathise with Billy Hayes, who, at the end of *Midnight Express*, throws up his arms on escaping from a Turkish prison. I half-expected a welcoming hug. Then the customs chief demanded a bribe.

His underlings slouched and smoked with the surly insouciance of their Romanian counterparts. The only differences seemed to be the colour of their uniforms, the modernity of their guns and the smell of the liquor on their breath.

'Open the back-side . . . This is for me?' (holding up a canister of tennis balls packed injudiciously near the top). 'Thank you' (flashing a smile which didn't reach his eyes). 'You may go now' (putting the booty on the ground).

It was disappointing but in a moment forgotten. On the road into Yugoslavia the sun was benign, the bumps infrequent, the hillsides stunning and our good spirits revived. North-east Serbia is one of the poorer areas of former Yugoslavia but the first village shop was stocked in more style than the diplomatic store in Bucharest. There were German salamis and oranges, and Swiss chocolate and peanuts, and a fridge which worked, stocked with Coca-Cola . . . We ate and drank all the way to Belgrade, paused for an hour and then started all over again.

Our host, the Belgrade correspondent, Michael Montgomery, took us out on the town and laughed at our child-like enthusiasm for a 'Four Seasons' pizza and American ice-cream.

'They are just in from Romania,' he explained to his colleagues. Belgrade was the real world and we stayed there for two ambrosia-sipping days.

Belgrade is not one of Europe's beautiful capitals. On the junction of the Sava and Danube it tops the Morava valley, the main invasion route from the north. In the seventeenth and eighteenth centuries such was the see-sawing between Ottoman and Habsburg control that it sometimes changed hands in alternate years. Belgraders could hardly consolidate one style of architecture before having to start all over again. The most irrevocable assault came in 1941, when in a few days the *Luftwaffe* left Belgrade in ruins. In Serbo-Croat, Belgrade is Beograd, meaning white city. The post-war creation of dreary 1950s blocks is more grey than white and has no pretensions at being anything other than East European.

In the 1960s and 1970s Belgrade was an important playground for the international spy agencies. In 1961 it hosted the first meeting of the Non-Aligned Movement (NAM), drawing thousands of journalists and political groupies. The session firmly established Belgrade as a whispering shop in the Cold War chess game and a bridge between East and West. Tito's death in 1980, and later the end of the superpower rivalry, eviscerated the NAM's ideal and made Belgrade's role redundant. But the legacy endured and in the summer of 1990 the city emanated an authority and style lacking in its Balkan neighbours.

We passed most of our time in the cafés in the Knez Mihailova main street, luxuriating in the snappy dressers, the denim, the leather, the exotic hairstyles: the sights and sounds of Carnaby Street. Brushes with classic communist inefficiency – the triple-queue system in shops, the first to choose, the second to pay and the third to collect – couldn't impinge on the materialist idyll. The climax came in a garage by the River Sava where I found a pump dispensing lead-free petrol. For the Oltcit, with its tinny fifteen-year-old engine, it was no use, but as a symbol of Yugoslavia's relative sophistication it was potent. So far had the federation emerged from East Europe that there was a market for lead-free petrol. 'Can Romania ever be like Yugoslavia?' I wrote wistfully in my diary.

On our last evening Michael touched on the political rumblings. A Fulbright scholar-turned-journalist, Michael had five years' experience of Yugoslavia and spoke with authority. He spoke of Serb nationalism and Croat counter-nationalism. He spoke of President Milošević of Serbia and President Tudjman of Croatia and he warned of dark times ahead.

'I'll be needing back-up here soon,' he concluded. I contemplated the menu and ordered another ice-cream.

I was on holiday – I was also very blind. I should have been looking at the characters with long beards and khaki-uniforms peddling nationalist trinkets and Chetnik (the Second World War royalist guerrillas) memorabilia in the Knez Mihailova. I should have been asking about the politician whose baby-face and frizzy grey hair adorned Belgrade's billboards. I should have puzzled over how the state was funding Yugoslavs' affluence. Then I might have appreciated the truth – that Yugoslavia was living on bor-rowed time.

Yugoslavia was always more myth than reality. The first Yugoslav state, which emerged from the debris of the First World War, was seen in the West as the dream solution to the Balkans. Before 1914 the South Slavs had been the bone of contention between the Great Powers. In the ante-rooms of Versailles, where the post-1918 world was carved up, the hope was that the new state, officially called the Kingdom of Serbs, Croats and Slovenes, under the tutelage of the Serbian monarchy, could contain those simmering issues. It couldn't. For survival the idea depended on tolerance, a concept with a poor pedigree in the Balkans; within two years the largest nationalities, the Serbs and the Croats, had fallen out. For the Serbs Yugoslavia satisfied their long quest for unification in one state. Regarding themselves as the liberators of their fellow Slavs from Austro-Hungary, they felt they deserved the bulk of the power. The Croats, who had been keenest to set up the new state, found that Serb domination was as galling as Austro-Hungarian. After parliamentary elections in 1920, the Croat deputies decided to boycot Yugoslav institutions. When they were enticed back, the crisis deepened. In 1928 Stjepan Radić, the leader of the Croatian Peasant Party, and two other Croat politicians were assassinated in the Belgrade parliament by a Serb nationalist. To bypass the parliamentary disorder, King Alexander dissolved parliament and set up what amounted to a centralized greater Serbian state. However, while restoring a measure of order, this further radicalized Croat nationalists, some of whom formed the Ustaše, a terrorist organization dedicated to forming an independent Croatia. In 1934 the Ustaše got their revenge when King Alexander was assassinated in Marseilles. In 1939, as the world drifted towards war, the Serb leadership in Belgrade made overtures to the Croats, restoring a federal system of government, and granted them a measure of autonomy. It was a move in the right direction but it was much too late. Within eighteen months (1941) Germany invaded, backing a Croatian puppet state and the dismemberment of Yugoslavia. Bulgarians, Hungarians and Italians all greedily took their share. The royal family fled into exile in London. The first Yugoslavia was no more.

Shattered in a civil war (1941–1945) which left over a million dead, the Yugoslav ideal emerged in 1945 for a second airing. To safeguard the foundations of his new state, Tito, a Croat, ruthlessly crushed nationalism in the name of federalism and international communism. In the mid forties he purged both the Serbian and Croatian nationalist movements which fought in the Second World War. In the late sixties and seventies he repressed a resurgent nationalism, imprisoning thousands, including the future president of Croatia, Franjo Tudjman. The second Yugoslavia worked, but Tito was the key. The rotating federal presidency, which took over after his death in 1980, was always struggling to restrain the old nationalist devils, lurking in the shadows. The political bickering which followed Tito brings to mind Thucydides' dry remarks on the effects of the death of Pericles on fifth-century Athens: 'In what was nominally a democracy, power was in the hands of the first citizen. But his [Pericles'] successors, who were more on a level with each other and each of whom aimed at occupying the first place, adopted methods of demagogy, which resulted in their losing control over the actual conduct of affairs.'

For the West it was convenient to indulge the fiction of Yugoslavia. After Stalin expelled Tito from the Soviet power block in 1948, Yugoslavia became a useful buffer zone, and even in the late eighties the West was willing to turn a blind eye to some of its idiosyncracies. As we sat chatting in our chic Belgrade restaurant, the myth was shakily intact. The southern region of Kosovo, the traditional Serb heartland with a 90 per cent Albanian majority, was run like a police state. In February 1989 Serbian police killed twenty-four ethnic Albanians when suppressing a civil protest. But the impression remained in the West that Yugoslavia was the progressive good guy of Eastern Europe. On paper the economy was emerging from the shambles of the eighties. In 1989 and 1990 the federal prime minister, Ante Marković, forged a path towards the free market. His run of success easily eclipsed the achievements of his reform-ist predecessors of the 1960s. In December 1989 he pegged the dinar to the Deutschmark and capped inflation, and in early 1990 he pushed through legislation to end the 'self-managing units'.

Political reform was moving in the same direction. The orgy of iconoclasm sweeping through Eastern Europe left Yugoslavia untouched and contributed to its image as the stable country in the region. There were no obvious symbols of oppression to overthrow; there was no equivalent of Todor Zhivkov, Bulgaria's hated communist dictator, to bring to court; there was no Berlin Wall to knock down; there were no Red Army troops to send home; there was no Securitate to hound. Yugoslavia appeared dignified, even dull, in its disposal of totalitarianism. In January 1990 the Communist Party voted itself into extinction. In April Croatia and Slovenia, the richest and most Western of the six republics, held their first democratic elections. The other republics were due to follow suit in the winter. If any state in Eastern Europe looked ready for closer integration with the West, it was Yugoslavia. But while communism *per se* had slipped away, it had merely ceded to a different authoritarian creed – nationalism.

The arch villain of this new philosophy was Serbia's

president, Slobodan Milošević. When the history books are written, Milošević will be favourite for the title of the man who killed Yugoslavia. His rise to power came in a climate of resurgent nationalism. In January 1986 the Belgrade Academy of Arts and Sciences issued their famous 'Memorandum' calling for the inclusion of the two-million-strong Serb diaspora in Croatia and Bosnia into a 'Greater Serbia'. But Milošević was the first post-communist politician to dare to bring this message to the top of the political agenda. He was the first to articulate it to the Serbian masses.

The key moment came in April 1987 in a small town in Kosovo, where an angry mob of Serbs was besieging the local Party headquarters, claiming oppression by the ethnic Albanian majority. A line of police barred the Party building. Milošević, then a party functionary, emerged, reproved the police and told the crowd: 'No one will ever beat you again.' Kosovo, site of a terrible Serb defeat by the Turks in the fourteenth century, is the Serbs' holy of holies. Milošević's speech was a clarion call which rang all over Yugoslavia. Throughout Serbdom it united the left and the right, appealing to the Serbs' traditional victim pyschology, reviving old dreams of all Serbs in one united Serbia. It resounded in Serbian beer cellars, where down-and-outs at last had a cause to espouse. It resounded at the Writers' Club in Belgrade, where intellectuals could now scribble crazed pan-Serb pamphlets at will. It resounded in the Alpine valleys of Slovenia, fuelling a desire to secede. Most momentously of all, it resounded in the crescent-shaped land that is Croatia, the old enemy, stirring a counter-reaction. By August 1990, after three years of bitter rhetoric between the two capitals, Belgrade and Zagreb, the Serb/Croat sore, which Tito had tried so hard to heal, was festering angrily.

Yugoslavia may have been nearing melt-down but, *en route* from Belgrade to the coast, we found the shortfalls of Romanian engineering and the delights of Yugoslav mechanics much more compelling. Our journey became a testimony to Balkan good nature. With each mile from the Yugoslav capital, the Oltcit developed a new ailment. There was a pattern to the break-down sequence. Each started with a whine, moved into a splutter and crescendoed with us stalling. But however remote our position, a Yugoslav St George would be with us in a couple of minutes, wielding a spanner, usually grinning at the state of the car. On one occasion, when we broke down on the coast road, two men swam out of the sea, clambered over the beach, fiddled in the engine, muttered something incomprehensible, swam back to their speed-boat, returned with spark-plugs in their mouths, and fixed the latest trouble. We quickly developed a Balkan esperanto, a mixture of English, Romanian and German, and a fond admiration for the Yugoslav people.

In this faltering way, we passed through three former Yugoslav republics dominated by three different Yugoslav nationalities. In 1992 the Belgrade-Sarajevo road became a Via Dolorosa for journalists and I came to know each twist and incline and the ethnic breakdown of every village. But in August 1990 the frontiers were faint green lines on the map and we assessed the locals by the strength of their coffee, not by their blood. We breakfasted in Belgrade, dined in Sarajevo, lunched the following afternoon in Mostar and slept the night on the Adriatic. It was all so easy. If someone had said that two years later it would take me four days to complete the same journey, I would have laughed in disbelief.

We hit Sarajevo mid-*korzo*, the magical Yugoslav ritual of the early evening, when bright young things promenade through the city centres, in an unconscious reminder of their proximity to Italy across the Adriatic. After Romanians, they all seemed so healthy and immaculately dressed.

'Can I help you? You need a room?' We spun round. The man from Yugotours wore pressed Levis and a Lacoste shirt. He could have been an advertisment for Sarajevo 1990, apparently the clean-cut city of the Balkans. He found us a room with his second telephone call.

'Just ring if you have any problems . . .'

The opening lines in our guide-book described Sarajevo

as 'Where East meets West and West meets East.' But the sizzling of *ćevapčići* (kebabs) in the old Turkish quarter seemed all that was keeping the city in its Balkan roots. Our landlord was positively Teutonic in his punctilious efficiency.

I have retrieved a post-card despatched home soon after our arrival in Sarajevo. The picture is of Sarajevo by night and the lens, focusing on the Miljacka River, has framed the city with the surrounding mountains. My message makes wry reading in the light of the tragedy which befell Sarajevo in 1992:

> Heaven is a place called Sarajevo, bars, shops, peace even beauty. I feel I could be paying a few more pampering visits Yugo-wards in the near future, particularly if the Romanian bread queues continue to expand and the comfort levels continue to sink. Everyone assumes we're Romanian because of our little car and the Romanian number-plate. Consequently police keep pulling us in. But there's great kinship with the handful of Dacias to have crossed the border. A consumerist splurge after months of nothing to buy and nothing to see. Heading down to the coast for a few days.

> Alec.

The Princip Museum offered a taste of the more conventional fustiness of the Balkans. Dedicated to Sarajevo's most famous son, Gavrilo Princip, the assassin of Archduke Franz Ferdinand, it felt like an unfrequented antiquarian bookshop. Princip and his associates from the Black Hand, which was called in Serbian 'Unification or Death', stared down from sepia prints. Their arrogant frowns, directed at the Habsburg judges, could equally have been despising the new breed of *Sarajlile* (Sarajevans), since in the Sarajevo of 1990 history and prejudice seemed a low priority. Princip's waistcoat lay in a corner and the museum was unattended. It took us twenty minutes to find the cement footprints marking the fatal spot where Princip took aim.

The sea was calling and we pottered on through the old

Turkish towns of Konjic and Jablanica, Mostar and Metko-
vić. The miles passed in a glorious haze with only a few
dimly-remembered snapshots. On Mostar's sixteenth-cen-
tury bridge, teenagers were diving from the arch into the
clear waters of the Neretva, sixty feet below. In the tower,
the keeper served treacly coffee and talked about Hajrudin
the bridge-builder, whose first attempt collapsed and who,
so the legend goes, had to construct a more successful
second or lose his head. So convinced was Hajrudin that his
second attempt would fail, that, after removing the supports,
he fled, and was later found digging his grave. In 1992
Hajrudin's span was a cherished target of Serb gunners on
the hills to the east and in 1993 it was under fire from the
Croats. Bracketed many times, it narrowly escaped destruction.

'*Mirhaba, mirhaba*,' the bridge-keeper said in farewell.
His Turkish phrase struck an authentic note. Rocking on
his stool, in his little skullcap, he could have been a *hodja*
from Hajrudin's day, when Mostar was the centre of a
sandjak (province) and ruled by a *beg* (governor).

We mumbled a reply, ambled back to the Oltcit and were
soon winding through the moonscape of dessicated rocks
that is western Hercegovina, one of Europe's harshest
terrains, a plateau as barren as Anatolia. Our guidebook,
full of the euphemisms of a state-approved work, made
veiled references to the savage fighting in Hercegovina
during the Second World War. Locals said darkly that
Hercegovina bred the toughest Serbs and the toughest
Croats. But to us none of this seemed remotely relevant.
The first island off the coast road was Hvar, the mythical
watering hole of the Cyclops. It seemed as good a destination as any other.

The ancients thought Hvar was among the Isles of the
Blest. Illyrian pirates retired there with their plunder. On
the northern point, the Venetians designed a jewel of a city.
After a few days I could appreciate why. We stayed in a
half-built villa twenty yards from the sea. The local shop,
our source of food, shut at midday. In the evenings we
retired to the neighbouring bay where a Croat professor was

studying Plutarch's *Lives* in her holiday home. The only intrusion was the whirr of cicadas.

After three days I woke with a twinge of panic that Romania might be hitting the headlines and I insisted on hurrying to the far end of Hvar for a phone. The deputy foreign editor was at his most tactful.

'Where did you say you are ringing from? Ah . . . Well, I suggest you go back to the beach and enjoy yourself. We're rather tied up with the Middle East right now. A man called Saddam Hussein has invaded Kuwait . . .'

News is a bug. Catching a vague rumour of a cholera outbreak in Romania, we lasted only three days on Hvar before pointing the Oltcit to Belgrade. On arrival we headed straight to the International Press Centre to hear the latest. Chuck Sudetich, the *New York Times* correspondent, whom I had met in Sibiu covering Nicu Ceauşescu's trial, was on the telephone. He was speaking with the fire of a journalist on a breaking story. He hung up as we entered.

'It's happening. There's trouble brewing down in the Krajina. Watch Knin. You watch Knin.' He left in a rush. Sophie and I looked at each other in confusion. 'Cry-something? Kerneen?'

With fond glances at the Belgrade food-halls, we crossed back into Romania a few hours later and spent the night in Timişoara revisiting my old haunts. The Hotel Continental was as dark and hostile as ever. Corneliu Vaida, the imaginative press spokesman of January, had been relegated to the ground floor of the old Central Committee building. Silviu and his crowd had left for the West. But Corina was still there and with a classic East European story. Earlier in the summer she had visited one of her British TV friends from the revolution, become pregnant and lost the baby. (Or so she said – with Corina it was always hard to distinguish the truth from fantasy.) Bitter and disillusioned, she had returned to take up a job at the German consulate, catering for the thousands of Germans queuing to return to their homeland. Engrossed in her gossip, we luxuriated in the latest Timişoara conspiracies, and forgot all about 'Kerneen' and 'Cry-something', an issue which seemed both complex and parochial.

Our reaction – or non-reaction – mirrored that of the international community. On the weekend of 17 August, a simmering dispute between Croatia and its 12 per cent Serb minority flared into the open when Serbs in the south-west Krajina region had an armed confrontation with the Croatian police. The victory of Tudjman's Croatian Democratic Union Party in the April 1990 elections, on a ticket of secession from Yugoslavia, had alarmed the Serb minority, stirring bitter memories of the last independent Croatia in the early 1940s, the fascist puppet state of the Ustaše. When Serbs started losing their jobs in Croatia's administration, unscrupulous local politicians started fanning the flames, and declared the Krajina an autonomous Serbian region within Croatia. Zagreb's road and rail links to the Dalmatian coast were cut by Serb paramilitaries. All autumn the disturbances spluttered away with neither side willing to back down. The Croatian president, Franjo Tudjman, was too arrogant to understand the concerns of the Serb minority. The Serbs, fortified by weapons and money from Belgrade, were too stubborn to consider compromise.

The relationship between Croatia and its Serb minority is the key to the Yugoslav crisis. The Krajina uprising in August 1990 was the opening of the Balkan Pandora's box and a dress-rehearsal for the war proper the following year. Preoccupied with the Middle East, the outside world didn't seem to notice.

The Gulf Crisis came at a bad time for the fledgling would-be democracies of East Europe. Iraq foreclosed on millions of dollars of debts and was barred by the UN embargo from maintaining its flow of cheap oil in barter deals. 'The East European economies are cracking even as their governments make attempts to change,' warned Jacques Attali, president of the European Bank for Reconstruction and Development, at the opening of the 1990 annual meeting of the World Bank and the International Monetary Fund. His cry went unheard. Western politicians and newspaper editors were diverting their attentions and purse strings to the Gulf and the liberation of Kuwait. In November, Bulgaria, until then the dozy card in the Balkan pack, had mass demonstrations and overthrew its neo-communist government. The event hardly featured in the foreign press. Presidential and parliamentary elections in Bosnia-Hercegovina merited a few paragraphs. Serbia's poll in December, returning Milošević to power, aroused only marginally more interest. The election to the Serbian parliament of Vojislav Seselj, a right-wing extremist who stood for a Greater Serbia and the expulsion of non-Serbs from Serbian lands, was regarded as a typically ridiculous Balkan joke. When in the autumn, for the first time since the revolution, Romania showed signs of making a break with the past and a split developed in the Front between Iliescu's hardliners and a reformist wing, it seemed hardly worth ringing London.

For Balkan correspondents the news doldrum had no obvious end. Taking advantage of the lull, I pursued a few off-beat ideas and revisited old friends. Back with the millionaire shepherds in the Carpathians, I found them resorting to DIY, as the local Saxon stonemasons had joined the German exodus back to Germany. East of Bucharest, communities were turning on local gipsies. Among the most bizarre episodes of the year Sapînţa, a tiny village in the northern region of Maramures, announced a second revolution and threw out the old communist officials – a sign that the Balkan peasant wasn't locked in the past. *En route* to Sapînţa on the Romanian-Ukrainian border, I gained a poignant testament to the Jews of Eastern Europe at a wedding where I met Adi, the last Jew in the town of Sighetu Marmaţiei. The Sighetu of Adi's grandparents' day was thronged with the gabardines and long beards of the believers and the street signs were all in Yiddish. In the 1930s the region had one of the largest concentrations of Jews in Eastern Europe, supposedly originating from the medieval kingdom of the Khazars. But in 1990 the traditions which had led pre-war travellers to raptures had been stamped underfoot and Sighetu exuded raw xenophobia. Adi, a gloomy man in polished black shoes and a shiny suit, was an outsider even at the marriage festivities. While the bridal couple and guests became drunker, the dancing more frenzied, and the smell of sweat and cognac and garlic more overpowering, Adi hopped awkwardly from one dance formation to another, ever on the fringes. Occasionally he stopped and stammered out snippets about his forebears' wealth. 'We are a very wealthy family. My father, she has golden hands and golden connections . . .' The whirring squeeze box, the rhythmic stamping and Adi's poor English grammar heightened the pathos of his tale.

In between these roamings there was time to settle in for a long haul and prepare for the Romanian winter. So I started Romanian lessons and moved from Popa Soare to a more central quarter of Bucharest. My new landlady, Doamna Lydia, ran a curious household. Viorel, her husband, was drunk by noon and insisted on addressing me in German, however often I said I didn't understand. After a few weeks he took to wandering into my room unannounced, chanting German hymns, which he punctuated with *'Mein Herr. Mein Herr'* and a slight bow. I was negotiating another flat when Romania had a final grab at the headlines – Michael of Hohenzollern, Romania's King in exile, made a bid to return home. Late on Christmas afternoon, accompanied by his wife, Anne of Bourbon Parma, and Princess Sophie, one of five daughters, he flew into Bucharest airport unheralded. Before the government knew what was happening, they were speeding towards Curtea de Argeş the site of his ancestors' graves.

The cloak and dagger style of Michael's return was the stuff of Restoration Comedy and an uncanny echo of episodes in Balkan royal history. The founder of Romania's Hohenzollern-Sigmaringen dynasty, Michael's great-great-uncle, Prince Karl of Hohenzollern, entered his kingdom-to-be in 1866 disguised as a Swiss drummer boy. The scandals which dogged his successors were matched only by the antics of their Balkan counterparts. Bulgaria's King Ferdinand, a Coburg, was legendary for his sybaritic tastes. In 1908 he revived the medieval title of Tsar and commissioned a theatrical costumier to design a set of Byzantine regalia. The loose-living and libido of Romania's King Carol II, who reigned from 1930 to 1940, scandalised even Bucharest's liberal upper classes. As heir to the throne, in September 1918 he renounced his inheritance and eloped with a commoner, Zizi Lambrino, to Odessa. When the marriage was annulled he continued to clown around, abandoning his next wife, Helen of Greece, for the red-haired divorcee of a Romanian officer.

However, these *Prisoner of Zenda* touches, loved by Western satirists, are offset by a darker tradition. The affections of Balkan peoples are notoriously fickle. Serbia has a particularly grim record. In the nineteenth century two rival peasant dynasties, the Karadjordjević and the Obrenović, battled for the throne while at the same time trying to throw off the Turks' yoke. Their bloody feud was set in motion in 1817 when the original Kara Djordje (Black George), a hot-tempered peasant with an appalling reputation for savagery, was assassinated, almost certainly on the orders of his rival, Milos Obrenović, a herdsman and Turkish place-man; his head was despatched to the Turks. There followed eighty years of assassination and intrigue, with both dynasties winning and losing the throne, until in 1903 King Alexander Obrenović and his queen had their throats cut by rebellious officers. The summary defenestration of their bodies into the palace courtyard in Belgrade marked the final victory of the Karadjordjević clan. In Romania and Bulgaria there was a less turbulent tradition, but abdications were almost as common as accessions. Bulgaria's eccentric King Ferdinand lost his throne after 1918. Romania's roué monarch, Carol II, was disinherited once, won back his throne by guile and was eventually forced to abdicate in 1940. He died in Portugal in 1953, unloved and in ignominy.

His son, Michael of Hohenzollern, experienced his fair share of such Balkan bouleversements. As a young boy, Michael reigned for three years under the regency of his uncle and the Patriarch while his father, Carol, was banned from the country. In 1944, in his early twenties, Michael was a key-figure in the coup against Romania's pro-German

dictator, Marshal Antonescu. Endowed with the determination of his legendary grandmother, Queen Marie, who in
1919 won the hearts of Western statesmen at Versailles
when she arrived with sixty gowns, eighty-three pairs of
shoes and the watchword 'this is no time to economise . . . a
concession could be lost', Michael tried to steer his country
away from the influence of Moscow. It was an impossible
mission. Communist provocateurs machine-gunned a royalist demonstration on St Michael's Day, 1947. A few days
later Michael was forced to abdicate at gunpoint. After a
spell of chicken-farming in the United States, he moved to
Versoix, Switzerland as an airline pilot – a bathetic end to
his career.

When communism started crumbling in December 1989,
of all the Balkan monarchs-in-exile, Michael was seen as the
best bet to regain his throne. But the long years in exile
seem to have dulled his old flair. Instead of returning
immediately in December, when the country was in turmoil,
he delayed until April, by which time Iliescu was firmly in
control. When Michael announced he would celebrate
Easter in his old kingdom, the Front panicked and refused
him entry, claiming his visit would destabilise the election
campaign. Then, after months of rumours and speculation,
came the Christmas 'flutter'. While his entourage subsequently described the visit as 'strictly personal', there is
little doubt that they intended to wait and see, in the faint
hope that a demonstration might grow into something.

The first I heard of the return of the king was over
Christmas dinner with the BBC. Owen and Mandy
Bennett-Jones had been planning the feast for months and
the provisions were the result of hours of scouring the
markets and a series of strategic food-parcels from London.
It was with the greatest reluctance that a group of us cut
short the festivities and headed into the freezing night in
search of the royal party. Our ill-humour wasn't helped by
the necessity of a spot of late-night petrol siphoning. Romania was going through one of its periodic fuel shortages and
the queues were a day long. Marc Champion's Volkswagen
worked but needed petrol. My Oltcit had petrol but, of

course, wouldn't start. There can be few more disgusting sequiturs for turkey and plum pudding than a mouthful of low octane fuel.

By the time petrol was trickling from the Oltcit to the Volkswagen, the Romanian security forces were drawing up plans to ambush the royal party. As if Michael was a common thief, they blocked the road with tractors and escorted the Hohenzollerns back to Bucharest's Otopeni Airport. By dawn on Boxing Day, when I reached Otopeni, Michael was in the air bound for Switzerland. His first visit home in over forty years had lasted barely eleven hours. He never even saw his old kingdom in daylight. A Christmas farce, it was a poignant postscript to the year's events.

A fortnight later the order came to head to Turkey – 'soonest'. It was bad timing. Tarom, the Romanian airline, was on strike and the train was blocked by snow. A friend promised to arrange a driver and a car. When the doorbell rang at the appointed time I was confronted by a doddery old man with, of all cars, an Oltcit. With one headlight and no windscreen wipers, we made slow time. Worse was to come. It was only at the frontier that the driver confided he had no green insurance card.

'I thought we could get one at the border,' he said lamely, before pocketing half the fee and returning smartly to Bucharest.

I ended up stranded just inside Bulgaria, hitching a lift in a Mercedes with a Turkish black-marketeer and his Romanian sweetheart. Fog and engine failure restricted the Mercedes to twenty m.p.h. I fear I was an annoying passenger. The Turk kept stopping to say, 'We sleep. We sleep.' I would let five minutes pass before tapping his shoulder and pointing at the road. It was 7 January, a year to the day after my arrival in the Balkans, and I did not expect to return – at least not to work.

7

Nappies and Napkins

July 1991, Slovenia

'This is the hour of Europe' – *Jacques Poos, Luxembourg foreign minister* en route *to Belgrade for peace talks, July 1991*

I RETURNED TO THE Balkans to the boom of a ship's fog-horn. Why the captain of the *Marko Polo* decided on this assertive signal was unclear. Even as the sun was climbing over the north Dalmatian coast, the day was clearly set for one of those cloudless visions beloved by generations of Illyrian seafarers. But the deed was done and the hoot set off a chain reaction of wails and counter-wails, echoing from the shipyards and bays which line the old Roman port of Pula.

Awake in a moment, I ran to the rail and watched the crew _____ to dock. Marko, a Yugotours guide and ac-_____ the previous evening in Trieste, joined me.
_____ _____nest sights in the world, the Adriatic coast. _____avia at its best ... or should I say, Croatia.' He laughed. Dr Zoran, the third man in our party, gave a loud yawn behind us and stretched his head above the deck bench, before relaunching his favourite lecture.

'And you still want to go there? Among all these crazy Balkan people? They will eat you. You are crazy, crazy.' The doctor, a Croat Italophile, slumped back to his make-shift berth. Marko, who called himself a Yugoslav, winked.

'He's a Croat and I'm a Serb. Better watch us carefully, hey.'

Ropes were snaking on to the shore and the *Marko Polo* was nosing against the quay, where thousands of Western holiday-makers were revving their engines as they waited to board. We trooped down to the hold and were out in five minutes – three people in two cars, the only passengers on a liner designed for fifteen hundred, the pride of the Yugotours fleet.

It was 4 July 1991 – ten days after Slovenia and Croatia declared their independence from Yugoslavia, a week after federal army tanks rolled into Slovenia. The Bosphorus, where in January I had ditched my black-marketeer's Mercedes for a taxi into Asia, was a thousand circuitous miles away, across the Dinaric Alps, down the Danubian plain and on over the Balkan and Rhodope mountain ranges. After six months in Turkey I was re-entering the Balkan peninsula from diametrically the opposite end. Driving through the dockyard, I feasted on familiar sounds and smells. Pula was the federal navy's main base and, while never under Istanbul's yoke, it oozed the inefficiency and indolence of post-Ottoman dominions. Half-dressed sailors were emerging from their quarters, inhaling violently on cigarettes. With imagination, I could smell stale cognac.

'You see, this has never really been the Balkans.' The doctor, bound for Rijeka and hitching a lift, interrupted my reverie. He was frowning at the federal Yugoslav flags flying over the port offices. 'Remove the red stars, sharpen the place up. Ecco Europa.'

I swerved round a succession of pot-holes and harbour junk which littered the road and thought of the immaculate motorway which had swept me from Venice to Trieste eight hours earlier. Abuse of the term 'Balkan' was fashionable throughout Croatia and Slovenia in 1991, where 'Balkan' equalled Yugoslav, equalled backward, equalled bad. Slovenia can with some justification disown the Balkans. Enclosed by Italy, Austria and Hungary, it fits snugly into the underbelly of Central Europe. Ruled by Western Europe from the ninth century until 1918, it has a most unBalkan tradition of political stability. Slovenes' only tie with the south is blood. Like the Serbs and Croats, Slovenes are thoroughbred Slavs, descended from the tribes which poured south in the fifth and sixth centuries.

However, Croatia's claim to aloofness from the Balkans is less clear-cut. The Kupa River, the traditional north-west demarcation line of the Balkan peninsula, neatly bisects Croatia's crescent-shaped territory. Croatia's turbulent history of intrigue and invasion is pre-eminently Balkan. Its much vaunted medieval empire stretched deep into Bosnia, the heart of the Balkans. The Istrian peninsula, hanging from Trieste like a lower lip, looks as if it's aching to swing towards Venice and away from the Balkans. It is a neat symbol of one of the key dynamics of the Yugoslav trouble. Croatia itches to belong to the West but is firmly rooted to the Balkans.

It was difficult leaving Pula. My intended destination was the Croatian port of Rijeka, where Istria joins the mainland. There I would pause to glean the latest news of the fighting. But my map of Yugoslavia, the back of a Trieste hotel brochure, showed Istria as a roadless blob – not the best way to navigate around a war – and Dr Zoran, who knew the region, was set on first showing me Pula's Roman ruins. My admission that I had studied Latin and Greek strengthened his resolve.

'There is no question. This will be the gilding of your education. You must see the *ampiteatru*. It is magnificent. We go there now, no?'

'Well, there is a slight problem. I'm here for the war. I have to talk to people, find out what is going on, send a report . . .'

'But we can talk to people in Istria. I know many people. You can stay here for a few days. You have anything like these buildings in England? I think not . . . And yet you want to go to the war?'

While determined to press on, I was all too aware that the doctor, with his immaculate English, was an invaluable find. For Russian-speakers, or better still, Bulgarian-speakers, the intricacies of Serbo-Croat are negotiable. But my Romanian could yield only a handful of Slavic phrases, presumably deposited on the left bank of the Danube when the Slavs headed south. Memories of abortive attempts to communicate with the islanders of Hvar crowded my mind. We reached a compromise. The amphitheatre had survived a Venetian attempt in the fifteenth century to transplant it to Venice. It would wait until 'next time', when I would stay in the doctor's Istrian holiday home, drink his wine and tour the ruins 'properly'. Meanwhile I would drive and he could talk about his beloved Istria, or better still the countdown to war in Slovenia and Croatia.

We were soon spinning through the Julian mountains, high over the Adriatic. It was a comfortable ride. The afternoon before, at Venice airport, I had found the Avis rep. apologetically wringing his hands as he was 'down to his last car'. Anticipating a Fiat bubble, I was ushered to an Alfa Romeo.

'It is OK? It is OK.?' the rep. asked anxiously (As if I was going to say no). 'You go far?'

'Oh, not too far' (lying comes easily on the brink of a war). 'Just a little tour, a bit of business, a bit of pleasure, you know, around and about . . . If I want to cross a frontier . . . into Austria, for example?'

The man was almost indignant.

'Why, no problem, Signor Russell. We are an international agency. You can go wherever you like . . .' And so twelve hours later I was driving to the war in a brand-new white Alfa Romeo with a quadraphonic sound system. For six months I had been writing about Turkey and the Kurds; my knowledge of Yugoslavia's crisis was limited to the previous few days' newspapers and tit-bits imbibed in Belgrade the summer before. On an empty road in an idyllic landscape, I settled back to enjoy the doctor's discourse.

My first lesson came in the doctor's opening spiel. We were not in Slovenia – as I had believed – but in Croatia. Ignorance is the bane of journalists arriving in any crisis. It was to prove particularly acute in Yugoslavia, which drew hundreds of Balkan first-timers. Mine was a harmless mistake. Croatia and Slovenia were effectively on the same side in the conflict and we were a hundred miles from the nearest flashpoint. But it was a timely lesson on the potential

dangers of misnavigation and it convinced the doctor I was
an innocent abroad. He launched into an impassioned lecture on the frontier vicissitudes of Istria.

After an hour, we had almost halved the distance to
Rijeka and were still in the early days of the fascist and
anti-fascist vendettas of the Second World War. When the
doctor branched off on to the role of the Lombard League
with Istria's exiled ethnic Italians, I steered the conversation
to more recent and relevant developments.

Events in Yugoslavia had moved fast since my balmy
summer holiday the previous August. In the eight months
in which Saddam Hussein prepared for, waged and lost the
Mother of all Battles, the disintegration of the Yugoslav
federation proceeded apace. The doctor, good Croat that he
was, concentrated on the turmoil in Croatia and peppered
his analysis with partisan catchwords. But, sifting through
his 'elitist' rhetoric, I gained a reasonably clear picture that
relations between Croatia and its Serb minority had deteriorated badly since Chuck Sudetich of the *New York Times*
had charged out of the Belgrade press centre. In the intervening months the rebellion of the Krajina Serbs had spread
like damp through a quarter of Croatia, prompting the
Croat security forces to respond with a reckless insensitivity.
By May 1991 the net result was about forty dead Croatian
policemen and an explosive frustration among right-wing
groups in both Serbia and Croatia. This was boiling up
towards the key issue in the Yugoslav crisis, the Serb-Croat
conflict. However, as the Alfa purred along the Istrian
peninsula, it was Slovenia that was on the TV screens and
Slovenes who were intriguing the world. 'WAR IN EUROPE',
ran the headlines of the Western newspapers, over pictures
of federal army tanks lumbering into action against Slovene
guerrillas.

'Britain,' I cautiously explained to the doctor, 'is unable
to grasp too much at once and wants to know first about
Slovenia – and then, of course, Croatia.'

For the doctor it was difficult to separate the struggle of
the two republics, which he regarded as 'democrats' fighting
against 'communists'. He harrumphed and muttered about

the old Habsburg/Ottoman divide. So I watched a few more miles pass, shared my experiences of the Hungarian/Romanian rift in Transylvania, commiserated on the difficulties of dealing with Orthodox people, and delicately pumped him for information. As a war-briefing it was unsatisfactory. The doctor was as ill-informed about the situation on the ground as I was. But his resumé of the key dates in the countdown to war was, I later learned, faultless. In a referendum on 23 December 1990, 90 per cent of Slovenes voted in favour of secession. On 25 June 1991 the parliament voted for and declared independence. On 26 June Slovenes took control of the international frontiers. The next morning federal tanks deployed to retake the frontiers and the war was underway.

The Istrian coastline, which pre-1991 was a favourite for Italians in search of unexploited and cheap sun, can vie with the best of Greece or Spain. The doctor grew nostalgic at the endless miles of beaches, the stacked deck-chairs and furled parasols. We pulled in for a coffee and he reminisced about his childhood, when Istria offered cheap state holidays for people from all over the Yugoslav federation. It was the Blackpool or Margate of Yugoslavia – only blessed with more style and, of course, more sun. As the driver, I felt entitled to ask at least one presumptuous question: 'So there were some good things about Yugoslavia?' He paused, caught between his reverie of Yugoslavia's carefree past and the fraught present.

'Well, it wasn't all bad.'

And that was it. In the first of hundreds of days reporting the Yugoslav crisis I chanced on the question few Yugoslavs ever liked to answer. 'Was the federation that bad?' The Croats and Slovenes are adamant the Serbs had the best deal. The Serbs rail that the Croats and Slovenes had the best deal. Both points of view have an element of truth. In the argument it is sometimes forgotten that Yugoslavia was a beautiful if elusive idea.

A bustling provincial fishing port, Rijeka felt like Oban in August, when crowds descend for the Highland Games.

The old Venetian streets were thronged with cars and people. There was no sign of the war. Indeed, throughout the year Rijeka would be a haven, assailed only by thousands of refugees fleeing the mania to the south and east.

'Look, we're miles away from all the madness,' said the manager of the Hotel Bunavia, gesticulating at a topographical map. He looked at me disapprovingly as if I, as a journalist, was the one who had made his customers flee. 'We have rooms free. Guests have a good time. What's the bother?'

The 'bother' was on the map a thumbnail's width above his finger. Rijeka was twenty miles from Slovenia. It was mid-morning, and time to jettison Istria's intoxicating escapism. I parted from the doctor, who made me pledge to omit his name from my reports, and headed north, placing my binoculars on the dashboard.

On the 'border' with Slovenia, three schoolgirls in psychedelic T-shirts were hitching. They giggled at the chance of a lift in an Alfa.

'*Dobardan*' (hello), I started in my best Serbo-Croat. They replied in Slovene and chattered incomprehensibly all the way to the first barricade.

Within a couple of hours I was in Ljubljana, an hour's drive from Klagenfurt, one-and-a-half from Trieste, and the focus of Europe's first war in over forty years.

The conflict in Slovenia became known as the 'Ten-Day War'. The Slovenian Information Ministry kept the drama to a maximum, day after day pumping out defiant statements about 'Yugoslav aggression'. But of the ten days, only six saw any fighting and in the overall context of the Yugoslav conflict, it was an overture. About fifty people were killed, including two foreign truck drivers and two Austrian journalists. A few lorries and buildings were destroyed. On day two, the Yugoslav Peoples' Army (JNA) recaptured the international frontiers. But that was their last effective use of force against the lightly armed but mobile Slovenian Territorial Defence (TO). Most of the JNA soldiers were unsure of their orders, reflecting the indecision prevailing in the JNA high command. 'We will ferret them [Slovenes] out of their holes,' said General Blagoje Adžić, the JNA Chief of Staff. It was one of the best quotes of the war and featured prominently on Western front pages. But the ferreting was never attempted. By day four, the JNA units in Slovenia were either blockaded in remote valleys or surrounded in their barracks and cut off from food and electricity. I arrived on day seven and the fighting was over.

Ljubljana's Holiday Inn was an international talking shop buzzing with the same mixture of camaraderie and competition I remembered from the Hotel Bucharest in early February 1990. This was a war you could reach in a few hours down the autobahn from Vienna and journalists had poured in from all over Europe. The Balkan gurus were all there, diluted by Danes, Swedes, Swiss, Norwegians, Japanese, each with a short-wave radio and several days' worth of war anecdotes. The names of Slovenian and Serbian politicians and generals, theories and conspiracies were reverberating around the garden café of the Holiday Inn. On the hour there were angry cries of 'hush, hush' as the distinctive jingle of the BBC World Service rose from scores of radios.

At the International Press Centre I was number one thousand one hundred and something to receive a laminated orange press pass. A grey monstrosity, the building reminded me of the Shell Centre in Waterloo and had the same air of corporate claustrophobia. It was a relief to find the next in the queue was an old friend and counsellor from Timişoara, *Le Figaro's* Jean Jacques Mevel. He was feeling equally shocked by the crowd. We rose at dawn and went in search of Slovenia.

We found it in a village called Kostanjevica on the fringes of the Julian Alps, where life was pursuing its placid, orderly pace. Or, to be more precise, we found it in a bar in a village called Kostanjevica, where the men were arranging linen napkins for lunch and the women were folding nappies for makeshift gas masks. We were a few miles from the Kracovo forest, scene of some of the fiercest fighting, and yet the main concern seemed to be that a picture due to arrive at the village museum had been lost, delaying their Cubist exhibition. Our questions about panic or jubilation met puzzled shrugs and courteous offers of drinks.

'Our government had to act, and it has,' was the closest one brandy-drinking carpenter would come to emotion.

'We never expected presents or generosity from Belgrade,' added his companion, sipping a fortified wine.

With its pristine flower beds, starched white napkins and imitation Liebfraumilch, Kostanjevica epitomised Slovenia. There was something stultifying and quintessentially Austrian about the villagers' attitude. I longed to shake the wine-sipper and tell him to celebrate. He should have been drunk – not laying out napkins. I longed for a touch of intrigue or of zest and instead was handed a copy of the National Anthem, which in rough translation read like a tract of the Pilgrim Fathers. I scribbled down the most memorable verse, the fourth.

> God's blessing on all nations
> Who long and work for that bright day
> When o'er earth's habitations
> No war, no strife shall hold its sway
> Who long to see
> That all men free
> No more shall foes but neighbours be.

There was a Balkan twist to Kostanjevica. While the phlegmatic villagers were continuing their daily business, some of the senior community figures had quietly disappeared, presumably to safer quarters. No one had seen the mayor or the priest for forty-eight hours. The curator of the Museum of Expressionism, a grandiloquent term for the village hall-cum-gallery, had pinned a sign to the door saying, 'Closed. Back soon.' Our guide shrugged and led us to the hospital, where the doctor bobbed politely.

'No, we're quite ready. We can clean up and tend to most wounds. We don't have much to say. We don't panic . . . You see, it's not very likely that tanks come here . . .'

I suppose I should have been grateful that the flames of

nationalism which were raging elsewhere in the old communist bloc, and particularly in the Balkans, could find no fuel in the Slovenian psyche. With an ethnically homogeneous population (90 per cent Slovene) and a compact hedgehog-shaped territory, Slovenes pursued independence with a marked lack of jingoism, in keeping with the very unremarkable course of their history. For five hundred years they were the ideal vassals of the Austrians, never rebelling, never complaining. In nineteenth-century Slovene writings there is barely a trace of the heady ideals of 1848. They only left the Austro-Hungarian Empire when, following the collapse of the Dual Monarchy in 1918, there was no alternative. In the same way, the Slovenes were quite happy belonging to Yugoslavia as long as Belgrade didn't dabble with their heritage or disrupt their natural thrift and industry. Under Tito such misgivings were allayed. But when in the 1980s the federal authorities impeded liberalisation, Slovenes, who with 10 per cent of Yugoslavia's population contributed 20 per cent of its GNP, started to question their membership of the federation. The more Milošević stymied economic reform and the more the federal budget was channelled into the security operation in Kosovo (a Serbs-only operation), the more the Slovenes thought of going it alone. Possibly the final confirmation of the necessity for this course of action came in December 1990 when the Serbian government siphoned off from the Yugoslav National Bank the bulk of the money supply earmarked for the federation in 1991.

The low-key reaction and lack of triumphalism at the bar in Kostanjevica said it all. The formation of a new state was not some climactic and ecstatic rite of passage as it was for Croatia. It was more of a business deal. Indeed the plague of 'exceptionalism' which infuses the Balkans seems to have wholly bypassed the Slovenes. Romanians, Serbs, Croats, Montenegrins, Greeks, even the bland Bulgarians and the self-effacing Macedonians, like to vaunt their historical mission and noble origins. In the most poignant instance of all, Albanians, nurtured on communist propaganda and wisps of a hazy past, are convinced that their dust bowl of a country is destined for greatness. 'We have always been a rich nation. Look at our medieval empire,' the Mayor of the east Albanian town of Korce explained to me in early 1992. 'Just give us a few years and we'll be rich again.' The only way Slovenes can be tempted to indulge in national pride is when challenged on the viability of their tiny state. A page at the front of the state tourist guide primly highlights all the countries in the world smaller than Slovenia. Even this is done in the gentlest possible way: 'If you have trouble pinpointing Slovenia on the map, perhaps we can help . . .' This is nationalism in its weakest possible distillation, a rare luxury in the Europe of the 1990s. As the brandy-drinking carpenter of Kostanjevica said, 'Our government had to act, and it has. That's all.'

The road back to Ljubljana was blocked by tank-traps. Three metres high, made of welded railway tracks and underlaid with mines, they looked like giant metallic porcupines. On the other side, a detachment of TO in sneakers, white socks and tracksuits were erecting more obstacles. We didn't feel like applauding. It took three hours to find an alternative way back to the Slovenian capital and the Alfa clearly preferred the Istrian highway to the backroads in the Julian Alps. Hot and exhausted, we returned to the Holiday Inn with a dented sump guard to find the story had moved to Brussels. The EC was sending in a 'troika' of foreign ministers for a third time. The fighting had shifted to Croatia. Apparently the 'War in Europe' story had been covered and most journalists were thinking of pulling out or heading to Croatia. Bar the odd cameo appearance, the US networks didn't return to Yugoslavia for almost a year.

A 'troika' sounds like an exotic carriage from the pages of Tolstoy. In the event three Russian coachmasters would have been about as useful in solving the Yugoslav crisis as the EC troika, who in early July scurried backwards and forwards from Brussels to the Balkans, waving bits of paper. The EC was the second body to take up the Yugoslav challenge. The Conference for Security and Co-operation in Europe (CSCE) had proved a non-starter at the outset. Its special 'fireman' emergency mechanism was unable to convene until five days after the outbreak of fighting. At a summit in Luxembourg the EC member states hailed it as their big moment. 'This is the hour of Europe,' declared Jacques Poos, Luxembourg foreign minister, as he left Brussels on the first mission. But the debates had already raised serious differences of interest among the EC states, a factor which was to cripple their mediation in Yugoslavia. Germany's pressure for recognition of the two breakaway republics kindled concern in France of a German sphere of influence spreading in Eastern Europe. Fears of setting a precedent for the fractious republics of the Soviet Union alarmed British diplomats. So the EC had little to offer but pieces of paper and rhetoric. Within forty-eight hours Mr Poos' fiery words were ringing hollowly all over Europe after the ignominious collapse of the first of many EC-brokered ceasefires in the former Yugoslavia.

On the troika's third visit, the weekend after my visit to Kostanjevica, an agreement was formulated and later signed on the Dalmatian Isle of Brioni, Tito's old holiday home. The Brioni Accord stipulated that the federal army was to leave Slovenia and EC monitors were to oversee the operation. The pre-war status quo was to be resumed and no mention was made of recognition. Talks on the future of Yugoslavia were to resume in six months, after the furore had died down. In private, officials conceded that the Slovenes' breakaway bid seemed to have worked.

Inasmuch as the Slovene war ended, Brioni was a breakthrough and it was hailed as a triumph of European peacemaking. But the back-patting was premature. The Brioni Accord failed to tackle the problem of Croatia where a far more intractable conflict was underway. Brioni also bred an undeserved complacency in the West. The federal forces did not withdraw from Slovenia because of the fulminations and finger-wagging of Western politicians. Nor were they defeated by the Slovenes. While surprised by the resistance of the TO in the Ten-Day War, they only deployed a fraction of their strength – a few thousand troops out of Europe's fourth largest army. The federal forces backed off to concentrate on Croatia. It was to take the EC ministers and delegates several months to appreciate the extent of their miscalculation.

While the Brioni diplomatic wrangling was taking place I was languishing in Ljubljana, among the last half dozen of the original press corps. There are worse assignments than Slovenia in high summer, which was like a holiday after Romania and south-east Turkey. I was back to the ice-cream and cappuccino culture of Sarajevo. Two of the most experienced Yugoslav reporters, Andrej Gustinjić of Reuters and Tony Smith of the Associated Press, whiled away the hours, filling me in on the political situation, showing me the best bars in town. But it's hard to relax on a 'non-story'. London was instructing me to stay put and 'acclimatise'. I was convinced the Yugoslav 'story' was over. My diary is full of grumbles that 'the war has ended' and 'I have missed the action'. I spent the evenings reading *Bonfire of the Vanities*, whose fast-paced account of New York life and in particular the description of the 'pimp roll', the distinctive swagger of the blacks of Brooklyn, goaded my disdain for the smug bourgeois ideals which permeated Ljubljana. It reminded me of a toytown. Everyone dressed well and no one seemed to swear. The president, Milan Kučan, whose diminutive size belied a razor-sharp political brain, was known for his habit of jogging in the early morning. The city's hardest-hitting graffiti was advertising a rock group called Babes in Toyland. The name seemed highly appropriate. When a colleague rang from the hotel lobby with news of a mad Serb soldier holding Slovenia to ransom, I was downstairs in a minute.

The story of Lieutenant Dragan Grujević, who mined a fuel dump at the village of Mokronog, could have been culled from the pages of a Ruritanian farce. A tough-talking Serb, Grujević shot his more conciliatory superior and was threatening to detonate himself, thirty-odd comrades and a considerable swathe of Slovene countryside, unless the Slovenes renounced their independence bid. At Mokronog (which aptly translates as Wetfoot), the sense of comedy intensified. In the farmhouses surrounding the fuel-dump the name on everyone's lips was Stefan Sindelić, a Serbian hero, who in 1809, at the end of an abortive uprising against the Turks, detonated a fort in the Serbian town of Niš, killing himself, three hundred comrades-in-arms and half an invading Turkish army. The local federal army commander said he had promoted Grujević over the phone from sergeant-major to officer. The regional police chief, Stane Smolić, apologised profusely that he had no news. 'You see, it's tricky getting through to him,' he said. 'He only has one line and it's almost always engaged.'

It was an amusing vignette and I left for Croatia the next day in good spirits. But in hindsight this was just the sort of story that distorted the true nature of the Yugoslav crisis. The Ruritanian absurdity of Lieutenant Grujević accentuated the historical image of the Balkans as a silly little place with silly little wars. In the context of subsequent events in Yugoslavia, the fighting in Slovenia was silly and little. But the issues involved were neither. By pushing ahead with secession against the wishes of Belgrade and by taking on the federal army, Slovenia had bolstered Croatia's leaders to pursue a similar goal – and for this the peoples of Croatia were by no means ready.

8

Romeo and Juliet

Dalmatia and the Krajina, July 1991

'Slovenia is a Disneyland compared with the conflict we could
have here' – *Hrvoje Hitrec, Croatian information minister*

I HAD A BEWILDERING and depressing introduction to
Croatia. The day after I drove down from Ljubljana, the
advance team of European Community monitors arrived in
Zagreb. Their mandate authorised them to concentrate on
Slovenia and to deploy in Croatia 'as appropriate'. They
came on a day when vicious fighting flared in three regions
of Croatia. But they promptly announced at a press conference that their duties would be in Slovenia only, where the
fighting had ended ten days earlier. For the Croatian authorities this was understandably something of a blow.

'Perhaps still too little blood has been shed,' said Mr
Branko Salaj, the Croatian negotiator with the EC. 'It
would seem that we have to come to an abyss for the
international community to intervene.'

The furore ended my pet Romanian theory that Balkan
press conferences never yielded good stories. The Croats,
who had organized the meeting for moments after the
monitors' arrival, probably to make this very point, hammed
up their outrage. The EC team was humiliated and their
leader, Ambassador Jo van den Valk, looked mortified.

'I'm rather sorry to sound so negative,' he said, wringing
his hands. 'I was not prepared for this crossfire of questions.
Our mission is willing to share its views at any time.'

But the orders from Brussels were orders and the essential
absurdity of the situation remained unchanged. Two days

later, looking like cocktail waiters in their natty white uniforms, the monitors drove north into the valleys of Slovenia, while Croatia slithered towards full-scale war. It was an unfortunate entrée for the EC's trouble-shooters. 'No better than ice-cream sellers,' said one Croatian news paper. The nickname stuck.

For the international community the middle two weeks of July were a make-or-break phase in tackling the Yugoslav crisis. The war in Slovenia was over and the conflict in Croatia was spluttering at a low intensity. One person died here; a car was attacked there. A few shots were reported in such and such a village. The deaths in Slovenia had given a foretaste of the dangers of Yugoslavia. There was no short-age of pessimists explaining the worse horrors to come in Croatia. Dire soothsayers were even talking about Bosnia. This was the time that the West should have tackled the more complex issue of Croatia.

With the benefit of hindsight it is easy to prescribe. Milošević and the rogue federal army generals should have been told that war in Europe was inexcusable and they should have been threatened with something more substan-tial than pieces of paper. In turn, Tudjman should have been told that he had to grant far-reaching rights to his Serb minority. Such action would not have ended the blood-letting. Many of the Serb-dominated regions of Croatia were too far down the road to war to put their guns down and Milošević's minions were already at work disseminating arms and alarm among the Bosnian Serbs. But in July 1991 most mixed Yugoslav communities still lived and worked together in harmony. The poisonous strains of ethnic hatred, which by the end of 1991 infected swathes of Yugoslavia, had still to reach full potency. Yugoslavia was on the brink, but not in the abyss. The West had to show a firm hand.

Such is retrospect. Such is the sort of thinking indulged by angry Balkan correspondents after a few bottles of wine. It is even shared, I suspect, by some Western politicians. With the passing of each month in 1991, 1992 and 1993 the situation in the former Yugoslavia has become bloodier and more intractable and the shame of the West has increased.

But the point is that nothing was done and in all honesty, on my arrival in Zagreb from Ljubljana, I was as blind to the scale of the impending nightmare as the functionaries in Brussels.

'I think they [the EC troika] have quelled a volcano that everyone is hoping will not explode,' said Dutch foreign minister Hans van den Broek. It was another of the great erroneous quotes of the war.

By early July, Western journalists in Zagreb were split into two camps. The electronic media colonized the Hotel Intercontinental, which was best able to cater for their satellite dishes, editorial suites and squadrons of engineers. The scribblers, or 'pencils', made for the Esplanade. Less upholstered but more Habsburg, with an ornate central staircase, period chandeliers and a suitably gloomy atmosphere, it became rather like a favourite armchair. Ensconced in its purple-velveted luxury I found it easy to discount the Croats' shouts of 'War! War! War!'

For three slothful days I led a nine-to-five existence. Every morning the Croatian Ministry of Information held a press conference with the latest from the 'front line'. So lurid were their allegations of Serb atrocities that I was reminded of my old friend Corneliu Vaida, the imaginative press spokesman in Timişoara. The accounts of eye-gougings echoed the rantings of the more extreme Romanian nationalists about the Hungarians of Transylvania. Via the most restrained titbits from the morning briefing and the reports of peace-talking in Belgrade, I fashioned a daily despatch. The latest from Bucharest seemed much more pertinent. In late June a delegation of Romanian miners had returned to the Romanian capital, this time to protest against the government. 'I'll clear up here and be back in a few days,' I wrote to Sophie. It was on a whim that I agreed to accompany two American colleagues on a trip to the market town of Glina.

There had been a heavy fall of rain and it was one of those sticky mornings when flies and mosquitoes clog your hair and it's hard to clear your head of the previous night's excesses. The Kupa valley, south of Zagreb, is rich farm country and the road to Glina wound past steaming hay-stacks and heaps of ripening fruit. *En route* my companions, the correspondent from the *Los Angeles Times* and a US radio reporter, gave me a 'fill' about Glina. A 90 percent Serb town on the edge of the breakaway region of Krajina, it had already experienced serious fighting. In September 1990 the Croat police launched an abortive raid to disarm local Serb militia. In late June, a fortnight before our visit, Serbs came down from the hills to the south and attacked the Croat police station, until the Yugoslav Peoples Army (JNA) intervened and formed a buffer zone.

The synopsis sounds innocuous in writing and it seemed equally bland in speech. 'Oh, right,' I remember thinking. 'So the Serbs came down and then the army moved in . . .' I filed the information away in my mind and concentrated on the joys of driving a powerful car on twisting rural roads. With the harvest coming early, the terrain looked rather like the Evesham valley in late August – only in Worcestershire you don't expect to stop every five minutes to be searched by men with shotguns. After four friskings by Croat checkpoints, each more panicky and smelling more of *slivovitz* (the Yugoslav variant of *ţuica*) than the last, we came to Glina and parked beside a federal army T-54 tank.

I use the term 'T-54' with an air of authority. But this was the fruit of a subsequent rummage in the bookshelves of a better-informed colleague. At the time, the T-54 was an ugly metal monster with a revolving gun, whirring tracks and a closed hatch. For several months the Yugoslav conflict was covered mainly by Balkan stringers. We could tell good plum brandy from bad, knew a bit about Byzantine conspira-cies and considered ourselves experts on paranoia – but the arcana of military hardware was another matter.

This was the first time I had seen a tank at close quarters and the Alfa suddenly felt very puny. But my Eveshamesque rhapsody endured a little longer. A war 'expert', after my day in the Julian Alps, I was still convinced that this was a Slovenia repeat, a matter of amateur fighters in sneakers and tracksuits, a provincial affair. The tank reminded me of the barricade outside Ljubljana, a hindrance to the day's work, to be directed out of the way if possible. My American radio colleague, who had a better-developed sense of self-preservation, grabbed my arm and pulled me towards the police station. We crunched over glass. Someone called out. We were surrounded by a crowd of soldiers shouting at us in Serbo-Croat. The idyll was over.

Milling around the back yard of the police station, moving with the jerky action of puppets, there were about sixty Croat National Guardsmen, reeking of *slivovitz*, communicating only in shouts, plainly terrified. Most were in their early twenties. The walls were peppered with bullet holes.

'If the army wants to fight us, let them,' said the commander, Captain Zlatko Krušic. 'We'll take them on and the fucking Chetniks.' (The Second World War Serb Royalist guerrillas, the Chetniks were purged by Tito. Their name was adopted in 1990 by some Serb irregular formations and used by Croats to denote all the Serb forces.) These were brave words but from a desperately frightened man. My colleagues did most of the questioning. I looked out the window, saw a tank barrel levelled in our direction and cancelled my intended query about why there were no look-outs.

Glina was doomed. Captain Krušic and his men were on one side of the square; the Serb mayor and cronies had barricaded themselves into the town hall on the other. JNA units with their T-54s were patrolling the middle ground. It was as if someone was waiting for a signal to begin – and yet the stand off was vaguely ridiculous. I felt I was with a group of children who had had an argument and could not make amends without losing face.

'Don't worry, Captain,' I said as we rose to go. 'We'll have a talk with the Serbs and see what they say. I'm sure it's not that bad.'

I writhe at the memory of my blasé bonhomie. It was 'that bad' – and worse. The Serb mayor, Dušan Jović, had gone mad.

'The Croats have formed the National Guard to massacre

us. If it wasn't for the army we would be dead men, and not just dead. You know what they did in the last war? They killed millions of us, slit our throats, bludgeoned our babies. Here in Glina sixteen hundred people died. Well, it will happen again. We were a peaceful town and then they came from Zagreb and took our jobs. We only have pistols. Adolf Hitler, Mussolini and Pavelić, they were all for Croatia. We face the new Ustaše (the Second World War Croatian puppet fascist state whose atrocities shocked even their German allies) . . . forging the Fourth Reich . . .'

It was the psychology of the miners of Bucharest in June 1990. Myth and mania had replaced reality. There was a hint of truth in a fraction of the mayor's ravings. After the victory of Tudjman's Croatian Democratic Union (HDZ) Party in the May 1990 elections, Zagreb had conducted a purge of Serbs from positions of authority. To the Croats the purge was a way of redressing the numerical balance. Tito had made Croatia's administration top-heavy with Serbs, as a way of both diluting Croatian nationalism and satisfying the pride of the Krajina Serbs. However, for Mayor Jović of Glina, the purge had shades of the Second World War – and the Balkan mindset had taken over. For Jović, the Croat soldiers cowering in the police station were neo-Nazi child-murderers. In his fevered brain it was kill or be killed.

In his khaki fatigues and with a handgun, Jović looked more like a bandit than a small-town mayor. We wanted to argue with him, to shout and scream, and instead we fawned and smiled and praised his *slivovitz* and mumbled sweet nothings about 'misunderstood Serbia'. We closed with the trite parting question. 'What did you do before the trouble?' His eyes brightened and back came possibly the most ludicrous line of the nightmarish morning. 'Gynaecologist. I used to be a gynaecologist.'

I returned to Zagreb and filed a lugubrious dispatch. For the first time I appreciated that Europe was on the brink of a horrible war. The people in Glina weren't talking about the rights and wrongs of Yugoslavia. They were talking about 'Chetniks' and Ustaše, the labels of the

Second World War. The horror scenario had come true in outlying regions and the political grievances were turning into an ethnic war. It was a hate culture, stirred up by the power mania of the Yugoslav politicians, Milošević in particular, primed by two of the traditional Balkan dynamics, prejudice and plum brandy, and now totally out of control.

The same night, talks in Belgrade ended with Yugoslav politicians reaching some vague agreement on a framework for the future. 'Irrelevant,' I concluded in the light of my experience in Glina. I retired to bed without sending an update. The next morning I heard that 'Fresh Peace Hopes in Belgrade' had squeezed my more pessimistic story out of the late editions of the paper. On reflection, I suspect the tone of my writing was at fault. Sarcasm never works in print. 'Only two people were killed yesterday . . .' ran one particularly angry paragraph. The editors had had the sense and good taste to apply their blue pencil. However, the experience strengthened my determination to go travelling, to understand more about the war. Many of my colleagues at the Esplanade were old Yugoslav hands with years of knowledge of the region. It was time to find out why a gynaecologist had turned gunman.

The headquarters of Croatia's rebel Serbs was a medieval fortress called Knin, fifty miles from the sea. In the regional capital, the Dalmatian port of Zadar, Croats were reported to have set fire to Serb holiday homes. It seemed a good place to start. Four hours after leaving Zagreb, I was lounging in a hotel room by the Adriatic enjoying a platter of Dalmatian prosciutto. My diary entry for the day records that my most important decision was choosing between taking a swim or a second cup of coffee.

In happier times the Hotel Zadar was a shrine to the Western package-deal. The rooms had whitewashed walls and bright blue towels. Tinted french windows looked over the sea, luminous posters in the lobby announced excursions, the restaurant menu ranged from schnitzel to spaghetti. On Saturday 20 July 1991 the register was empty, the bar was closed, the staff on half-time and I was the only guest. But with a stretch of the imagination you could almost hear the shouts of children and the ghosts of holiday-makers past.

In this ambience it was easy to metamorphose into a tourist. When the porter interrupted my journal-writing to say I had a phone call in the foyer, I padded down the corridor in sandals with a towel round my waist. Mario, the receptionist, wouldn't mind.

The porter was wrong. It wasn't the telephone. I had a visitor. Professor Ljubomir Radić, Zadar University's Professor of English Literature, man of letters without equal in north Dalmatia, was sitting by the bar, waiting for me. He stood up at my arrival. 'Er, hum, the *Daily Telegraph*?'

There was nothing to be done. I stepped forward as if I always held interviews in beach-gear, shook the professor's hand, concocted some fantastic story about telephones and retreated to my room for a quick change.

Professor Radić was my contact in Zadar – or at least he was a friend of a friend of a friend, whose telephone number I had been given in Zagreb. When I arrived in Zadar I rang the number to find friend number one spoke no English but knew someone who did. The 'someone who did' only spoke French, and poorly, but knew the French professor, who in turn knew Radić. Swept down the chain, I never had time to explain that I was only looking for an interpreter – not for an interview. The net result was the top literary professor in Zadar cutting short his Saturday afternoon siesta – and me foregoing my swim – for a meeting whose reason neither of us really understood.

As if holding a grandiose tutorial, we sat looking over the Adriatic, two people on a terrace designed for a hundred, one in late middle age in jacket and tie, the other in a crumpled short-sleeved shirt, the cleanest my wardrobe could muster. Mario brought some coffee and juice. The professor cleared his throat and began.

He spoke for almost an hour. Starting with culture he moved on to history and finally to politics. In his precise, clipped tones he covered Zadar's glory years as an independent city state, the centuries under Venice and then the nineteenth-century *bouleversement*, when the French, Austrians and Italians bickered for Zadar's control. He ranged from Anastasia, the patron saint of Zadar, to St Donatus of Fiesole, one of those mad Irish priests who roamed the world in the Dark Ages, and built – or at least is believed to have built – Zadar's Church of St Donat, one of the most unusual churches in South-East Europe.

It was a virtuoso performance and, to my shame, largely wasted. The only part which held my attention was a reference to the sack of Zadar by the Fourth Crusade, which stirred the memory of a distant history lesson and seemed wryly appropriate to the crisis in Yugoslavia. The essence of the story is that in 1202 the Doge of Venice, a notorious schemer called Dondolo, did a deal with the leaders of the Fourth Crusade who agreed to storm Zadar in return for transport to the Holy Land. Such was the success of the joint venture that two years later the partnership repeated their skulduggery and sacked Constantinople, Venice's trade rival in the eastern Mediterranean. So within two years the 'warriors of Christ' pillaged two of the cultural jewels of Europe. It has to be one of the more ignominious episodes in the history of medieval Christendom, making a mockery of the crusading ideal. In 1991 Serbs and Croats liked to present the conflict as a crusade against each other's faith. The Serbian Orthodox Church, as corrupt as its neighbour in Romania, preached hellfire sermons about the 'Vatican Conspiracy'. 'Croat Catholics have something in their blood that makes them always want to kill,' Father Filaret, an Orthodox priest known by Serbs as their 'Mother Teresa', told me. 'We know what is their game. Some of them are like devils and devil's daughters.' The Croats in turn professed the moral superiority of the Catholic culture over the Orthodox, a view which had a bloody climax under the Ustaše who regarded Serbs as apostates and slaughtered up to 300,000 who wouldn't convert. If any Croats should have been cynical about such rhetoric it was the Zadaris, whose ancestors were put to the sword by soldiers with red crosses on their tunics. But with the professor in full-flow on the Dalmatian heritage, it was not the time to indulge in such thinking.

His oration ended as the sun dipped over the Adriatic. Mario brought a bottle of Posip, one of the driest and best of the Yugoslav wines, and the professor asked to exchange roles.

'You do the talking. It is my turn to ask the questions.' Normally this is a twist to be avoided. Journalism is about listening, not talking, and the added danger of airing your views in a war zone is that your banter has a curious habit of reappearing in the local paper, dressed up as a triumphant vindication of the local grievance. However, my meeting with the professor was more of a symposium than an interview and so, after a sample of the Posip, I agreed to the request. His first question went straight to the jugular.

'Tell me, Alec, in all honesty do you think a British journalist with no Serbo-Croat and on his first visit to Croatia can ever hope to understand let alone report on the conflict?'

There was no easy reply. The answer was no, but yes. No, a non-Balkan could never fully understand the Balkan mind and a lack of Serbo-Croat was a disadvantage. Yes, only outsiders could write about it without prejudice. It didn't seem fair to reprove this humanist with the taint of Balkan barbarism, so I cast my mind back a few days, forgot the warm Adriatic breeze and Zadar's marble balustrades and told the professor about my encounter with the gynaecologist of Glina.

He appeared to like the story. Maybe my presentation of Mayor Jović pandered to the Croat stereotype of the 'Serb fanatic' – a character stretching back to Princip, the young assassin of Sarajevo in 1914. Maybe he thought I was being sympathetic to the Croat Captain Krušic. If so, in a way he was right. I did feel sorry for Krušic. He and his men were the fall-guys of Glina; of the Serbs, who were about to attack; of their own government, who insisted they stayed at their posts; of the West, which was ignoring their plight; even of the journalists, who arrived like emissaries from the outside world, sighed, wrote a story and left. But I also felt sorry for Mayor Jović, whose brain was so addled by his masters' propaganda that he had given himself over to the dark side of the Balkans, although this was a subtlety I suspected the professor did not grasp.

By the end the professor was leaning forward in his chair, nodding at some of the details, tut-tutting at others. By early July no Croat in his right mind went to places like Glina – just as few Serbs dared visit a Croat heartland like Zadar. The consequent dearth of first-hand information about the other side thrust both peoples into relying on their state televisions and contributed to the rapid polarisation of Yugoslav opinion. Both Belgrade television and Croatian Television (HTV) reported at their respective presidents' bidding. Their hyped trash demonised the other side and talked up the war. While the professor was intelligent enough not to believe all of HTV's rubbish, my story was a rare opportunity to hear first-hand about the Serbs.

'Very interesting,' he cried. 'I have the answer for your study. [Did he think I was a student?] Ive, the Mayor of Zadar, is a friend of mine. I will ring him tonight and you will see him tomorrow. It will be the interview of your career. Then you will understand everything.'

Nothing was easier in my mind than to justify another day in Zadar and postponing a visit to the Serbs' headquarters in Knin. We sealed the decision with a second bottle of Posip and I tottered in search of Mario, the master of ceremonies for the night ahead.

If the Zadar of 1202 was anything like its late twentieth-century successor, I can understand why Doge Dondolo was covetous. My night in Zadar was without doubt one of my most hedonistic in three years in the Balkans. Mario laid down one rule: 'Don't mention the war.'

We couldn't escape from the crisis, not even in the Olympic Club, a Hippodrome lookalike where young blades strutted round the dance floor in designer combat fatigues, impressing the girls with their hand-grenades and knives. But this machoism meant nothing to Mario, who said he hated guns.

'Besides, these aren't the real fighters. The real fighters are on the front line facing the Chetniks.'

'Chetniks?'

'Well, OK, Serbs.' We talked about rock-and-roll and London and the States. Of course we returned to Yugoslavia because you couldn't talk about the West without talking about the West's reaction to Yugoslavia and Mario, like every young Croat, was perplexed by the West's refusal to 'welcome his country into the club'.

Then Mario's wife arrived and we drank and we danced and drank some more and suddenly it was nearer dawn than midnight and Mario was offering one more cocktail. I was poor company over breakfast when the professor called to escort me to the mayor.

We drove to City Hall in the professor's bubble car. Hurtling through the narrow avenues, scattering worshippers on their way to Mass, I felt like a bit part in a 'Monsieur Hulot'. All the while the professor was chattering away, pointing out Zadar's sights, including the church of St Donat, which reminded me distinctly of a Martello tower. The door was locked and the caretaker asleep. Half an hour late, we heard a puffing and panting and the sound of bolts being removed. The door swung open. It was the mayor.

His face has faded from memory but I do remember his dapper grey suit and his magnificent sculpted office, draped in Croatian heraldry. The red and white chequerboard, which symbolised the glory days of King Tomislav in the tenth century, and the not so glorious days of the Ustaşe, had been readopted by Tudjman and his party the HDZ for the May 1990 elections. It was everywhere in Croatia in 1991 and it emblazoned the mayor's possessions, his stationery, desk, visiting cards and walls.

Mayor Ive Livljanić was as urbane as the professor and shared his fascination with history. He said much that was reasonable and courteous – and yet there was something disturbing about his obsession with culture. Zadar, with its 83 per cent Croat majority, was not the innocent city that its elegant marble plazas suggested. The previous night Mario had mentioned the 'troubles' in April, when young HDZ activists charged through the streets, looting Serb-run shops and the offices of Yugoslav companies. The mayor deployed the classic nationalist's tactic of using culture as a euphemism for nationalism and talked about the fight for democracy against 'Bolshevism'. He was, I now realise, the HDZ personified – desperate to be thought of as Western and liberal, but not quite succeeding.

Although not fascist, as the Serbs claimed, Croatia in 1991 was far from democratic. President Tudjman, a former communist general, had no conception of the meaning of the words 'liberalism' and 'democracy'. For Tudjman, as for Iliescu, Milošević and their authoritarian confrères who have since sprouted all over the ex-Soviet Union, these were mere slogans. Like most ex-communists, Tudjman totally failed to understand the concept of minority rights. Croatia's Serbs required gentle massaging. They needed a reassurance which might have kept them from the clutches of the unscrupulous politicians in Belgrade. Instead, Tudjman behaved in a clumsy and authoritarian way, insisting that Latin script replaced Cyrillic. (Cyrillic was traditionally used by the Serbs and Latin by the Croats.) This provision was later revoked, but not before the Serbs were talking uneasily about the parallels with the Ustaše state of 1941.

Croat friends rightly point out that Tudjman's peccadilloes do not justify the carnage wrought by the Serbs – just as there was no comparison between the urbanity of Livljanić of Zadar and the mania of Jović the gun-wielding gynaecologist of Glina. In the early stages of the war the number and scale of Serb atrocities easily eclipsed any horrors done by the Croats. However, too many Croats blinded themselves to the realities of their state. Unlike Slovenia, Croatia cannot claim immunity from the Balkan psyche. The Serb/Croat dispute was not 'evil' pitted against 'good'. One of the most depressing aspects of the war was watching Croat soldiers sinking to the psychotic levels of men such as Jović.

Mayor Livljanić closed the interview with an impassioned blast against the 'terrorists' of Knin and a plea for the West to beware of the horrors looming on Europe's doorstep.

'My appeal would be to the world not to wait and waste

time,' he said. 'The longer they wait the worse the bloodshed will be.' Within three months he would be leading the defence of Zadar against a three-pronged attack and his words would be sounding hollowly across the Adriatic towards Italy and Western Europe. But on that hot Sunday morning, as I left his office, I was quietly sceptical about his alarmist rhetoric. After bidding farewell to the professor, whose name I pledged to change in print, I was all the more determined to visit Knin, to see what the Serb 'terrorists' had to say in reply.

Second time round, Zadar-by-night paled. We visited the same bars, danced to the same songs and watched the same young bucks parade with their fancy weapons. I felt sated on the good life. Mario was also depressed. A bomb had exploded in his suburb that afternoon – or at least someone said that a bomb had exploded in his suburb.

'I decided today that I too will fight if I have to.' There wasn't much to say. Like so many young Yugoslavs, Mario was locked into his own struggle, an identity crisis between his Yugoslav youth and the new dark forces calling from Zagreb and Belgrade.

The following morning Mario handed me a parcel of trashy paperbacks, the cast-offs of visiting British tourists.

'We won't be needing these for a while. Take them. If the Chetniks lock you up, you may want something to read.' I laughed but he didn't laugh back.

'*Bok*,' he shouted. 'Croatian for cheers – but don't say it in Knin. They'll gouge your eyes out if you do.'

On the map the Maslenica channel, which separates the Zadar peninsula from the mainland, is a hair's width strip of blue, so faint it's hardly visible. In the Middle Ages it was on the fringes of the Venetian and Ottoman Empires. In July 1991 history was turning full circle and the Maslenica Bridge, a key road junction for Zagreb, was once again a frontier zone.

Purring over the bridge, I reflected on Mario's parting words. In the Hotel Esplanade dining room tales of the 'terrible Serb' had spiced several late-night conversations.

On the edge of the Krajina the anecdotes seemed less far-fetched. Twenty miles from Zadar the road divided. To the left stretched the route to the north, towards Zagreb and Austria and normality; to the right was Knin and the Balkan hinterland. I pulled over. In Glina I had craved the independence of travelling alone. On the edge of Croatia's heart of darkness, I wasn't so sure.

Behind me the sun sparkled over the Pag peninsula, a vision as ethereal as anything on the Aegean. In front nothing moved. The parched hills had a brooding intensity, reminiscent of Kohistan in north-east Pakistan. There each community is a private fiefdom subject to tribal law, and travellers still sometimes disappear. In the winter of 1989, when I was cycling through the region, every morning locals clustered around with dark stories about the village ahead. 'They will kill you and rape you and kill you again . . .' Each time the same mental battle had to be re-hearsed: 'I know they are exaggerating, but what if on this particular occasion they are right?' On the fringe of the Krajina I faced the same decision.

Maybe a smart executive appearance would help? I fumbled in my bag for a tie, wrapped it round my neck, looked in a mirror and pulled it off again, cursing my superstition. I was coming from the direction of Zadar. That was all that would matter to the Serbs.

This was one of the last times I crossed the lines alone. It's hard to justify why you drive down a particular road, which may have a gun waiting at the other end. On this occasion I was curious and still a little naïve. I put on my favourite cassette, settled into the seat and swung the wheel to the right – besides, I had promised London a piece from Knin.

My first hitch-hiker of the day was a toothless Croat peasant with no English. I dropped him off near the unofficial no-man's land. He crossed himself hastily and scuttled over the road.

The Serbs of the Krajina are the Spartans of the Balkans – as they never tire of saying. It is a reputation which has suffered in the early nineties. Throughout the Yugoslav conflict there has been a distinct lack of valour in the Serbs' tactics. Their run of victories first in Croatia and then in Bosnia were won by big guns blasting away at civilian communities. Infantry have only deployed to butcher stragglers. Usually they have sat on hill-tops with bottles of plum brandy, watching and waiting – hardly in the spirit of Leonidas and the three hundred at Thermopylae. By early 1993, after eighteen months witnessing the results of the Serbs' war machine, I found their ritual beating of the breast and incantation of a noble warrior past hard to stomach. However, there is no disputing the martial lineage of the Krajina Serbs, whose presence in historic Croatian lands is at the heart of the twentieth-century Yugoslav crisis.

The Serb connection with the Krajina stretches back to the late seventeenth century when Bishop Arsenije led thirty thousand Serb families north from the Ottoman Empire after the failure of a rebellion against the Turks. In return for freedom of worship, the migrants became part of the Habsburgs' warrior elite, the *Grenzer*, deputed to guard the Empire's eight-hundred-mile eastern border, a buffer zone known as the Military Frontier (*Vojna Krajina*, in Serbo-Croat). Although some Serbs had crossed into the Empire in previous centuries, most of them were latecomers to the job. When the Habsburgs set up the Military Frontier in 1578, the southern frontier was the Julian Alps (including Kostanjevica, the nappy and napkin village of Slovenia) and the bulk of the *Grenzer* were Croats and Germans. Arsenije's mass migration in 1690 decisively shifted the ethnic balance.

In the style of the Free Companies of the Hundred Years' War, the *Grenzer* led a boisterous existence. On the fringe of two great powers, the recurrent instability bred typical frontiersmen, hardy, proud and contemptuous of authority. They took orders directly from Vienna, bypassing the Croat authorities in Zagreb. But even the Emperors must sometimes have despaired of keeping them under control. According to one local legend, one Hungarian *boiar* (nobleman) whose land abutted the Military Frontier made the mistake of upsetting the *Grenzer* with demands for taxes. The *Grenzer* promptly strapped him on a bench straddling the border; poured money into his hands, which were suspended over his property, and gave him a sound thrashing on his bottom, which was suspended over theirs. Thus they felt they had dispensed the provisions of both sets of laws.

For Vienna the *Grenzer* were a valuable adjunct to its power, a body of tough soldiers and a counter-weight to the regional governments. In the First World War the Krajina Serbs stayed loyal to Vienna and fought with suicidal bravery against their fellow Serbs from Serbia. Of the Habsburg army that invaded Serbia in 1914, a quarter were Krajina Serbs – a telling statistic in the light of Belgrade's propaganda that the Serbs have always been fighting together for unity and freedom.

However, for the long-term stability of the Balkan peninsula the Military Frontier posed a problem. In the eighteenth and nineteenth centuries, as the Empire squeezed the Turks south, so the Military Frontier expanded until it covered almost half of the territory of the medieval Croatian kingdom. For the Croats, who had some autonomy in Zagreb, this was insufferable and they petitioned Vienna for the right to govern the Krajina, while the Serbs campaigned to retain their independence. The issue was left unresolved in the two Yugoslavias. But when in 1941 and again in 1990 the Croats moved towards independence and tried to assume full administrative control, the old *Grenzer* spirit stirred once more. Some of Yugoslavia's most savage fighting in the Second World War occurred in the Krajina. It was an ugly precedent for 1991.

In Sparta there was an elite within the elite, so it is with the Krajina. The toughest Krajina Serbs live in the Lika region, north-east of Zadar, and around the town of Knin. In 1914 a Habsburg detachment of Lika Serbs was hard-pressed by the Serbian army.

'Surrender. Don't die stupidly,' shouted the Serb commander.

'Have you ever heard of Serbs surrendering?' came back

the reply. Knin was the engine room of the 1990 Krajina rebellion. It is also one of the driest, hottest and most barren parts of the Balkans and renowned for the horny-handed simplicity of its people. In the autumn of 1990 and the spring of 1991 a succession of visiting correspondents ended up the wrong side of a Knin shotgun while the gap-toothed bearer debated whether to douse the offender with petrol. I was almost disappointed when I drove into Knin, parked beside the Radio Station and no one paid the slightest attention.

The first Kninska Serb I met had wide, goofy eyes, a puppy-like smile and a T-shirt down to his knees. Almost eighteen, Igor Matijaš spoke immaculate 'cop-movie' English and his baseball boots would be the envy of any self-respecting beach-bum in the West. His main ambition was to go 'cruising girls' on the Dalmatian coast, and over a chilled orange juice he talked about his Croatian girlfriend, Marija, 'with the smoky-blue eyes, and, phew, what a figure!' Igor was, I soon realized, the reason why journalists had to keep crossing the lines; anyone less like the stereotype Knin goon of Croatian street-talk was hard to imagine. I recruited him as my interpreter on sight.

Igor's baggy T-shirt set the casual tone for my stay in Knin. It was hard to know what the fuss was about. Knin seemed a typical sleepy, grey, dusty Balkan town, probably a bit duller than most, enlivened for most of its inhabitants only by the fire of the local *loza* (a variant on *slivovitz*). I stayed in the old people's home – the only hotel closed in the 1970s – where the dopey caretaker uncharitably brought to mind a Romanian saying, 'Who ever saw a green horse or an intelligent Serb?' I went to sleep to the drunken chanting of two soldiers in the room next door.

There are two jewels to Knin's crown, one ancient and one modern. While the most devoted rail-buff might find it hard to enthuse, Knin railway station, connecting Zagreb and north Croatia with the Dalmatian coast, is 'the strategic key to an independent Croatia', as Igor's father, a prominent local journalist, explained with a sly smile. The second 'jewel' needed no introduction. Knin's tenth-century fort dominates the town from every angle. The focus of scores of battles, most recently in 1944 between the Partisans and the *Wehrmacht*, the castle also symbolised the antiquity of Knin, the coronation site of the medieval Croat kings. For Tudjman, this was the lure. A Croatia without Knin would be like a Scotland without Scone.

Both the station and the fort deserved my attention. The first symbolised Knin's significance to Zagreb, the second was the headquarters of the Krajina forces, led by an Australian mercenary, Captain Dragan, and including the *Kninjas*, the women warriors of the Krajina. However, Igor had no doubt which to visit first.

'The railway station? What on earth do you want to do there? Anyway, there are hardly any trains these days . . .'

There are times when it's not worth arguing with your interpreter. A sweltering day in Knin was one of them. We drove to the fort and spent the best part of a day there doing what besieging armies have done for centuries – waiting at the drawbridge. The Falstaffian-shaped sentry, a Partisan veteran, was Balkan man at his most obtuse.

'You can't go up unless you have permission.'

'OK, so where do we get permission?'

'From the commander in the fort.'

'Fine. Up we go.'

'Hold on a moment. Not until you get the permission.'

'But you just said we have to go there to get permission.'

'Well, you'll have to wait until the commander comes down.'

'So, how often does the commander come down?'

'Oh, every few hours.'

Igor liked the Alfa. While I fumed he was quite happy listening to the sound system. For an hour we sat, sweated and watched the sentry stamp up and down, clad in a thick worsted Second World War uniform, seemingly impervious to the sun. A disturbing thought came to mind.

'The commander, is he in there?'

'Commander Frankie? No. He left hours ago. He's out on exercise. But he should be back in a few days.' We retired down the hill in poor spirits.

The next morning 'Sergeant Balko', my nickname for the previous day's stalwart, was off duty and the drawbridge was down.

'But mind how you go,' said the replacement sentry. 'These are not your average young ladies.'

In the keep the women were training under a Lieutenant Šenka, a manageress from the local honey factory. While Igor and I were entertained with endless 'protocol' cups of coffee and an inspection of the mascot bear, which had been captured from a nearby Croatian national park, the *Kninjas* debated whether to talk to the *Daily Telegraph*. Eventually a lieutenant with the code-name Brija was despatched into our presence. Endowed with a petite and most unBalkan figure, she stood to attention, saluted, pledged her patriotism and left. Our audience was at an end – two days' wait for two minutes.

Mixing portly Partisans, a medieval fort and the 'Amazons' of the Krajina, the two days wove into an amusing story. But they brought me no closer to understanding the role of the Krajina Serbs in the Yugoslav crisis.

Igor's father, an archetypal Balkan hack with the belly of a wrestler, the writing style of an anguished poet and a cigarette perpetually on the go, knew that Milan Babić and Milan Martić, the two leading figures of the 'Serbian Republic of the Krajina' were in town and suggested I applied for an interview. It was sound advice. Babić, the dentist turned irredentist president, and Martić, the police inspector turned 'Interior Minister', were the men of the moment. Their swift rise to power in 1990 reflected the speed of Croatia's descent to war. However, I shrank from the prospect of yet another Balkan political interview with the inevitable attendant history lecture, map discussion and bigotry. Instead we walked down the road to the headquarters of Radio Knin, a.k.a. 'Krajina Ministry of Information'.

With the hindsight of two years I regret the missed opportunity. Babić bears a large share of the guilt for the carnage in Yugoslavia. He was the trail-blazer in a new era of Balkan Bonapartism, whose career was a role-model for the

Bosnian Serb leaders and other strongmen lurking in the shadows. In the spring of 1990 Babić, while a former member of the Croatian Communist Party, was a relative nonentity, applying to join the Serbian Democratic Party, the newly-formed political movement of the Krajina Serbs. By December he was backed by Belgrade and was masterminding the Krajina Serbs, turning a movement for minority rights into a provocative demand for territorial autonomy. It's unclear if Milošević approached Babić, or vice versa. But once the link was made, Milošević's henchmen pumped munitions into the Krajina, turning the local shotgun culture into a ruthlessly efficient military machine. The terrible crime of Babić and Martić was to exploit the simplicity of the local Serbs by whipping up insecurity about the new Croatian government with wild talk about a rebirth of fascism. History has proved Babić was more of a cause than a symptom. In February 1992 he defied pressure from Belgrade to accept the UN peace accord and Milošević had to replace him with a more compliant puppet. Babić was shot in the head in mysterious circumstances, survived and 'retired' from politics. Martić, his sidekick, ran his own private army, the *Martićevci* (literally Martić's mob). A rural policeman, he became the first Yugoslav warlord – setting an unfortunate example.

The 'Information Minister' was a very different style of man. Lazar Macura, Knin's English and Italian professor, had smooth Mediterranean features and a melodious voice. While his politics were as extreme as his superiors', he softened the effect with a veneer of sophistication. He ushered us straight into his office. He had, he said, some interesting news.

'You are just in time. I have to tell you something. "Operation Wasp" is underway.'

'Operation Wasp?' (This was the first I had heard of such a move.)

'Yes, yes. Today we start to clear out any Croatian forces occupying the Krajina communities. We have given enough ultimata. It should take us two months maximum and then Krajina will be free.'

Thus I learnt of the imminent Serbian offensive – not that I knew this with any confidence at the time. Indeed, Macura's revelation posed an interesting dilemma. His candour ran against all the norms of warfare. No serious commander tells a journalist anything of strategic significance. But 'Operation Wasp' sounded eminently plausible in view of the tense standoff in Glina and other communities. I filed the story, unsure whether I was rewriting Serb propaganda, or whether I had an exclusive insight into the next phase of the war. When I returned to Macura's office, he started to spout ridiculous stories about Kurdish and Romanian mercenaries fighting for the Croats, and I began to suspect the former. Having spent a year in Romania and four months with the Kurds, I felt both qualified and sufficiently angry to shout down this lie. Macura didn't seem the slightest concerned.

Igor and I were planning an afternoon off when an Irish journalist walked into the office wanting to investigate the effect of Second World War atrocities on the new conflict. It seemed an interesting idea. In the Second World War the various Yugoslav militias slaughtered each other with a savagery surpassing the occupying SS forces. Some of the worst and best-documented atrocities were committed by the Ustaše, whose leader, Ante Pavelic, was fixated with the creation of an ethnically pure Croat state. The most reliable estimates suggest that at least half a million Serbs, Jews, gipsies and Croat political opponents were killed in this loathsome quest.

After the war the Serb-dominated Partisans revelled in the chance of revenge. Tito tried to bury this bloody history, forbidding worship at mass graves, and allowing the sites of massacres to be marked only with neutral signs to the 'fallen martyrs'. However, in 1991 the Serb politicians and media sought to rekindle the folk memory of these horrors and Knin was a centre for this rebirth of history. These last details I learned from Lorna of the *Irish Times*, who had had the idea. As I had a car, we agreed to work together on the story. Macura knew of an 'authority' on atrocities, a priest by the name of Dane Korać. Within minutes we were winding into the mountains in pursuit.

Father Korać lived in a neat cottage on the edge of the village of Gračac. The Balkan priest personified, red-cheeked and rotund, Father Korać was the mirror image of Father Buja, the millionaire shepherd father of the Carpathians. He had a mouth full of home-smoked ham and he signalled for us to come round to the back. The idea of a tour to the nearest mass grave filled him with delight.

'And then we can finish the meal,' he shouted to his maid. 'Bring it along after us.' We ended up swigging his home-made wine and sharing his lunch a few hundred yards from a gloomy grotto, which marked the site of an Ustaše massacre. The previous Sunday the father had officiated there at a ghoulish liturgy attended by several thousand Serbs. 'Of course, you can't see any of the bodies now,' he said. 'But the Ustaše hurled hundreds down that cliff, hundreds all swept underground.' He chuckled when asked about the Croats.

'Oh, they're not that bad. Of course you can't be too careful. I mean, you never know what might happen if they get uppity. Look at 1941 . . .'

Here was prejudice but no paranoia, and in village after village it was the same story. At the fourteenth-century monastery of Archangel, south of Knin, a group of sculptors from Belgrade were holding their annual retreat. Over yet another hearty meal, I heard the standard Serb complaints about Tudjman and the Slovene leader, Kucan: how they were traitors, how they had destroyed Yugoslavia, how Yugoslavia had always repressed the Serbs . . . but this was the equivalent of bar-stool bickering, not the blind hatred of the gynaecologist. They were soon joking away with the monks, one of whom, a Father Benedict, made one of the more astute comments of my time in Croatia: 'For nearly fifty years there was pressure, pressure, pressure to keep the lid sealed on. After that you must go slowly, very slowly. You cannot lift the lid overnight.'

I returned to Knin that night, slightly drunk and with the glimmer of an understanding. Knin was like the eye of the storm. In these 90–plus per cent Serb communities there was minimal tension. People could joke and talk about Croats at their ease. The problems came in villages with a fifty/fifty ethnic split, or on the borderline between Croat and Serb-controlled territory, where rival propagandas were hard at work.

The receptionist at the old peoples' home was operating at new heights of efficiency – I had a telephone message to call London. One of the joys of working west of the Danube was the Yugoslav communications system, and I was connected to London first dial. The news was mildly alarming: I was a wanted man, or at least I had a wanted car. It was almost a month since I had cruised down the Venice–Trieste motorway and the man from Avis was ringing the *Telegraph* daily pleading for details about his beloved Alfa.

'Tell them it's in Yugoslavia, in the headquarters of the rebel Serbs,' I said, joking. 'Oh, and that it's still just in one piece.'

The message was duly transmitted. The Italian apparently gave a strangled moan. More pertinently, the *Telegraph* switchboard was besieged by calls from London's expatriate Croat community, complaining my work was pro-Serb. I would like to think the accusation was unjust. But it pricked my conscience. It was time to swap sides again and write from the other side.

On my last night in Knin, Igor was looking a little glum. He had failed to speak to his girlfriend Marija and the lines were down to Sibenik, her hometown. It was his eighteenth birthday the next week and they should have been on the beach celebrating – but there was no way he, a Serb, would dare to cross the lines into Croatian-held territory.

Around our table a gang of street-children were playing war. In previous years the Germans were the enemy in such games, now it was the Croats. 'Bang, bang, bang, Croat man!' they shouted. 'You're dead!' Their cries were a painful reminder of the new social realities. There was nothing to say. Then Igor leaned forward, smiling.

'But, who knows. When it's all over, maybe we'll be able to get together again ... and in the meanwhile we'll just keep trying.' It was a moment of great hope. As I write, the hope has been shattered in two years of civil war and it's impossible to feel much sympathy for Knin, so much destruction and killing has been done in its name. Knin remains untouched by a single shell, while swathes of Croatia are devastated as if by a monstrous scythe. But the meeting with this latter-day Romeo, who was plotting trysts, despite the war, was for me a final confirmation that, while some Serbs disliked and even feared the new Croat regime, the drive for the war was coming from the politicians and not the people.

Split seemed very insipid after the burlesque atmosphere of Knin. With Macura's prediction of an imminent attack nagging at the back of my mind, I had no regrets at the idea of foregoing a visit to the Palace of Diocletian, Split's most famous son. The Alfa had been dragging its sump-guard since the Julian Alps. Prompted by the anxiety in Venice, I stirred a mechanic from his siesta on the outskirts of Split before heading on down the coast, stopping only for a nostalgic meal overlooking the isle of Hvar, Sophie's and my holiday refuge of the summer before.

By nightfall I was on the outskirts of Medjugorje, the Lourdes of the Balkans. It was like entering a forgotten world. As I parked I almost knocked over a tall, owlish woman on a bone-shaker.

'Och, I'm sorry! Please do excuse me ...' she said, wobbling on her way. She spoke in English; the accent was unmistakeably Morningside.

Medjugorje is venerated by Catholics as a shrine to the Virgin Mary, and a group of pilgrims from Scotland and Ireland were in residence. In faded flowery frocks and baggy empire-building shorts, they could have stepped off a Victorian daguerreotype. I was so relieved to be away from the Serb v. Croat argument that I joined the evening discussion group. They fell on me as a possible convert and were most disconcerted when I confessed I was a journalist.

'Well, I suppose journalists can live here,' said Phillie uncertainly. Phillie was a red-headed Dublin banker who had 'seen the light' and was vowing never to leave.

'Oh, of course he can,' interrupted a southern Irish lilt on my left. After a few cups of Earl Grey the unsavoury nature of my profession was forgotten. The most vexing question was how and when the Virgin Mary would intervene in the Yugoslav crisis. The owner of the Irish lilt, a Kerry primary teacher, whispered that Our Lady was due any day.

'It may sound a little strange. But if you leave the weeds alone, then perhaps they may follow in the right path.'

The only sense I heard was from the Franciscan monks attached to Medjugorje's Church of St Jacob, a sparkling white building funded by the millions of Catholic pilgrims pouring in over the previous decade. The monks had no illusions of the danger of the conflict. Medjugorje is in the heart of the hardline Croat region of western Hercegovina, but it is close to the fracture line with Serb-dominated territory across the Neretva river. Twenty miles down the road was a Stygian glade with the remains of twenty-five priests slaughtered by Partisans in 1945.

'Catholics and Orthodox don't have to fight,' said Father Slavko Barbarić, 'but religion is being sucked into the conflict and rapidly becoming its most dangerous inspiration. The wounds from the last war were not healed and now they are coming out. It was not an ethnic fight and now it is becoming one. We can only hope and pray.'

That night the Krajina Serbs launched an offensive against Glina. Captain Krušic's police station was devastated. Scores of Croats were reported killed. In the neighbouring village of Struga, elderly Croats who survived the onslaught were forced to walk as a human shield in front of Serb fighters as they attacked the next Croat position. Stragglers falling out of line were shot out of hand. It was one of the earliest examples of the savagery which was to mark the actions of the irregular Serb forces and which was later aped by their Croat counterparts. It set the tone for the months of horror to come.

Egon Scotland, correspondent of *Suddeutsche Zeitung* and one of the few experienced Western journalists then working the Balkan beat, chose that particular day to pay a visit from Zagreb. He was driving along the approach road into Glina when a Serb checkpoint opened fire. Shot in the thigh, he died on the way to hospital.

The July lull was at an end. Sergeant 'Balko' of the Knin drawbridge had been wrong. When I had called on Knin castle, Captain 'Frankie' had not been training, but finalising the plans for the offensive against Glina. More interestingly, I realized that Lazar Macura, the Krajina 'Information Minister', had spoken the truth when he tipped me off about Operation Wasp. It was an early lesson in the bizarre frankness which has characterized episodes of the Yugoslav war. Regular JNA officers tended to stay tight-lipped, remembering their Cold War training. But once they were out of the regular army, serving on one side or other, they were willing to chat away, revealing invaluable details. Croatia's conflict of 1991 was savage, even complex, but seldom subtle.

News of the assault on Glina rescued me from a series of rashly-pledged commitments to the Celtic pilgrims. After a dawn walk to the hilltop where the Virgin Mary is believed to have made her first 'visit', I left, advising the pilgrims to return home. They smiled sweetly and called me 'a dear child'.

'Don't you worry your little self about us,' trilled Phillie. 'Nothing can happen here, you see ... you'll be back. Everyone comes back to Medjugorje.' The tall Scotswoman wobbled past on her way to church. I shook my head and plotted a course for the north. It was almost a relief to be returning to the war.

Ten miles out of Medjugorje I was stopped for speeding. The policeman strode over, waving pieces of paper and opened with a blast of Serbo-Croat. But when he realized I was a journalist he softened his act. A former waiter from Mostar, he spoke immaculate English. He was much happier talking about the latest developments from the front.

'Crazy people,' he concluded, shaking his head. 'But you watch how you drive. This is Bosnia not Croatia. You have to keep to the law.' He waived the fine and I promised 'next time' to pay a visit to his holiday house by the sea. I never asked him which nationality he was. It didn't seem appropriate.

The traffic was heavy and I spent the night in Sarajevo. Michael Montgomery had heard rumours of arms-shipments going from Belgrade to the Bosnian Serbs and recommended a quick look at the Bosnian political situation. The Holiday Inn, a yellow and green monstrosity on the main highway, was serving an excellent rump steak. But it seemed a long way from the war. 'I am in the wrong place at the wrong time,' I wrote in my diary. I left for Belgrade at dawn and was there in three-and-a-half hours.

9

A Slavonian Rhapsody

August 1991, Osijek

'When is a war not a war? When it's in the Balkans' – *Ivo, a young Croat officer sitting by the Danube in Vukovar, August 1991*

'The risks are not always worth the rewards' – *Paul Jenks, British photographer in Osijek, a few months before he was killed by a sniper*

THERE WAS A time when a flare-up in the Balkans set generals all over Europe frantically sticking pins in maps and foreign ministers reaching for their attaché cases. From 1875, when Hercegovina rebelled against the Turks, prompting Bismarck's legendary comment that the Balkans weren't worth 'the healthy bones of a single Pomeranian grenadier', until 1914, the history of Europe was a catalogue of Balkan crises. A buffer zone between Austria-Hungary and Russia, the peninsula became the chess-board for the world's balance of power. Even Britain, which with its mighty overseas Empire had no obvious sphere of interest in the Balkans, devoted its finest diplomatic brains to the region, lest the old enemy, the Russian bear, made a breakthrough towards Constantinople.

Saki, himself an old Balkan hand, the *Morning Post* correspondent for the war of 1902 and the Macedonian crisis of 1903, beautifully articulates this Balkan-mania in *The Cupboard of the Yesterdays*, where a 'wanderer' describes to a more prosaic companion the lure of the Balkans.

'When I was a child one of the earliest events of the outside world that forced itself coherently under my notice was a war in the Balkans . . . It seemed a magical region, with its mountain passes and frozen rivers and grim battlefields, its drifting snows and prowling wolves . . . There is a charm about those countries that you find nowhere else in Europe, the charm of uncertainty and landslide, the little dramatic happenings that make all the difference between the ordinary and the desirable.'

However, seventy years later, when the Balkans again erupted into the headlines, the mood which had inspired fictional characters like the 'wanderer' had evaporated. Lack of interest was the hallmark of the West's reaction to the 'grim battlefields' of Croatia in 1991. For over half a century the Balkans had been a backwater. The EC focused on negotiations for the Maastricht Treaty. Financiers looked to the richer pickings of Central Europe.

For the Western public, indifference was fostered by confusion. There was no official declaration of hostilities between Zagreb and Belgrade, no ultimatum, no rolling of drums. Like a leaky tap, the fighting was now on, now off, and by August it had settled into a cyclical pattern. The Serbs attacked a Croat position; the EC issued a condemnation; the federal authorities called a ceasefire. After a few days of posturing at peace, the sequence started again with the next Serb assault. No one seemed sure if this routine counted as war or not and so journalists, politicians and the public continued to talk about the 'Yugoslav crisis' just as we talk about currency crises or job crises – and the depressing cycle continued, each time bloodier than the last.

When I reached Belgrade the fighting in Glina died down. The Serbs had ejected or killed the Croat forces and a ceasefire was agreed. I was ordered to stay put. Meanwhile in Sarajevo tens of thousands of people were marching through the streets in a peace rally. This was the first major public plea for peace in Yugoslavia and I had driven straight past it.

*

For a few blissful hours Belgrade seemed unchanged. The French patisserie on the Knez Mihailova continued to dispense the only true croissants in the Balkans. In the International Press Centre, a hundred yards further down, phone lines, coffee, gossip and even news were available on request. In the catacombs of the medieval fort, Yugoslav rock music, which had championed East European youth culture for twenty years, thudded away as expansively as ever. Milorad, a Serbian journalist friend from Knin, took me on an all-night tour of Belgrade's nightspots, where the rarified costumes and hairstyles matched the best of North London.

However, this cosmopolitan lifestyle, which had so intoxicated me on retreats from Romania in 1990, palled quickly. There was a new surliness to the Serbian capital. Recruitment squads for the JNA were roaming the suburbs looking for draft dodgers. Thousands of young men were in hiding, fearing the midnight knock on the door. The liberal heart of the city was in mourning for its missed opportunity in March, when President Milošević had faced the most serious challenge to his power. In three days of protests the opposition had massed in the streets demanding the dismissal of the head of the television station and more open government. But the moment had passed. The Serbian opposition were hopeless politicians, reminding me of the Romanian protestors of University Square in 1990. A mixture of idealists and dreamers, obsessed by history and orthodoxy, they were no match for an arch-opportunist like Milošević. The net result of Belgrade's March protest was two dead, a few cosmetic changes and 'Slobo' more strongly entrenched than before. Rallying the masses, he behaved like a model Stalinist, warning of the dangers of 'vampiroid fascistoid forces of the Ustašas, Albanian secessionists and all other forces in the anti-Serbian coalition which threaten the peoples' rights and freedoms.'

Belgrade's sullen apathy was reminiscent of Bucharest after the miners in June 1990. Nowhere exuded this more than the Hotel Moskva, Trotsky's haunt for the Balkan Wars. A diehard haunt of intrigue and commie inefficiency, the Moskva was vintage Eric Ambler. The switchboard connected you to the laundry when you wanted room-serv-ice and to the reception when you wanted an outside line. In the dining room, the stained tablecloths, overflowing ashtrays and low-wattage light bulbs reminded me of the dire days of the Hotel Continental in Timişoara in January 1990. Orders stopped at 8 p.m. sharp and the *maitre d'* shouted abuse if guests arrived any later. For the first time I appreciated that one of the principle linguistic legacies of the Slavs on the Romanian language was in the swear-words. The *maitre d'*'s more pungent insults were all too familiar from the street markets of Bucharest.

In the lobby unsmiling Yugoslavs sat slumped over cups of coffee. I liked to imagine they were brokering arms deals or fixing money frauds. More probably they were govern-ment stooges or just passing the day with tobacco and caffeine, as is the Balkan way. Shrouded in smoke, they seemed rooted to their tables. Their ennui was infectious. The only news to file was about EC diplomats shuttling between Belgrade and Brussels. The most alarming moment of the week came when I was waiting at Belgrade airport for the latest EC mission and the Alfa disappeared. I was rehearsing for the umpteenth time a grovelling conversation to London on the lines of 'You know that nice Italian car ... well ...' when I learned it had been removed by the car-park authorities. In those days breakfast became later and later and my despatches shorter and shorter. I sweated, festered and fumed.

It took a diversion on the Adriatic to rouse me from my torpor. Sophie caught the night train from Bucharest to Belgrade and we flew down to Dubrovnik, where we were two of the four resident foreign tourists. The other two were the *New York Times* correspondent and his wife. 'Heaven is a place called Dubrovnik,' I wrote in my diary. 'Fortunate is the foreign correspondent with the Adriatic beat.' Niko Concul, the manager of the Hotel Argentina, implored us to explain to Britain that the war was irrelevant to Dubrovnik. 'We are something different here,' he said. 'Something special.' Emerging from the emerald waters of the Adriatic on to the Argentina's terrace for a plate of prawns, I was inclined to agree.

For thirty-six hours we shopped, slept and swam, oblivious to the fighting which had erupted in east Slavonia, the easternmost of Croatia's four troubled areas. The night we returned to Belgrade the federal authorities announced a ceasefire. Paramilitaries were to retire from the front line at dawn. The JNA would supervise the operation. It seemed a good time to re-take to the road. Sophie returned to do battle with the bureaucracy in Bucharest, where she was setting up development projects. I emblazoned 'PRESS' in slanting twelve-inch letters on the Alfa, using masking tape procured by the hotel porter. The result was a tragedy for the car's sleek outline, but I felt satisfied that I had taken a token precaution. All that remained was a search for a travelling-companion. Stefan Bosch, a Dutch radio reporter with a mop of blonde hair, a diffident smile and a curious shuffling gait, volunteered. Unsure of the wisdom of two amateurs travelling to war in the same vehicle, I accepted. We left at dawn.

The Road of Brotherhood and Unity was intended to symbolise all that was good about Yugoslavia by linking Zagreb and Belgrade with a six-lane highway. Like so many Yugoslav ideals, it was never quite realized. The project faltered when both capitals refused to fund the central stretch. In 1989 the EC, keen to improve the main land route into the Balkans, voted a large loan and work was due to re-start when the war intervened.

After luxuriating in the first hundred kilometres, we turned off for east Slavonia. Within three hours of leaving Belgrade we were on the left bank of the Danube, the border of Serbia and Croatia, barely five miles from the village of Dalj, the latest flashpoint.

By the side of the road hundreds of JNA squaddies lazed in the sun, playing cards, smoking, asleep. It was a picture of tranquillity. One flaxen-haired private cracked open a beer and chatted about the aspirations of his football-playing son.

'Maybe this is peace – maybe not. But, God knows, I want it. I'd love to bring my young Dragan over to London to see Arsenal play . . .'

In his ill-fitting uniform and with his sagging paunch, Private Zivo Djorjević looked and spoke like a typical happy-go-lucky JNA squaddie. The Bosnian beer was clearly closer to his heart than combat. But his peace-loving message did nothing to dispel the impression that the truce was no more than a breather, a chance for a few beers.

Tanks were parked in the cornfields with their barrels protruding from the crop. A few hundred yards further down the road were bands of Serb paramilitaries. Bearded and draped in bandoliers of ammunition like the Balkan *hajduks* (bandits) of legend, they were drinking and talking with the JNA soldiers.

'What about Dalj?' we asked one group of soldiers.

'Dalj?' came back the innocent reply. 'Oh, it's been liberated from the Ustaše. It's all safe now.'

'So, can we go there?' we asked.

'Er, no, there's still a few problems with snipers. Much too dangerous right now. But it was a heroic fight, we were nearly massacred.' Waving and shouting they cheered us on the way, gesturing the traditional three-fingered Serb salute.

The atmosphere was reminiscent of a half-time break in an autumnal game of football – and in this particular match the Serbs clearly felt they were several goals ahead with victory in their sights.

'So the army is neutral, eh? the old bastards . . .' I looked at Stefan with new respect. It was one of the few comments he had made all morning.

By August 1991 the JNA had metamorphosed into little more than a Serbian army, or at least a Serbian armoury. The high command disputed this charge and claimed to be Yugoslavs preserving Tito's federation. In the Slovenian war the JNA's thrust to retake the international border crossings from the Slovene Territorial Defence fitted the generals' Yugoslav rhetoric. But when the army tamely ceded defeat in Slovenia and the fighting spread to Croatia, the absurdity of this claim grew. The talk of saving Yugoslavia became an excuse for the consumption of the outside world and for the consciences of some of the senior officers. The specifics of the JNA's relations with Milošević have never been clarified. In a few regions the JNA did genuinely try to mediate between the Croat National Guard and the Krajina Serb's militia. In Belgrade there was constant speculation that faction X was with Milošević or that faction Y was against him. However, in most areas, particularly in East Slavonia, the JNA openly backed and fraternised with the Serb paramilitaries.

Some generals fought to save their pensions and prestige – Yugoslavia was their paymaster and *raison d'être*; some helped the Krajina Serbs out of a kinship – the JNA officer corps was over 60 per cent Serb; some fought out of hatred of the Croats – General Blagoje Adžić, the JNA Chief of Staff, lost his family in an Ustaše massacre; a few fought because they were so indoctrinated by their own propaganda that they genuinely believed they were saving Yugoslavia. For the people of Croatia the end result was the same. Thousands of young conscripts like the beer-swilling Zivo were thrust into a war which they neither understood nor wanted, and the ordnance of what was reputed to be Europe's fourth largest army was available to Serb irregulars on tap. In Glina, Dalj and scores of other communities they could attack Croatian settlements with a devastating superiority in firepower.

It took Stefan and I five hours' hectic driving alongside the Hungarian border to find a way across the lines into Croatia. Sarvaš, the village down the road from Dalj, was still in the hands of Croat fighters. When we arrived it was late afternoon and we had been travelling all day. With our deadlines pressing we had only a few minutes to garner information. For once the pressure on time was a relief.

Sarvaš was a shambles. The Catholic church had taken several direct hits. The corner shop opposite was gutted. One house in two had been hit by a shell, leaving rafters gaping in the air like upturned spillikins. A dead pig was lying in the middle of the road. My eyes and brain went on auto-pilot and recorded each separate image like a camera-shutter, shifting in a moment from one to the next. In front of me was a bullet-scarred signpost pointing to Dalj. Down the road was a deserted sandbag emplacement. A few hundred yards further on was a small wood. Was that movement in the trees or was it the wind? If it was a person, he or she was moving very furtively. Where were all the people?

There was a whistle from behind the church and a shout in Serbo-Croat followed by one in Australian English.

'Hey, you! Get down!' Stefan and I looked at each other and in the same moment I slammed the car into gear. Round the first corner we skidded to a halt against the sandbags of a Croat National Guard outpost; five minutes later we were at the brick factory which served as their headquarters. These were the first Croat troops I had seen since Glina. Fortifying themselves with hunks of salami and plum brandy, they were resigned to their deaths. Mario, an expatriate Croat from Australia who had returned in the spring, laughed when asked about the ceasefire: 'You know how long the last one lasted? Half a day. The one before? Two days. What do we think about this one? What sort of journalist are you?'

'Why don't you stay the night with us and see what really happens on the front line?' That was Drazen with three days' stubble and a strong reek of liquor. There was no mistaking the challenge.

'Another time, another time,' I said, relieved to have a genuine excuse. 'The most important thing is to get to Osijek [the regional capital] for a phone so we can send a report.'

Mario was one of hundreds of emigrés who had returned to help 'the motherland'. Australia and Canada had large Serb and Croat communities which often proved '*plus royaliste que la reine*', refusing to tolerate criticism of Milošević and Tudjman. In Sydney the rival Yugoslav peoples fought gangland wars. However, while there was no doubting Mario's commitment to Croatia, a spell in the lines had clearly dented his ardour. He seemed grateful for the chance to talk English, and during a quick guided tour of the brickworks I asked him about Dalj. There was a short silence and he swore softly.

'It was a massacre. We lost over sixty dead, gunned down like dogs. Don't believe what our leaders say. They fucked up too. They left those guys there like sitting ducks and then the Chetniks went in and blew them away.

'Oh, and another thing, I heard a interview on the BBC. Some poncey British politician was talking about the threat of Yugoslavia descending to all out war. Well, you tell him to come down here and see if this is war or not.'

Amid the shell–craters and damaged houses, the gleaming white Alfa looked like an exotic butterfly. We turned at speed and roared down the road to Osijek, cursing the Yugoslav politicians, hating the Balkan mentality and most of all loathing the indifference of the West.

'*Buna ziua. Buna ziua. Ce faci? Ce faci?*' In my haste to secure a telephone at the Osijek Hotel I almost failed to register I was being addressed in Romanian. I spun round and was met by the lanky cadaverous figure of Radu Sighetu, a Romanian photographer and old friend from Bucharest. My anger faded. It was like returning home.

After I filed a piece – burning, I hoped, with pessimism about the prospects of the ceasefire – we retired to the bar across the road, and indulged in escapist nostalgia about Bucharest.

Radu and a Bulgarian colleague, Oleg Popov, were among half-a-dozen photographers based in Slavonia. I worked with them for a bucolic fortnight. Traipsing the hayfields, watching the harvesters swap scythes for shotguns, I took rudimentary lessons in covering a war, still nursing the naïve hope of young reporters that by writing you can change the world.

One of the many ironies of the Yugoslav war is that the plains of East Slavonia have – or at least had – an envied reputation in the Balkans for ethnic harmony. Historically Slavonia has proved too flat and open for the guerrilla warfare which has characterized South-East Europe. From the janissaries to the *Wehrmacht*, invading armies steam-rollered across Slavonia on their way to tougher resistance in Bosnia or the Julian Alps. The one great historical battle fought in the vicinity was a disaster. In 1526 King Louis II of Hungary took to the field at Mohacs, thirty miles north of Osijek, against the all-conquering army of Suleyman the Magnificent. According to his chronicler, the king knew it was folly but was egged on by his archbishop and nobles. The flower of the Hungarian nobility fell under the Ottoman scimitars. Louis was crushed to death by his horse in a stream in Baranja, the wedge of Slavonia north of Osijek.

In the centuries that followed, the Slavonians concentrated on filling the bread-baskets of Central Europe. Cushioned by the Military Frontier to the south and east, they eschewed warfare for bourgeois profit and the region prospered. The Habsburg Emperors encouraged colonists to emigrate there from all over the Empire. It seems hardly a coincidence that Bishop Josip Strossmayer, one of East Europe's great moderates of the nineteenth century, was Slavonian born and bred. Advocating religious union between Catholics and Orthodox, Strossmayer was one of the earliest Yugoslavs and won the political argument of the day against the extremist Party of Rights, which aspired to a Greater Croatia. Strossmayer's hope of South Slav unity was eventually scuppered not by Slav chauvinism but by the Hungarians, who saw talk of Slav unity as subversive to their hegemony. He left politics in disgust and retired to his episcopate in the south Slavonian town of Djakovo where he died in 1905. His ideals briefly flowered again at the start of the royal Yugoslavia in 1918. Strossmayer represents the dream, the hope that liberalism and ethnic harmony can flourish in the Balkans. But by August 1991 Strossmayer was out of favour even in his home town, Osijek.

At the extremity of Croatia's crazy long finger of territory, east Slavonia is closer to Belgrade than Zagreb. When relations between the two cities worsened in the late 1980s, the Serbs of East Slavonia were easily accessible to the proselytism of Serbia's extreme nationalists. While Serb-dominated villages around Osijek were subjected to the steady drip of anti-Croat chauvinism, liberal Croats were ousted from authority by Tudjmanite nationalists. For the local peasantry there was no middle course. You were either with Zagreb or Belgrade. Slavonian Serbs started losing their jobs. Weapons were brought in from Belgrade. The result was a patchwork of paranoid village-states, barricaded by haycarts, defended by straw-chewing yokels and terrified of strangers.

The ceasefire held for two weeks after I arrived in Osijek. For those with neutral passports, steady nerves and a fast car, the Slavonian lanes were negotiable and the village sieges, stretching twenty miles north and south of Osijek, became the focus of my daily work. It was an extraordinary beat. The landscape was pure Bruegel, ripening cornfields, red-faced peasants, wooden carts, scythes, large hunting dogs, swarming flies and steaming barrels of beer. However, the atmosphere had the menace of *Straw Dogs*, Sam Peckinpah's classic of the 1970s about a bloody village feud in a remote part of Cornwall. Every day shots were exchanged between different communities or even between different halves of the same community. My knowledge of war-zones stemmed from two months with the Turkish Second Army on the Iraqi border, where the only activity came from the tea boys and the loudest noise was the braying of donkeys. I willingly ceded to the experience of the photographers.

Writers and photographers traditionally make poor colleagues. While the latter search for the key moment, writers require more time to compile material. In war-zones the distinction amplifies. The most striking pictures are from the front line. But writers have to weigh up the raw immediacy of battlefield copy with the better access to information from behind the lines. An office briefing will invariably yield a more balanced overview than a rushed chat with some psyched up squaddie.

Consequently photographers deride 'scribblers' as armchair journalists, and writers disdain 'snappers' as reckless fools. In Zagreb one old-hand correspondent had advised me to stay clear of the 'monkeys'. 'Only get you in trouble,' he said, reaching for another drink. His advice was well-meant but the Osijek team numbered veterans of wars in Africa, the Middle East and Central America. Aware that the Yugoslav war was in its formative stages, they regarded those August days as a period of reconnaissance. Often three or four days passed without their taking a single picture.

'Better to make friends, take your time and wait for the big story,' explained Chris Morris, the unofficial team leader, a New Yorker on assignment for *Time* magazine. 'Working in wars is about making the right decision at the right time,' he said. 'Always talk to people. Always follow your own instincts. If the road feels bad then don't go down it . . .'

With immaculately groomed blond hair flowing down to his shoulders, a soft drawl and an array of smooth designer outfits, he seemed an unlikely combat photographer. But his advice made sense.

And so make friends we did. Each morning we set out past the south Osijek checkpoint into no-man's land, skirting the most notoriously volatile villages, smiling and waving in others, chatting when we could find an English-speaker, dispensing cigarettes, consuming endless glasses of *slivovitz*. On one occasion in the village of Trpinja, a Serb-dominated community on the fringe of hardline Croat territory, we even ended up playing table-football with the local goons. Although it was late in the afternoon and I was frantic to return to Osijek to call the *Telegraph*, the challenge seemed imprudent to decline. Claiming experience in my college bar, I was selected to uphold the honour of the '*straini novinari*' (foreign journalists) along with Jon Jones, a photographer with the Sygma agency, the only other British journalist in our party. It was a bizarre, not to say alarming, contest.

Trpinja was one of the most frightened and unstable Slavonian communities. Our opponents had the lazy-eyes and hair-lips of decades of inbreeding. They also had hand-grenades in their belts and shotguns strapped to their sides. Every goal was the cue for a slug of *slivovitz* and a cheer from the Worzel Gummidge lookalikes gathered around. Jon and I held a rapid council of war. The main dilemma was whether these proud Serb patriots would appreciate Britain upholding its pride – or whether it was better to cede gracious defeat. We decided on compromise and fought hard for a draw. By the time we were allowed to leave, the old Anglo-Serb alliance had, at least in the village of Trpinja, been revitalized; honour was even at two games all; the bottle of *slivovitz* was empty and we had a guarantee of safe passage whenever we wanted.

The table-football connection with Trpinja was a tactical coup. For several days we passed through the tiny village, always stopping to talk with Boro, the headman, never rushing the sentries in their painstaking search of our cars. Slowly the trust grew and the menace of the inarticulate sentries with their frayed jeans and sawn-off shotguns receded. The hillbillies of Trpinja were not desperadoes by nature. They were peasants who wanted nothing more than the simple life. Slavonia, like so much of the Balkans, is steeped in a subsistence rural mentality. Boro explained that his people were more worried about the harvest than the war and were reaping the crop with a gun at their side. When he offered a guided tour of the harvest war, one or two of the photographers looked interested. I glanced at the surrounding cornfields rumoured to be laced with mines and politely shook my head.

One morning skirmishing was reported around Trpinja. No amount of shared table-football games could have induced me to drive down the open stretch of road from Osijek to Trpinja after a night of shooting. So we decided to take a side route, via the village of Vera. One member of our group had heard of someone passing through Vera recently without any problems. After a quick consultation of the map, which was ringed with symbols representing 'friendly', 'hostile', 'Serb', 'Croat', 'unsure', etc., we were off. A hundred yards from the first houses a tractor and an upturned cart blocked the road – the standard Slavonian checkpoint. Blithely confident, we slowed to a halt.

From the moment we stopped something felt wrong. Our

cheery '*Zdravo, zdravo*' and then '*Dobardan*' met silence. All we could see was a medley of gun-barrels poking out from behind the barricade. It was too late to reverse, so we stayed there for half an hour, chatting, sweating in the mid-morning sun while the outpost pondered our fate.

We can't have looked too threatening. Cameras and notebooks were locked in the car boots. Our cars were plastered with international-press stickers. Bright 'unmartial' T-shirts were the dress of the day. A gap appeared in the blockade and a voice in heavily-accented English told us to enter – 'slowly'.

Our interlocutor was a Serb who had lived for two years in Chicago. The 'doctor', as he introduced himself, had appalling teeth and was wielding a vicious-looking Second World War Russian machine-gun, familiar only from the cinema. He had recently returned to his home village and seemed upset by his fellow villagers' paranoia.

'I don't know what is going on. I'm sure it will be OK but no one can understand what you want here. They assume you must be spies and they don't like spies.' The two Americans in our party, Chris Morris and Ron Haviv, were soon chatting to him like an old buddy. The rest of us walked behind, unsure if we were honoured guests or under arrest.

Our reception in the café reminded me of arriving in a rural British pub a few years ago after a car-breakdown – conversation stopped and all eyes turned towards us. There was one crucial difference between Berkshire's Headley Arms and the Vera café. In the latter everyone carried arms. An old man sitting in a corner broke the silence. Waving a rifle, he started banging his fist against a table.

'They are from HTV [Croatian Television]. We must shoot them all. I've had enough of journalists.'

His outburst was the signal for a village debate. In an instant the village was in uproar as locals divided into two camps – those for and those against the old man's proposal. While the 'doctor' pleaded our case, a group with Tommy guns and 303 rifles blocked the exits. When a sharp-eyed loafer in dungarees noticed that one of our cars had

Ljubljana number plates, the mood shifted away from the doctor.

'I told you,' shouted the old man. 'They are in league with those fascist Slovenes. They have been sent by Kučan [the Slovenian president]. We should shoot all these people or they will kill us.'

The 'doctor' was helping with some rough and ready translation. Then the old man turned on him; the translation ended and we were left groping for an understanding of the progress of the debate. From the venom of the old man's rhetoric and the 'doctor''s hangdog expression it seemed that he too was accused of being an outsider.

It was one of those occasions when you are desperate not to catch anyone's eye and when any move might be the wrong move.

So we sat and waited as the shouts of 'Ustaše' rose and fell. In the distance I could hear the sound of a tractor humming. I mentally cursed the fact that at breakfast we had separated from Igor the Bulgarian, who spoke tolerable Serbo-Croat, and then in the same moment I reconsidered. Igor was working with an Austrian photographer. We were better without them. To carry an Austrian or German passport in a region which dwelt on memories of the Nazi occupation was a death warrant. A few weeks before, a German diplomat passing by train through the region was forced by Serb paramilitaries to strip to his underpants.

Chris produced a 'to whom it may concern' letter from our friends in Trpinja. This apparently was not good enough. The two Serb-dominated villages were only six miles apart and yet they were like separate islands. The son of a friend of the old man was missing in the Croat-controlled town of Vukovar. We had come from Osijek the regional centre of HDZ. That was all that mattered.

The tribunal seemed a long way from a decision when a haycart rumbled down the street, spilling its load in its wake, setting the dogs barking in a cloud of dust. A few people wandered out to check on the rumpus. Someone laughed. The tension eased. The waitress arrived with a tray brimming with coffee and *slivovitz*. Slowly the circling

Kalashnikov barrels became less prominent. The old man was left muttering in the corner. The 'doctor' waved us through. Eight hundred yards further on was the blessed relief of no man's land. We paused for a deep breath before moving on to the next checkpoint and potentially the same reception all over again.

In hindsight the morning in Vera was laughable, a great source of dinner-table anecdotes and a good story for the commuters on the train to Waterloo the following morning. But we had been lucky. The day before our showdown in Vera, an old friend from Bucharest, Vladimir Ivanov, a correspondent from *Le Figaro*, was shot in the arm by Serbs near Glina. His assailants disinfected the wound with plum brandy and sent him on his way, warning they had orders to shoot on all-comers.

From the early stages of the fighting, the Yugoslav war claimed a heavy toll of journalists' lives. By the end of 1992 over forty journalists had been killed in eighteen months of conflict, a statistic which beggars comparison even with Central America and Vietnam. The high figure reflects the fluidity of the front lines. In a war fought from hedgerow to hedgerow no amount of experience can guard against the chance shell, the ill-placed mine, the ricocheting shell-fragment. However, it also reflects an uglier aspect of the war. For many of the combatants the press were targets. Former communist cultures have never found it easy to understand the role of the Western media. Accustomed to their own journalists who – with a few brilliant exceptions – slavishly adopted the official line, many Yugoslav fighters could not believe that Western journalists were genuinely independent. Regarded as the agents or representatives of our governments, we were tangible targets for anti-West sentiment.

Initially most of the intimidation came from the Serbs. Stewing in their own propaganda, they considered themselves the injured victims and felt betrayed by the outside world, particularly their old allies France and Britain. The Serbs also had the most to hide. When the Krajina militia attacked Glina, a machine-gunner firing at Croat civilians from the back of a lorry saw a photographer, swivelled his gun and opened up, screaming 'Shoot the journalists.' By contrast the Croats appreciated the importance of winning over public opinion and treated journalists more judiciously. However, by the end of the year the balance was shifting. The Croats felt betrayed by the West in their 'struggle for freedom', and in the Osijek forces, who were led by a neo-Nazi killer, Branimir Glavaš, there was an especially strong vein of anti-press sentiment.

Among the Osijek team of photographers in August 1991 was a young British free-lancer, Paul Jenks, who wrote as sensitively as he took pictures. After completing a post-graduate photography course in July, he drove to Croatia with his girlfriend in a battered Renault Four. Together they roamed Slavonia without any financial back-up, and emerged with excellent pictures and some of the more prescient and witty comments over dinner in Osijek. In Croatia's dark autumn of 1991 Paul worked tirelessly in Slavonia to record the effects of the Serbs' offensive, and he wrote a moving piece for the *Daily Telegraph* about the reasons for working in Yugoslavia. 'The risks involved are, however, not often commensurate with the rewards,' he concluded. 'While many journalists are attracted by the danger of being in a war-zone, night-time bombardments and hidden snipers provide little in the way of photo opportunities.' In January 1992 he was killed south of Osijek, while investigating allegations of Croat-on-Serb atrocities. Initial reports that he was shot by a Serb sniper have been discounted. It now seems more likely that he was killed by mercenaries, working for the militia in Osijek – the city whose plight he had been publicising for month after month.

The Vera encounter induced a degree of caution. Each morning we looked at each other over cups of grainy coffee as if to say, 'Why are we doing this?' Each morning the daily grind continued. The dividing lines between danger, voyeurism and journalistic curiosity are narrow. Operating in the fields of Slavonia was tremendously compelling and provided striking copy. But there was another factor driving us on. By zigzagging through Trpinja and Vera we had access to both sides of the lines. We could cross from Osijek to the Serbs' stronghold of Borovo Selo, to the Croat-controlled town of Vukovar all in the same afternoon. During this phoney war of plum brandy and partial cease-fires, this was tremendously important. We were the only people who had access to both sides. While it was possible, we had to keep crossing backwards and forwards. It was only by visiting both sides that I appreciated that the political conflict of the Krajina was turning into an old-fashioned war of territorial aggression.

In Belgrade and Zagreb each side regularly accused the other of launching offensives and bombardments. Whenever fighting occurred the Serbs accused the Croats of starting it and vice versa. From a hotel room it was easy to dismiss both sides as being equally at fault. Time and again reports appeared in Western newspapers quoting Belgrade Radio, which said that the Croats had attacked, and then quoting Zagreb Radio which said that the Serbs had attacked. By quoting both sources, as a professional you have covered your reputation. 'I only said "according to . . ." ' you can argue, if your information is later disproved. However, by blandly quoting both sides, the Western press often failed to communicate the actual situation on the ground. In the Balkans normal rules of journalism don't apply. In a society where people are inveterate liars it's not good enough to trust in quoting officials and, when I look back at some reports I filed from Belgrade, I wince. During my week 'festering' in the Hotel Moskva I wrote with heavy scepticism about a Croatian Radio report of a Serbian attack on a Croatian town. In my piece I made sure to remind the reader that many such reports had been proved false before. When it appeared on the front page the word 'attack' in the headline was in inverted commas. My caution may have been justified at the time, but a fortnight later in Osijek I realized that the Croatian account had been correct: the town had been attacked by Serbs and my cynicism was un-founded.

This failure by the Western press to differentiate between 'solid reporting' and the dissemination of lies was compounded by our inability to appreciate what we were seeing. Because both Tudjman and Milošević were former communists-turned-nationalists with a similar disregard for the ways of democracy, no journalist wanted to come down on either side. After a few days in Osijek I visited Dalj, where sixty Croats were killed for the loss of three or four Serbs. Whatever the rights or wrongs of the war, the Dalj incident was brutally straightforward. The Serbs launched a dawn raid against the police station with rockets, mortars and heavy machine-guns and then gunned down any resisting Croat National Guardsmen in the school sports stadium. So fearful was I of losing the balance that I wrote a report which would have fitted neatly in a Serbian newspaper. I quoted the Serbian mayor who said, 'Now we can all live together again. Of course it is tragic, but it's good to start again.' I compared the village setting to a sleepy landscape in Hardy's Wessex. I described the killing in the impersonal third person or passive 'more than sixty Croats were killed . . . so intense was the fighting', as if it was perpetrated by some amorphous beings. I totally failed to make the point that this was the bloodiest incident in the war and that the Serbs were responsible.

The Croats were no angels. Tudjman shares the blame for the build-up to war. In an attempt to gain world sympathy, the Croat National Guard deliberately provoked a number of the Serbs' assaults. However, the Croats were losing the war and this point was not reaching the readers – at least not in my pieces. Two days after visiting Dalj I went to the Serbian village of Borovo Selo where locals were outraged about a recent Croatian attack. They showed me two shells embedded in a garden, a house with shattered windows and a roof with tiles blown off. I scribbled furiously in my notebook and wrote a story about the Croats shelling Borovo Selo. The next day I visited the Croatian half of Borovo on the edge of Vukovar: every house was badly damaged, several people had been killed and ammunition was running low. There were two sides of the story but they were not equal.

In the evenings, weary and yet with the adrenalin still

flowing from the day's escapades, we sat on the terrace of the Hotel Osijek, overlooking the River Drava, gazing through a haze of mosquitoes towards Baranja, supposedly the last resting place of King Louis II. This was the time for reflection, reminiscence, anger, sadness and sometimes a touch of bravado; each day brought a fresh and ridiculous story. Jon Jones, my table-football partner from Trpinja, drove to a front-line Croatian town, found the place deserted but the telephones working and spent the whole night calling friends all over the world from a cellar in the middle of a battlefield. I went with Alex Sutton, a young British photographer, to the village of Tenja and found the Croat troops drunk, stoned and enacting an *Apocalypse Now/ Rambo* fantasy. It was the day after a battle. They were barely four hundred yards from the Serbs and they were preparing a barbecue. 'Popeye', a computer-programmer-turned-sniper in a bright-red sunhat, shuffled out the door cackling to himself, waving a bottle of McGibbons whisky. A round hummed down the street. No one looked up. 'Sure, this is Vietnam,' joked one young guardsman called Boris. 'This is hell. Just we have no jungle . . .' The absurdity of war is absolute.

Slavonia's phoney war ended in the second week in August when the Serbs launched a heavy bombardment on Osijek. I remember the moment with clarity. Dragana, the slender blonde interpreter at the Osijek Press Centre, had been stalking me all week. One night we had a meal at the Chinese restaurant where she poured out her fears for the future as well as her problems with her husband. Then came the invitation to dinner at home. On the fourth request I felt duty-bound to accept.

When I arrived, sweat-stained and exhausted after a long day in the hayfields, she announced lightly that her husband and family were away in Zagreb. The table was laid with candles and a traditional Croatian dish. She was wearing a mini-skirt and a low-cut top. I was frantically trying to work out how best to extricate myself with least embarrassment, when the shelling started. It came like a low roll of drums and at first I assumed it was thunder. Then came an explosion closer to hand and suddenly the Habsburg skyline was lit up like a fireworks display. Pushing back my chair I ran to the balcony.

As a precaution I had given the foreign desk Dragana's number. On cue the phone rang. I had never been so relieved to hear the voice of the *Telegraph* switchboard. They connected me with the man on night duty.

'Alec? We've just had some Dutch journalist gabbling away on the line saying Osijek is raining shells and your hotel is rocking to its foundations. What's going on?' The embarrassment at London having to call me with the news of an attack on my hotel was easily outweighed by the relief at having a reason to leave. I stammered my excuses to Dragana about 'the pressures of the job' and ran back to the hotel.

In the lobby Jon Jones, Ron Haviv, Peter Northall and others were gathered, discussing their tactics for the night ahead. At last the ceasefire was over. They looked like excited schoolchildren planning to go truant. After the weeks of reconnaissance, at last the story had begun. I ran for the stairs, remembering a veteran's advice never to use a lift during a bombardment, and promptly felt rather stupid when everyone else made for the lift. After filing an update, I lay awake listening to the shells and musing on the absurdity of being able to telephone England directly from the war zone. I was wondering if I should be lying under my bed when I fell fast asleep.

Several hundred mortar shells and rockets landed on Osijek that night. It was one of the first serious attacks of the war and yet the net result was a few holed roofs, a burnt warehouse, some cratered roads and a destroyed tobacco kiosk. No one was killed and only a few people lightly injured. In hindsight the night-long barrage brought an abrupt end to the ceasefire and ushered in a new phase of more blatant Serbian aggression. But in the context of the peripheral damage it was difficult to convey the importance of the story. In daylight, with people venturing on the streets, I felt unconfident of my judgement and followed the lead of the commentators in London, who continued to talk lovingly about the ceasefire. For my photographer friends it was an impossible day.

'It's all right for you,' said one. 'You can scribble about whatever you like, but how do you make a trashed kiosk look dramatic?'

During the attack it was clear that many of the shells were coming from the JNA barracks and so I went to see the commander, a Lieutenant-Colonel Branko Kučković. He looked me straight in the eye as if I was an importunate recruit.

'Your eyes must have deceived you,' he said. 'Why should we want to do such a thing?'

'Why indeed, Colonel,' I replied, shaking his hand. 'That is what I will never understand.'

Two days later I turned on the World Service to hear that Mikhail Gorbachev had been detained in his Black Sea villa. I was about to leave with a Spanish colleague for the front line where the fighting was escalating by the hour. We shrugged our shoulders and retired to the hotel for a leisurely breakfast. For a fortnight the news was all from Moscow and, while the fighting raged in Yugoslavia, the world's television crews flocked to the Soviet Union. Within a few weeks the break up of the Evil Empire was a *fait accompli* – an irony in view of the fact that for months British and US diplomats had been citing the dangers of the disintegration of the Soviet Union as a reason for not recognizing Slovenia and Croatia.

It's good to have a cast-iron excuse for a holiday. Sophie was flying into London from Bucharest. After a cheery parting with the Osijek team, I departed for Venice, where the man from Avis nearly kissed my hand in delight, before retiring to south Devon. Within forty-eight hours of reaching Mothecombe beach, I was at Riga airport negotiating with the KGB my visaless entry into the Soviet Union. By the time I returned to Yugoslavia in October the brick-factory in Sarvaš was in the Serbs' hands, Osijek was suffering a nightly bombardment and the Hotel Osijek had been devastated by rockets and abandoned.

10

'Pivo with Ivo' – Portrait of a Siege

Dubrovnik, October–December 1991

'What is this obsession with old buildings? Just because the medieval quarter still stands, are the Serbian attacks acceptable? I suppose if the centre of London was flattened you would say "Oh, that doesn't matter, just as long as the Tower is in one piece."' *Zeljko Sikic, President of Dubrovnik's Council*

BOUGAINVILLEAS, imitation shutters and flashing lights – Opatija has all the trappings of a pretentious resort. Ever since an Austrian doctor in the last century decided that the then Istrian fishing village would make a good money-spinner, the great and good of Central Europe have descended there in search of a health cure. It's a stuffy and precious place, normally the last place in the Balkans I'd choose for a weekend off. But in October 1991 the guest-houses were deserted, the shrubberies untended and the prevailing tranquility was an Elysian dream compared with the Slavonian battlefields I had just left behind.

With Ed Vulliamy, the Rome correspondent of the *Guardian*, and Davor Huić, a Croatian journalist, I spent a night at Opatija while *en route* to Dubrovnik. Away from the ditches and mud around Osijek, we were in excellent spirits. An amusing encounter in our hotel with a young Croat refugee confirmed our new holiday mood. Fifteen-year-old Krino Turić was Yugoslavia's Jim from *Empire of the Sun*. A born survivor, with a cigarette butt always on the go, he thought Opatija was 'super' and intended to spend the next few months drinking *pivo* (beer). As for his month under siege in the east Croatian town of Vinkovci, he seemed chirpily unscarred. 'Whenever there was a lull I used to sprint outside to see if any kiosks were hit . . . Scared? Not me. I would stand there and gawp at the fighting. No one would shoot a nutcase like me.'

Amid the grimness of the war, Krino was a refreshing reminder of the versatility of human nature. Chuckling at his tales we spun on south. Ed, a true Renaissance man, had a bag of Beatles cassettes and a fund of anecdotes on anything from the mafia to the Risorgimento. Davor Huić, our interpreter, a former philosophy lecturer, was one of that special breed of interpreters with insight, humour and dedication. The Balkans has few roads to rank with the Dalmatian highway. In the autumnal sun, the deep blue of the Adriatic and the jagged contours of the Dalmatian mountains are better defined than in the dog days of summer. 'The Magical Mystery Tour' played all the way to Zadar.

It was in the late afternoon that we switched on the BBC World Service to hear that a ceasefire had been agreed around Dubrovnik and a ferry with EC monitors and journalists on board was already on its way to breach the siege. We were three hundred miles north – and our friends and rivals had stolen a march on the biggest story of the war to date.

World opinion is a fickle creature. In the autumn of 1991, in the wake of the failed hardline coup in Moscow, Balkanisation spread across the Soviet Union and almost unnoticed the federal Yugoslav army (JNA) went berserk. The cornfields of Slavonia turned to mud and the bucolic touches of Bruegel gave way to the raw horror of the Western Front. Suddenly there was war in Europe – messy, dirty war, with splintered trees and trenches and rubble, and young people brought up on rock-and-roll dying in their Levis and not knowing why, and peasant women in smocks fleeing in panic to neighbouring towns, and terror and confusion and disbelief, above all disbelief.

This was the most savage fighting in Europe since the Second World War. By October, three, four, maybe five hundred thousand refugees were on the move. Federal tanks and planes and artillery were pounding half-a-dozen Croatian towns. It was a dirty war of sieges and slaughters of stragglers. East of Rome, north of Athens, south of Vienna, in the heart of Europe, thousands of people were dying, and in the West, like rabbits caught in headlights, the politicians were strangely silent.

Part of the problem was bewilderment. After the clean-cut images and aims of the Gulf War, the Yugoslav struggle was alien and complex. The fighting had five main theatres, in each of which the JNA had different war aims. On one front the fighting was about ethnic rivalry. On another it was about territorial aggression, a.k.a. Greater Serbia. On a third it was about tribal vendettas. On a fourth the fighting was spawned by the culture of violence. With commentators struggling to explain this maze, interpretations differed, and the big picture, that the JNA was running amok, was obscured.

However, more culpably, the international community indulged a blinkered – maybe wilfully blinkered – vision of the issues at stake. On the brink of signing the Maastricht Treaty, Europe was obsessed with federalism and seemed determined to ignore the reality – that Yugoslavia had ceased to exist. The politicians rehearsed like a mantra the view that the Serbs were protecting their minority in Croatia. Time and again they implied that, by opting to secede, Croatia somehow deserved its pummelling by the JNA. The more they waved paper, the more confidently the federal generals pursued their assault.

Every fortnight a fresh outrage by the JNA spurred the diplomats into action. At the start of September with much fanfare the EC peace conference was convened in the Hague under Lord Carrington. Its first ceasefire fell apart within a few days. Two weeks later the Dutch foreign minister, Hans van den Broek, summoned a meeting of the West European Union to discuss sending in ground troops. In years to come this would be seen as another key moment for the international community. But the EC big players seemed more concerned with jockeying for position within the new post-Cold War Europe than with brokering, let alone enforcing, peace in their backyard. The Dutch and the French were reported to be keen. The Foreign Office was not – as some reports have suggested, in order to stymie the emergence of the West European Union as a rival to NATO. And so the posturing continued, until in early October the JNA made potentially a crucial tactical mistake and turned their gun-barrels against the coastal resort of Dubrovnik.

Dubrovnik was only the latest in a string of Croatian towns under attack. Novska, Nova Gradiska, Karlovac, Petrinja, Osijek, Sisak and other nondescript grey little towns had been pummelled throughout the previous month. But Dubrovnik, Byron's 'Pearl of the Adriatic', was different. A tourist destination with few peers, this was a place people knew and cherished. It also had the finest preserved medieval walled city in Europe, whose survival was all the more important following the destruction of the Ionian town of Zante by an earthquake in the 1950s.

Plagiarising the argot of the Partisan struggle of the 1940s, the Serbs said that Dubrovnik had to be 'liberated'. Medieval maps were pinned up in Belgrade showing Dubrovnik under the control of Serbia's fourteenth-century king, Dušan the Mighty, whose empire stretched from the Danube to the Aegean. But no amount of obfuscation could confuse the fact that their assault against a city with a 90 per cent Croat population was a clear-cut case of territorial aggression. The world focused on Yugoslavia with an intensity unsurpassed since the Slovenian war.

After spending September in Gorbachev's dying empire and then a spell covering Romania's latest bout of anarchy, I returned to Yugoslavia in mid-October to find the siege in abeyance. Then on 23 October the JNA renewed their offensive with a joint sea and land assault, advancing to within a mile of the city walls. The medieval quarter was reported to have been hit repeatedly. UNESCO and other cultural heavyweights competed in a chorus of outrage. The editor of *The Times* was said to be asking daily about the state of Titian's *Assumption*, the jewel in Dubrovnik's collection of art treasures. For correspondents the race was on to enter Dubrovnik.

It was a long and depressing haul south. The Maslenica bridge, where just three months before I had stopped to reflect while *en route* to Knin, was down, necessitating a detour. By nightfall we were still two hundred miles short of our goal, at the old Venetian port of Sibenik. The Hotel Jadran, the only hostelry in town, oozed the philistinism I had always imagined in Toad Hall under the weasels. The bar was full of drunken Croat soldiers in designer Rambo-fatigues. Britain, which throughout the summer had backed the Yugoslav federation, was not, it appeared, their favourite country.

Invisible behind his candle, the manager grunted strangely when we asked the price of the rooms and he handed us keys without comment. We understood soon enough. The windows in the rooms had been shot away and the bedboards were patchworks of bullet-holes. A week before, the Federal Navy had cruised offshore and sprayed the town with anti-aircraft rounds. I slept on the floor, with the bed between me and the window. Presuming our progress could only improve, we left for Split soon after dawn and on arrival headed straight for the headquarters of the EC monitors. With barely suppressed glee, their spokes-man announced that the boat to Dubrovnik had just sailed. Yes, there were journalists on board . . . No, we couldn't catch it . . . Weren't we a little slow off the mark? He had a lot of work pressing, so if there wasn't anything else . . .?

A bright young Canadian Croat in the Press Centre had a few words of cheer. He had heard something about another ferry bound for the Isle of Korčula, halfway between Split and Dubrovnik.

'When?' we asked frantically.

'Oh, sometime this afternoon or maybe tomorrow . . . that is, of course, if it comes; you know how it is.' More in frustration than with a clear sense of purpose, we took to the road. By the time we reached Korčula, Davor had fallen into a deep introspection, troubled by the suffering of his fellow Croats, petrol vapour was wafting from our spare jerrycan of petrol and the Beatles had been replaced by a funereal Croatian rendition of Mozart's clarinet concertos.

We were a paranoid bunch that night in the Hotel Korcula. Another dozen journalists had arrived, hoping to breach the siege. Whenever one of us left the restaurant, all eyes turned as if the absentee knew something the others didn't. Ed rang his foreign desk and heard that Maggie O'Kane, who was free-lancing for the *Guardian*, Phil Davison of the *Independent* and Jon Jones, my table-football partner from Slavonia, had smuggled themselves on board an EC launch and werealready inside Dubrovnik. The mood round the table darkened.

Maybe it's the climate: the Isle of Korcula has a record of beguiling the British. In the Napoleonic War the Royal Navy established a fort overlooking the old Venetian harbour. When Fitzroy Maclean, Churchill's liaison officer with Marshal Tito, landed on Korcula in 1943, he forged an instant bond with the islanders and after the war was awarded honorary citizenship. I too fell for its charms. A few hours wandering around the old Venetian quarter quite dispelled residual guilt about not reaching Dubrovnik.

We spent the morning with the local dentist, Josif Krstulović, who regaled us with Korčula's history. With a hint of pride he explained that south Dalmatia had never followed the lure of Croat nationalism. In the Second World War the Croats of Korčula had been a centre for the Serb-dominated Partisans. In 1991 the island still had a communist mayor, one of the last in Croatia. I sketched a few notes heavily laced with question marks. 'A Croatian stronghold for the Partisans?' 'A communist mayor in Croatia?' Yugoslavia's history and politics seldom square easily with trite generalisations.

Nora, the Krstulovićs' teenage daughter, was talking exuberantly of holidays past with her Serbian actor friends, when we were interrupted by the sound of activity from the quay. The *Liburnija*, the promised ferry, had arrived and was trying for Dubrovnik.

There were only a few minutes for a host of decisions. I left my Avis hire car and most of my luggage with the Krstulovićs. After much soul-searching Davor too decided to stay behind. His bravery was never in question. But with the JNA searching all ships entering Dubrovnik, for a Croat young man to try to enter was tantamount to an invitation to a stint in a Serbian detention camp. For Davor the risk was particularly acute. In 1981, after three months of military service, he went on hunger strike. Before being discharged he was interrogated and tortured for two days. It was not an experience he wished to repeat.

By the middle of the afternoon we were cruising south, playing cat and mouse with a pair of federal gunboats on our tail. With the crew shuffling around the markings, one moment flying the EC pennant, the next no flag at all, and with the captain alternating between bravado and the direst defeatism, we paced up and down the decks playing and replaying the endless unanswerable questions. Should we be apprehensive? Would the JNA turn us away? Why should we expect them to let us in? Suddenly we were coming into harbour.

The port authorities guided us in by torch-light. Apart from a few watch-fires flickering from the Serbs' positions in the hills, the city was shrouded in darkness. I was reminded of Byron's lines on the Assyrian coming down 'like a wolf on the fold'. The ramp was lowered and we drove on to the quay, hitching a lift with another journalist. The car behind us flashed its indicator lights and a flash of tracer shot into the sky, one, two, three times, as if to say 'Welcome to Dubrovnik.'

In a long and eventful history Dubrovnik has depended on its wits to survive. From its inception as a city-state in the eleventh century, the merchant fleet of Dubrovnik (or Ragusa as it was called then) competed with Venice for the Mediterranean. What they lacked in manpower, the Ragusans made up in seamanship and guile, extending a network of client colonies over the Balkans. When in extremis, they relied on their city walls. In the twelfth century Ragusa did a deal with the local pirates, whom they supplied with weapons in return for immunity from attack. In 1430, when the Turks were taking everything in their path, the Ragusan Senate negotiated a special arrangement with the Sultan, offering tribute in exchange for trading rights – a deal which the Ragusan intelligence service had been working on for years. Fifty years later a tribute set at 12,500 ducats was paid for recognition of Ottoman suzerainty.

The finest test for Ragusan diplomacy came in April 1667, after a fifteen-second earthquake destroyed three quarters of the city. With a fifth of the population killed and the walls ruptured, the city was defenceless and forthwith a Venetian fleet came charging down the coast to deliver the *coup de grâce*. Then came the moment which lives in Dubrovnik's history. As the Venetians prepared to land, a Ragusan ship (argosy) put off from the shore. On board was Nikolica Bunić bearing a letter 'on behalf of the Prince and Senate' – even though Dubrovnik had lost both in the disaster. Thanking the Venetians for their 'concern' in coming so swiftly, Bunić assured them everything was under control. Expecting submission, unsure how to proceed, the Venetian admiral backed away – Ragusa was saved.

I learned these snippets in a late-night chat with Vedran, a refugee from down the coast, several days after my arrival. Bunić, he told me, was the quintessential Ragusan. A few years after his confidence trick on the Venetians, he was sent to negotiate with the Pasha of Bosnia who was demanding a 'loan' of 150,000 ducats, in effect Dubrovnik's submission. Bunić's instructions were to 'Promise nothing, give nothing, suffer everything ... There you will meet a glorious death. Here the land will be free.' Like Regulus, the hero of republican Rome, who went to prison in Carthage to meet a certain death, Bunić left for Bosnia and died in captivity.

It is a tradition of which the city is rightly proud – although, in an area as unstable and militant as the Balkans, it carries attendant risks. Later adversaries have proved less pliant than the Turks. In 1806 Napoleon ignored all pleas for a parlay; his troops marched into town and overthrew the republic with barely a shot fired. The worst of all humiliations for the proud *Dubrovčani* was when two years later the French officially abolished the tiny state and an NCO strode into the Senate to announce the terms. In October 1991 once again an army was on the outskirts and once again the besieging commanders showed no sign of wanting to talk.

Dawn, a few hours after our arrival, found Ed Vulliamy and me standing at the south Ploče gate of the old quarter, alongside Teo and Srećko, two young barmen turned fighters. In the half-light the city walls glowed a delicate salmon pink. We stopped for a moment to admire the view. Teo directed our gaze the other way, towards the Žarkovica hill, barely a mile to the West.

'There they are, they only came yesterday: three tanks, a couple of trucks and some 120mm mortars. Not a lot but more than they need to finish the job.' Through binoculars the Yugoslav flag was just visible, with its red star flickering in the sea breeze.

The worst part was the waiting. The *Liburnija* arrived on day two of a ceasefire and, at a cursory glance, Dubrovnik appeared to have weathered the storm. By midday a piano was tinkling in a secluded courtyard, boutique owners were dusting down their windows and the *Dubrovčani* were strutting along the Stradun thoroughfare in their designer best. Apart from the planks and sand-bags protecting the most valuable monuments, a few chipped edifices and the odd pile of rubble, the old city was little changed since my holiday in August.

However, while the lull was appreciated, no one expected it to last. In the thirty days of the siege, the federal troops had followed a grim sequence of attack, pause, attack, pause. With the gunners now in sight on the hill-top, uncertainty gnawed like a cancer. Dubrovnik had become a goldfish bowl. Each day you faced the same dilemmas. Shall I go out now or shall I go out later? Shall I walk down this road or shall I walk down another? If they hit this spot once, what are the odds they will hit it again?

Most mornings were punctuated by the odd shell landing in the suburbs. When the hours passed without any shooting you started to crave the relief and certainty of a shell-burst, a signal to run for cover or jump into action. 'Its a psychological nightmare,' explained one Croat commander. 'In the phases like this, we all start jumping at the mere banging of a door. It's as if we are walking on air.'

The day began at 7.00 a.m. with the howl of the all-clear siren. I used to wake at five to the hour, lying in wait for the signal, brooding on the day ahead. But at least for the journalists the pressures of the job meant there was little opportunity to reflect on the danger. For the civilians, sitting at home or in shelters, with no electricity, little water and nothing to do, time passed very slowly.

By late October Dubrovnik's peacetime population of thirty thousand had been doubled by refugees fleeing the JNA'S advance. Most had stayed in their homes until the last moment, had waited until the shells were literally landing in their gardens or backyards. Now their very sanctuary was under attack. On our first night in the city, Ed and I visited the catacombs under the Revelin Fort. Dusty room after dusty room was filled with the fugitives, under blankets, on deck-chairs, squatting, crouching, silent in despair. In the light of a single bulb, they could have been lifted from footage of the Underground in the Blitz.

'We're all going mad. We just sit around and reminisce about our possessions and wonder how much the Serbs have left.' That was Anna, of the striking blonde hair, a school supervisor with a high-pitched laugh. 'Escapism? You must be kidding. All I want to do is wash my hair. But I can't, so I sit here and feel sorry for myself.' Ivo, a chubby-cheeked banker in a leather jacket and designer shirt, launched into a peroration about his four-berth cruiser, which was sunk in one of the first bombardments of the war. 'A beautiful boat . . . nestling neatly under an awning . . . why? why? why?'

For the soldiers defending Dubrovnik there was something derisory about these suburbanites, fussing about their hair and their yachts. Dubrovnik was a long way from the

Biblical scenes of misery in Slavonia where thousands of peasants daily streamed out of villages on foot, in carts, dragging livestock in their wake. Ed and I were escorted back from the Revelin Fort by a young fighter from Vukovar. He made as if to spit in the direction of the catacombs.

'Where I come from, if you give a man a gun he treats it like a Mercedes,' he said. 'Here they're only interested in the sun, the sea and themselves. If they care so much about Croatia, why aren't they up on the hills defending their homes?'

In the summer of 1992, when the siege of Dubrovnik was lifted, Croats from more hardline regions were contemptuous of the *Dubrovčanis'* apathetic resistance. The more I heard these criticisms the more I warmed to Dubrovnik, whose history is a testament to the triumph of reason over man's baser instincts. For centuries it was a beacon of hope in the Balkans, a haven of arts and morality. Dubrovnik's orphanage and old people's home date back four hundred years. Slavery was abolished in the mid-fifteenth century, three centuries before William Wilberforce. In the early 1990s the city still stood for the same values and was refreshingly clear of the nationalism ablaze in Split and Zadar.

'We are not Balkan,' said Srećko, my barman friend at the Ploče gate. 'We do not understand this violence and hatred.' It was the message of Bunić, the legendary envoy. It fell on unreceptive ears.

If the siege unfairly tarnished the reputation of the Dubrovcani, it was harder still on the city fathers'. Sieges have provided the stage for some of history's most inspirational commanders, but Dubrovnik was led by a clique of small-town politicians better suited to organizing cultural festivals than rallying morale on the barricades. Unfortunately for them, while all their inclinations seemed to be to end the fighting, but there was intense pressure from the government in Zagreb to hold out. The sieges of Dubrovnik and Vukovar were wonderful public relations boosts for Croatia's cause. It was never explained why relief forces failed so abjectly to lend any support.

Rendered at times inarticulate with their responsibilities,

Mayor Pero Poljanić and his councillors wrung their hands, agonised and sent faxes to the West – including to Prince Charles, who politely declined an invitation to visit. Not once did they broadcast a confidence-boosting speech to the city. Not once did they inform residents of the latest negotiations. In the Middle Ages the Republic's *Knez* (Rector) emerged from his Palace only on feast days, and then only to endorse the decisions of the Grand Council of nobles. The Dubrovnik of 1991 had no nobles and the fabric of society slowly crumbled.

Early in the siege, the authorities banned the sale of alcohol in public places in an attempt to keep the fighters sober. This only deepened Dubrovnik's collective despair. In a fit of panic, one group of residents tried to take down for safe-keeping the statue of the patron saint, St Blaise. Hours later St Blaise was still there – minus a finger, broken off in an argument about how to move the statue. When stocks of water ran low, residents besieged the Seminary of Ignatius, whose monks they accused of hoarding supplies. Breaking down the door they shouldered the rector out of the way to fill their urns. This was less than a month after the siege had started. It was a sad insight into how swiftly a community can lose its soul.

Local legend records that in times of need the Catholic Church has come to the aid of Dubrovnik. When the Venetians were about to attack in the tenth century a vision of St Blaise is supposed to have warned a priest who in turn alerted the Rector. On our second morning in the old city Ed and I encountered a mutinous priest who was clearly keen to rekindle those days. Father Stanislav Lasić was the priest of the cathedral. After a few words in the shade of the Titian – the editor of *The Times* could relax, it was intact – he hurried us down a side-street to his home. A fiery talker, over a glass of *slivovitz* he expounded his belief that the politicians were cowards and that Dubrovnik should indulge in more fighting and less talking.

'The city made a big mistake. We should have brought in arms to defend ourselves . . . It was obvious we were in a critically dangerous position, surrounded on all sides. But we didn't even try to organize sufficient resistance. Serbia is waging a war on Catholic values. We have to defend ourselves.' There was a knock on the door. He broke off to issue instructions to two young men with black headbands and Kalashnikovs.

Father Lasić's stance had a disturbing ring of the 1940s, when the Catholic Church was grossly compromised with the Ustaše regime. The Ustaše claimed that Orthodox Serbs were lapsed Catholics. In April 1941 the first reaction of the Archbishop of Zagreb, Alojizije Stepinac, to news of the formation of the Ustaše puppet state was 'joyful'. Even when the Ustaše's massacres of Serbs reached their height in 1943, Stepinac failed to break off relations with their leader, Ante Pavelic.

This dark strand in the Croatian Catholic Church was to have an ugly reawakening in 1992, when the Yugoslav war moved from Croatia to Bosnia-Hercegovina and Catholic priests abandoned any pretence at 'turning the other cheek'. However, Dubrovnik in 1991 was the wrong city for such militant sermonising. The Dubrovcani were sun-worshippers, yachters, bar-goers – not zealots. The younger soldiers liked to wear rosaries and crosses on their tunics. The Bishop of Dubrovnik, Zelimir Puljio, dismissed their obsession as a temporary phenomenon.

'This is a fight like David and Goliath,' he said. 'People turn to us like an infant to his parents. When you are afraid, you cry, mama. People are not more or less religious than before. They are showing their fear.'

After Father Lasić's un-Christian remarks about the Serbs, it was reassuring to find the Bishop such a model of restraint, and for an entertaining half-hour we forgot the siege, discussing a range of issues. We had arrived with a stand-in interpreter, Ljubomir, to find the Bishop spoke English fluently. After chattering away, we were about to go when there was a stream of Serbo-Croat from Ljubomir mixed with a few phrases in English. He was, he explained, anxious to join in, but he couldn't understand. We replayed the conversation – with the Bishop translating.

*

Life under siege had its compensations. In every military situation it is axiomatic that someone somewhere fashions a luxurious lifestyle. Within the whitewashed confines of the Hotel Argentina conditions were positively cushy. By early November there was a hard-core of twenty Western journalists in residence and we shared the hotel with several hundred refugees, six EC monitors and the Honorary Consul. Sara Marojica, née Scowgey, was a one-time actress from the Midlands who had married a local. At the start of the siege a shell destroyed their house, forcing Sara to flee to a cave, where she survived for three days on vegetables and brandy. Her gregarious good humour enlivened many a long evening and her 'It's a long way to Tipperary' was incomparable, drawing rapturous applause from the Argentina's staff.

Of course there were trifling inconveniences. The restaurant menu had jettisoned some of the exotica I remembered from August. With the generator shutting down at 9.00 p.m. it was candles thereafter. Buckets of sea water were delivered for ablutions. Guests were kindly requested to keep their curtains drawn and stay off the balconies after dark. But these were incidentals. The monkey-faced barman in his dinner jacket served cocktails and span glasses with the aplomb of the old days. Breakfast was served on starched linen tablecloths. 'On the balcony, sir? Oh, was that a shell? Would you rather inside?' Dinner was three courses, and always with wine. Those in need of distraction could take to the sea.

A pre-breakfast dip became a ritual for a select band of guests. Among the keenest was a charming Danish EC monitor, George Petersen, a Special Forces officer who was married on the eve of his departure from Copenhagen. The only disincentive was the *bora*, the fierce Adriatic north wind – although even on calmer days you had to pick your moment. One gloriously sunny afternoon Missie Beelman, the correspondent from the Associated Press, took to the waters just as the JNA launched an impromptu raid. For three hours the unfortunate Missie was pinned down, half in and half out of the sea. On her safe return, she did not, I fear, receive the sympathy she deserved.

With too little to do and too much wine to drink, tempers rose, and in the evenings Yugoslav political arguments spluttered and fizzed around the table. The EC monitors, who dined in a separate section, were the most frequent target of the invective. But the arrival of Dr Kathy Wilkes, a professor from St Hilda's, Oxford, deflected some of the flak. A personal friend of Mayor Poljanić, she appeared to be on a crusade to share the city's suffering. Her pro-Croat arguments stood no chance in the hurly-burly of the night-time discussions.

But whenever the complement became too claustrophobic and thoughts turned to home, you could escape to the old city, watch the sunset from the ramparts and dream of wide open spaces. A picket of Croat volunteers with their girl-friends manned the St Ivan's Fort. Pipe, their commander, and Vuk, their number two, were amateur soldiers and welcomed new company. We drank 'Dr Schiwago' vodka in plastic cups, laughed and joked, as ever pledging eternal friendship after the war. At nine there was a curfew and, shortly before the hour, I would wander back up the hill, tripping and sliding in the blacked-out streets.

A whisper of a rumour told of the police chief who imposed the curfew in October ordering his soldiers to fire on all unidentified comers. The next night, so the story went, an unmarked car approached a checkpoint at speed and the sentry, as instructed, opened fire. The driver was killed – it was the police chief. While the story was probably apocryphal, it did not seem worth breaking the curfew.

With the world focused on Madrid for the Middle East Peace talks and Britain obsessed by the mysterious death of Robert Maxwell, Yugoslavia slipped down the news ratings. Occasionally the war disturbed our reverie. The Argentina was half-way between Mount Zarkovica and a Croat gun position. One Monday lunchtime the terrace was caught in the cross-fire and the delicate whir of passing bullets sent us smartly for cover. When my office in London called me an hour later and signed off with a jolly 'keep your head down', I replied a little tartly that I was, and that indeed my whole body was down, as two gunboats were steaming past my window. However, as the days passed, the manoeuvres of the gunboats lost their menace, the air-raid siren became less intrusive and it was embarrassing to hear concern voiced over the telephone for our well-being. I began to regret leaving my luggage on Korčula.

The only weight on my mind was the presence of Davor, my interpreter, who had arrived a few days after the *Liburnija* in a 'peace flotilla' of fishing boats. In early November the federal navy tightened up the blockade and insisted that all boats which left Dubrovnik had to be searched. I had nightmares of a private re-run of the *Killing Fields* in which Davor was left stranded on a smoking quay, while the journalists were lifted to safety.

On the evening of Thursday 7 November the federal army issued an ultimatum, ordering Dubrovnik to surrender or 'face the consequences'. The city authorities flatly refused and played down the threat. I was inclined to agree. The warning sounded like classic Balkan bombast. The next day a group of journalists left on a refugee ferry, along with Davor, whom they promised to escort back to Zagreb. With my conscience appeased, I headed down for a swim with Andrej Gustinčić of Reuters and Peter Green of UPI, only to be driven smartly upstairs by a burst of machine-gun fire. A short while later the telephone and telex lines went down. 'Maybe it's time to stock up with food and candles,' I speculated in my diary. 'Could this be it?' The next morning the battle for Dubrovnik restarted in earnest.

Why the JNA decided to relaunch their attack is not clear. To take Dubrovnik they needed infantry. The course of the war in Slavonia had shown that the JNA foot-sloggers had no stomach for hand-to-hand fighting. Even if they had been able to muster the necessary men and morale, a ground assault would have incurred heavy casualties and almost certainly failed. Further, the JNA commanders must have been well aware that of all the battlefields in Croatia, Dubrovnik was the one which most outraged the West. But logic seldom played an important part in the JNA's strategy.

The commanders in the south Adriatic were ardent Serb nationalists. Throughout late 1991 and 1992 they seemed to operate on their own agenda, frequently attacking when their leaders in Belgrade had signed a ceasefire. In the late summer of 1992 I was in the Montenegrin capital, Podgorica, and several Montenegrins told me proudly that their commander during the siege of Dubrovnik was a car-park attendant, who had an old grudge against the city. It was as good an explanation as any.

Maybe that sunny breakfast on Saturday 9 November the gunners were bored of waiting. Maybe they were hung-over. Maybe they were angry at the news of the EC sanctions on Serbia which had just been imposed. Maggie O'Kane was the first to suspect we were in for trouble. At dawn she and Paul McGeough of the *Sydney Morning Herald* were half-way up to the Croat frontline on Mount Srdj, when they turned to look out to sea and saw the standard two gunboats had been reinforced by two more. When all four started cruising towards the coast and training their guns on beach-hotels, Maggie decided to postpone her trip and retired to the city, leaving Paul to go alone. By midday the gunners had settled down behind their assorted weaponry and were blasting away.

For a few blissful hours the attack seemed stylised and unreal. The initial shelling focused on the Napoleonic forts on Mount Srdj and on the isle of Lokrum, the two main Croat positions. Feigning to analyse the strategy of the gunboats, which were darting in and out like formation dancers, I watched the attack with Pipe from the battlements of St Ivan's Fort, counting impacts and judging distances as if commentating on a race. Pipe tapped me on the shoulder and handed over his binoculars.

'Your Richard the Lionheart is said to have been ship-wrecked there on his way back from the crusades,' he said, pointing towards Lokrum, half a mile offshore. 'He swore that the fort will never fall.' I nodded and assiduously scribbled down more notes. Every few seconds a grey puff of smoke rose from the cypresses covering the island, followed by the sharp crack of the detonation. It was like

watching a *son et lumière* from the ring-side seats and we
lay back against the rampart with the sun in our faces.

Even when a federal fighter-bomber circled overhead
before dropping two turnip-shaped bombs on Mount Srdj,
it was hard to accept the booms and puffs of smoke were
genuine. Then in the early afternoon the gunners lowered
their sights on the old city. With a roar like an express train
a shell hit the rampart. Pipe ran into the fort for his rocket
launcher. Vuk cocked his rifle. It was time to withdraw.

Alive with camaraderie and awash with supplies, the
Argentina was nonetheless a hopeless headquarters to cover
the battle from. Halfway between Mount Žarkovica and the old
city, it was in the thick of the fighting and cut off during
the day. Worse still, it had no link with the outside world.
There were three satellite phones in Dubrovnik: the first
was the closely-guarded property of the EC monitors, the
second was in the harbour master's office at Gruž Port, the
far side of town and unreachable, the third was in Mayor
Poljanić's office. On the Sunday, the second day of the
attack, three people, including Phil Davison of the *Independent*,
were wounded in the hotel reception and the EC
monitors relented, allowing us to send a pooled (joint)
report. However, the clear understanding was that this was
for the last time. The same evening a group of us slipped
down to the old city and set up residence in the city hall.

With Dr Wilkes determined to send faxes to Michael
Foot and other old friends of the city, with the engineer
responsible for the satellite phone tearfully convinced that
all journalists were Serbian spies, and of course with the
Serbs themselves doing their best to disrupt proceedings, it
required a combination of patience, diplomacy and guile to
ensure the transmission of our dispatches. All the while
Poljanić stalked up and down the long corridors pursued by
the ghosts of Rectors past. One of the few times he could be
persuaded to speak, he muttered 'horrible, horrible' – a line
which he was mortified to learn was printed all over the
world. Judging from the distaste etched on his face, I
suspect that he would almost have preferred that his city

fell, than that he had to suffer the presence of half a dozen irreverent journalists at such proximity. My abiding memory is of the president of the City Council, Mr Zeljko Sikić, staring ruefully at a mound of typescript which was waiting to be sent.

'I would do anything to stop you typing. Why do you type so much?' he pleaded. 'You type much faster than we can send. Imagine you were in Biafra. What would you do there? You would not be able to send reports. You should tell jokes, or something, not write more reports.'

Some reports went a day late. Some never went at all. Sometimes you had to hold the hand of the engineer and coax him into trying the telephone. But even if unreliable, the system worked and it left us free to concentrate on the practical difficulties of covering the siege.

In one of the finest first-hand accounts of a medieval siege, Francisco Balbi da Correggio, an Italian soldier poet, describes in graphic detail the Ottoman barrage of the heavily-fortified base of the Knights of St John in Malta. For over three months in the summer of 1565 the pride of Suleyman the Magnificent's army and navy bombarded the Knights' fortifications with basilisks and culverins, using chain shot and incendaries, often blasting away without any prearranged plan. The federal attack against Dubrovnik bore marked similarities. There was little refinement, little subtlety. It was all about noise and smoke and bludgeoning. Even within the city walls, whose three metres of stone were designed to withstand such a pounding, the buildings trembled at each explosion and the surrounding hills amplified the sound, until the whole valley seemed to be exploding. Towards the end of the siege of Malta, when the Knights were prostrate with fatigue, Balbi wrote that it seemed 'as if the world was coming to an end'. In Dubrovnik, while few of the federal shells were high explosive, suggesting the JNA wanted to intimidate more than destroy, there were moments when, as in Malta, it seemed 'as if the world was coming to an end.'

The safest time to walk around was in the middle of the night, when the JNA gunners rested from their lanyards and a few brave spirits emerged from the shadows, like rats from their holes. On the second night of the attack, Paul McGeough and I crept through the darkness in the maze of alleys off the Stradun, crunching over the layer of rubble and chippings. The only light was from candles, the only movement from the odd cat in search of food. Conversations were held at a whisper. Apart from the occasional shell from an assiduous or malevolent gunner, the only sound was the chiming of the seventeeth-century clock. Balbi would have recognized the medieval scene.

By one or two a.m. defiance started to replace defeatism. 'You wait,' said one voice, addressing me from the gloom. 'They'll lose thousands if they try to come into the city. We'll fight them with our bare hands.' While shaken, the city was not cowed. In a testament to the medieval masons, many of the projectiles bounced off the city walls, leaving pockmarks no bigger than dinner plates. In the first two days there were fewer than thirty casualties. Matko, as the voice introduced himself, was convinced that his city would never fall. After a brief chat, squatting by a pile of mealie bags, we picked our way on to Pipe's outpost, heartened by the show of defiance.

However, to appreciate the full horror of the attack, you had to leave the sanctuary of the city walls and take to the road. Paul McGeough had a battered Renault 4, rented from the local Radio Station. With a push and a prayer it usually started. As the sun came up we would roll it along the south stretch of the Stradun, puffing and swearing, with the odd furtive glance at Mount Zarkovica. Then, after idling through the old city, we hurtled out the Ploce Gate like a greyhound off the starting blocks, screeching round the corner to the left, up the hill, past the row of burned out cars, dodging the unexploded shells in the road and on to the hospital, the Gruz docks, the refugee hotels, for a whirlwind assessment of the damage, before spinning round and back, highlighted for a moment on the Lapad ridge – a final tightening of the stomach and we were home. On a good day the commute was over in forty-five minutes, before the gunners had even stirred from their beds. It was a risk. But it was doing the job. It was also very compelling.

Day and night became a continuum. The hectic routine started at dawn and ended with a late-night scramble for food and shelter. The second and third nights of the attack, I slept under a table in Poljanić's office. On the fourth, Paul and I timed our return badly. The federal gunners had decided to launch a late-night salvo to coincide with the start of the curfew. At five to nine we found ourselves wild-eyed and panting outside the twelfth-century nunnery, in search of refuge, frantically ringing the bell, praying the nuns weren't taking shelter in the cellar, first whispering, then calling, then shouting, until, blessed relief, as if to medieval pilgrims, a nun opened the door and ushered us inside.

Their treasures were in cases in the cellar. Their church was abandoned. The day before, a shell had ploughed through their top window, scattering surplices, impacting in a sculpted bedstead. But, for the Sisters of Sigurata, nothing could disturb their daily rhythm. Dispensing a supper of ham and drinking water – a banquet after forty-eight hours of biscuits and whisky – they displayed an unflustered serenity born of fifty years' seclusion. 'Of course, the shell was a shock for all of us. We are praying especially hard for the Serbian fighters that they do good and not bad,' murmured Sister Babić. 'Milk? I know you English like milk in your tea.'

If the Montenegrins had read their history books they might have saved themselves – not to mention the *Dubrovčani* – considerable trouble. In 1806, in tandem with their Slav allies the Russians, Montenegrin forces advanced up the coast and bombarded Dubrovnik, but were unable to evict the occupying French army. In 1991 the tactic again failed. On the afternoon of Tuesday 12 November, the fourth successive day of shelling, the barrage crescendoed, and just as suddenly faded. Like spoiled children denied a treat, the besiegers closed their assault with a salvo on the old harbour, spitefully picking off fishing boats with incendiaries, one by one, until the waters were covered with charred wrecks, blackened planks and yachting memorabilia. At 7 p.m. a handful of sailors ventured out to scupper the surviving boats. Dubrovnik was quiet.

As a child I was told the story of my Irish great-uncle, who, after surviving four years on the Western Front, was killed in 1918 at a level crossing a few miles from home. The moral of the story applies equally to war-corresponding. Emboldened by the activity of Dubrovnik's sailors, Paul and I ventured over to the city post office, where Ivo, a telecommunications engineer, had repaired a phone line. Ivo was the true hero of the siege. On the first night of the attack, the day after the phone lines had gone down, he had headed into no-man's land, traced the fault and carried the offending shell-shattered junction box down to the city. The following night, after a day of repair-work, he repeated his journey – with the result that one telephone was working.

The mayor's phone had been restricted to filing reports. For the first time in almost a week we could speak to our families. Uplifted and exhilarated that the noise had stopped, we pledged to buy Ivo a *pivo* (beer) when the siege was over and laughed heartily at our simple rhyme. Another Ivo – all the workers of the PO seemed to be called Ivo – had a bottle of brandy. We toasted Ivo as the next mayor of Dubrovnik, called England once more and left.

We were picking our way down the main highway, musing on the idea of the Ivos running the city, when there was a gentle whirring high and to the right, like a rising pheasant. I cocked my ears, thought nothing of it and moments later came a massive explosion from the adjacent street. There was another whirring and another explosion, closer, louder and a third was whirring, surely on top of us. Lying face down in rubble and broken glass, I felt very vulnerable and for the first time seriously queried the point of covering a war.

It's hard to be objective when you are besieged. In late December in London, a senior colleague politely asked me if I had been afraid when I composed my reports, implying that my emotions had carried away my writing. The comment rankled. I have since re-read my despatches of the siege many times. Over one of them the front-page headline

was 'LIKE THE BARBARIAN HORDES ADVANCING ON ROME
THE FEDERAL FORCES HAVE ABANDONED ALL RESTRAINT.'
I stand by my comparison. When a reporter applies pen to
paper, fear and anger have to be kept under control, but
there are times when passion is essential to communicate
the force of a story. This was Europe 1991 and an army was
randomly shelling a city of minimal strategic significance
and with a large, defenceless civilian population. The fixation of the West with Dubrovnik's old buildings, at a time
when the east Slavonian town of Vukovar was being bombarded literally out of existence, smacked of Western cynicism at its worst. However, the siege of Dubrovnik was
nonetheless a terrible crime and all the more important
because it was a conduit for conveying the primitivism of
the JNA. In Belgrade the proud and *puissant* federal
generals were furious at being compared with barbarians.
At a dinner a few days later they ranted that the *Daily
Telegraph* was taking sides. On the day of the worst attack,
when a shell was landing every few seconds, these same
generals blithely swore that not one puff of dust had been
moved in the old city.

The fight for Dubrovnik was a different war from that
raging in Slavonia and the Krajina. This was a battle of
spite and jealousy. Ethnic hatred was important only in the
propaganda-befuddled minds of the federal privates –
Dubrovnik's resident Serbs were among the most determined to ward off the besiegers. Most of the besiegers were
reservists from Montenegro, the smallest and toughest republic in the old federation. Regarded by Serbs as blood-
brothers, Montenegrins pride themselves on their hardy
warrior lineage. Traditionally their forte has been freeboot-
ing. Tim Judah of *The Times*, an old friend from Bucharest
days, spent several days with the federal forces as they
plundered their way towards Dubrovnik in the early days of
the siege. As soldiers emerged from the duty-free at Dubrovnik's Cilipi Airport, with trolley-loads of whisky and
cigarettes, Tim asked their commander what the JNA's
policy was on looting. There was a slight pause before the
officer replied stiffly that the goods were 'the gift of the

grateful people of Cilipi.' The longer the conflict in Yugoslavia lasted, the more opportunities there were for the dross elements in society to come to the forefront and have their way.

After the bombardment the JNA had the temerity to cry 'foul play' at the Croats for firing from around the old city. Journalists had a duty to record that the Croats were using the old city in their defence. But to follow the Serbs' apologists' line and suggest that this in some way morally equated the two sides was absurd. The defenders of Dubrovnik had two light field guns, a handful of mortars and a few hundred men, pitted against the ordnance of one of Europe's best stocked armouries. Throughout the siege the JNA demonstrated that nothing was sacrosanct. Their treasured targets were two refugee hotels, the Plakir and Tirena, which by the middle of November had been hit by hundreds of shells. The nearest Croat military position was the Hotel Neptun, clearly visible eight hundred yards away, untouched. 'We are Athens to their Sparta,' said the Bishop of Dubrovnik. I had heard and dismissed that particular comparison many times before in Croatia. In Dubrovnik for the first time it seemed apt. It was the scenario of the miners of June 1990 in Bucharest all over again, dark against light, the triumph of Balkan barbarism.

For the *Dubrovčani*, the worst of their ordeal was over. Twenty-four hours after the end of the bombardment an unofficial ceasefire came into effect. For the next month the federal gunners held off from their lanyards and the people could take to the streets. While the blockade was to drag on until May 1992, Dubrovnik had to face only one more heavy attack. I wish I had known this two days after the barrage, as I watched the EC monitors, most of the journalists and several thousand refugees abandon the city.

Silhouetted against the still-smouldering harbour, with scores of wounded huddled on the car-deck, sick and elderly crushed against the gunwales and guards beating back those without passes to leave, the departure of their ferry was etched in the darkest images of the Second World War. In driving rain, as flames still licked from the blackened skeletons of nearby warehouses, there was not even a semblance of control. Windowless cars and ambulances skidded to a halt beside the ferry, disgorging panicked residents. Standing on the quay as the *Slavija 1* left, I was beset by doubts about my decision to remain.

That night Sara Marojica, the British Honorary Consul, defiantly hoisted the Union flag over the Hotel Argentina to replace the EC pennant. But the hotel felt curiously vulnerable without the EC monitors and the inevitable rumours were circulating that, with the 'ice-cream sellers' gone, the Argentina was the next in line for the assault. The Croats had abandoned Mount Srdj, effectively leaving Dubrovnik open to a *coup de grâce*. The hotel bar was filling up with demoralised Croat soldiers. It seemed only a matter of time before the city fell. When I entered the hotel restaurant to see half a dozen strange people, it took me a while to appreciate that they had breached the siege. My astonishment was all the greater when I learned who they were.

Dr Bernard Kouchner, the flamboyant French Minister of Humanitarian Action. Margarita Boniver, the Italian Minister of Immigration, and Stefan de Mistura, a UNICEF special envoy, made a colourful addition to the Argentina's complement. They had outstripped the federal navy in a UN hydrofoil and had come to Dubrovnik to broker a truce. Dr Kouchner, a co-founder of *Médecins sans Frontières* in 1971, was no ordinary politician. While he loved to court the media, he was also a passionate opponent of conventional diplomacy and, over breakfast on the hotel terrace, he would rail against Europe's bungled handling of the break-up of Yugoslavia, sparing neither his colleagues in Paris nor his equals in Europe.

The arrival of these illustrious blockade-runners was at first overshadowed by terrible news from Slavonia. Vukovar, the Stalingrad of Croatia, had finally fallen. In eighty-eight days under siege half a million shells are estimated to have fallen on the town. The buildings were flayed until they looked as if they were suffering from monstrous leprosy. Trees were jagged stumps, barely a handful more than a few feet tall. Vukovar was not taken, it was destroyed. It was without a doubt the worst atrocity of the war. For the people of Dubrovnik it was a salutary reminder of the ruthlessness of their enemy.

We were alerted to the scale of the tragedy in Vukovar's desperate final hours, when Dr Kouchner received a pathetic appeal for help from the director of the hospital. 'Help us! Help us! Gangrene is breaking out. Vukovar is a kingdom of death and destruction!'

Transmitted by a radio ham, it was the last message to leave Vukovar and it stirred Dr Kouchner to greater efforts for Dubrovnik. His masterplan was to broker a separate peace for the city and make the region a demilitarised zone, a most appropriate solution in view of Dubrovnik's peace-loving history. The first stage was to cross the lines to broker a truce. For the six remaining journalists, the chance to meet our attackers was not to be missed.

We arrived in the no-man's land suburb of Mokošica as the JNA troops 'liberated' it from the other direction. Once Dubrovnik's ritziest suburb, two miles west of the main city, it had been pounded by the JNA for the previous month. No building was untouched, no street uncratered. In ones and twos, encouraged by the UN flag fluttering over our minibus, the residents emerged from stairwells and cellars to cluster around Dr Kouchner, begging to be evacuated. Then the twos became tens and the tens became hundreds until we were surrounded by people begging to leave. A mother and father plucked at my arm and pushed forward their daughter.

'She is our only child. Take her to the city, take her away.' We were all in tears and yet there was nothing to say. We turned away.

For the federal soldiers, who had expected a heroes' welcome, it was rather embarrassing. There they stood, shuffling their feet, in a hotch-potch of uniforms: chubby grandfathers, smooth-faced teenagers, a handful of irregulars in Chetnik badges and shaggy hats, a real-life unit of Dad's Army. They looked distinctly ordinary, simple maybe, wild certainly not, and yet, and yet . . .

A federal sergeant was standing back from the crowd. I asked him why his men were shelling Dubrovnik.

'What shelling? We're trying to save the city from the fascists.'

'But you're destroying Dubrovnik, bit by bit, street by street.'

'You don't understand. They are destroying the city and then pretending it is us.'

'They? Who are they?'

'The Ustaše.'

'The Ustaše? But what about the destruction here. These burned out houses, that devasted shop. Who did that? The people of Mokošica?' Sergeant Miloš Laudanović was a painter with a fair-grasp of English, not your average squaddie. I could see he was troubled and briefly I waited for a ray of light, of reason. He frowned and back came his most Orwellian comment of all . . .

'We have to protect these people,' – the logic that had killed Vukovar.

There was no point in pursuing the argument. Montenegro, the smallest Yugoslav republic, with 600,000 people, had the most tightly controlled media in the old federation. The official line was that Croatia had to be rescued from fascists – an appeal to the heart of the Montenegrin soul. Throughout the nineteenth century Montenegro was a bastion of free Slavdom and Christianity in the heart of Turkish territory. In 1991, as the implosion of the Yugoslav economy started to affect the sturdy Montenegrin hillmen, along came another noble cause to follow. Fascism was on the march. Ergo, tear, rend and destroy. When in 1992 I visited the Montenegrin capital and asked about Dubrovnik, an old man took me to one side. 'Don't believe what you hear about that place. They were burning tyres to simulate fires. It fooled the foreign press but it didn't fool us.'

By the end of the afternoon in a candle-lit bomb-shelter, negotiations to evacuate the residents were proceeding smoothly. Then there was a sudden burst of firing. A few bullets whined past Dr Kouchner. The federal soldiers ran for cover and started shouting and waving their weapons. The deal was off and Dr Kouchner and de Mistura retired to Dubrovnik. They would try again the next day. I think we all knew that the plan wasn't to be.

With the negotiations dragging on and the siege settling back into its old sluggish rhythm, one by one the journalists and the politicians slipped away. By the end of November, like party-goers who crash out rather than leave a good party, Maggie and I were the only two journalists left.

We started making stupid decisions. When flares lit up the city, we no longer froze with the due scrupulous care. When walking up the hill we no longer hugged the walls. When the Renault had a puncture we clanked our way from one side of the city to another, in noisy defiance of the federal snipers. At the same time our standards started slipping. If we had a puncture in daylight, we would cruise along the rows of abandoned cars until we found an intact Renault 4, pull over, jack it up, swap wheels and drive on. The wine in the Argentina tasted bitter. In the corridors I could no longer look the refugees in the eye. It was as if we were sated, punch drunk on suffering. We were waiting for the signal to go but too weary to make the move.

All month I had been planning to stay in Dubrovnik until the end of the siege. But the atmosphere was subtly changing. Units from HOS, the militia of the extreme-right Croatian Party of Rights, had slipped through the blockade and were manning the defences. They demanded accreditation and refused interviews. Pipe and others had been relieved of their posts. The last agony came when we crossed to the Montenegrin port of Cavtat under a UNICEF flag and watched the two rival delegations embrace like old friends. For five weeks the leaders of Dubrovnik had been forced to skulk in cellars, now they were chatting away with their tormentors as if nothing had happened. A JNA colonel appeared with a case of Cabernet Sauvignon, presumably looted from the Cilipi duty free, and they all disappeared upstairs for a good meal and I knew I had to leave, that I could no longer bear the absurdity of the war. A colleague had given us the name of Pepo, a policeman, who could arrange transport out by fishing boat. Half an hour after returning from Cavtat, Maggie and I were huddled in the bottom of a blacked-out motor boat.

It was the final irrational, crazy decision, born of anger and frustration and fatigue. We could have – should have – waited until the next refugee ferry. Instead we crept through the federal navy's blockade with a unit of Croat National Guard and the body of a twenty-two-year-old soldier, draped in autumnal flowers, homeward bound from the battlefield of Srdj. The skipper, Juro, a merchant sailor, chattered away as he started the engine. 'We have an Englishman aboard and a lady, we will be lucky tonight.' We fingered the holes in the woodwork in silence.

On two occasions everyone groped for the hold as a coastal battery opened up, off-target. A voice warned, 'Stand clear of the gun' and without warning the boat surged forward, crashing against the waves; even the helmsman was crouching below the gunwales. Finally land came along-side, greeted absurdly by a burst of music from a stereo. It was one in the morning, pouring with rain and we were out, breathing lungfuls of fresh air.

At last we could jump in the air and shout and sing and dive into the sea and ignore the shadows. After a night in the boatman's cottage, we were given a lift to Korcula where the car was waiting in pristine condition. The first bath and shave and clean clothes in five weeks passed in a haze, as did a sequence of meals. On the long, straight road north, nothing could puncture our euphoria – and yet it was desperately fragile.

At Split we bumped into Ambassador Bondioli, the head of the EC monitoring mission for Dalmatia, who was travel-ling north. When he suggested we join his convoy, we accepted with pleasure and north of Zadar we all stopped for lunch. The former ambassador in Yemen, Bondioli was a witty conversationalist. With the chef preparing a platter of fish, we listened with equanimity to his tales of the war.

We heard how he swapped his Cartier lighter for a JNA general's attaché case. 'You see? It is magnificent, no?

Look, goddammit ... *ecco* ... you can read here. Major General V. Vuković.' We heard about a British monitor, a Mr Taylor, negotiating for a Serbian colonel's ears. We heard about the prowess of the drivers. 'These are the heroes. Write this down. Write this and then send it to me.'

However, as the first bottle of Posip ceded to a second and the second to a third, the ambassador's musings became less palatable. The wine stirred bitter memories of the despair pervading Dubrovnik after the monitors left and it also revived our anger at the arrogance of the West. Bondioli sensed our change of mood.

'You journalists don't understand,' he cried. 'Ever since we left the city there has been a ceasefire. If we were still there, maybe the fighting would be going on.' Maggie or I interjected wrily that, if that was the case, then to ensure peace the monitors should leave all the war-zones. Bondioli pounded the table.

'Goddammit! No comment! No comment!' The rest of the meal passed in uneasy silence.

Individually the EC monitors conducted their duties with diligence, integrity and bravery; in 1992 five were killed, four when an EC helicopter was shot down, one on duty in Mostar. But collectively they were a sop to the conscience of the West, filing endless reports about the breakdown of ceasefires, all the time careful to avoid blaming either side. Two monitors conceded to me privately that any field reports offering frank criticism of the JNA were sanitised before they reached the Hague. Bondioli epitomised the mock-seriousness of the operation. In early October he carved a niche for himself in the annals of the war when his stentorian voice was heard outside the town of Vukovar, competing against a storm of shells, demanding a medical convoy be allowed through. But he seemed hardly the man to arbitrate in Europe's bloodiest war for almost half a century. He drove on alone.

Zagreb was full of drunken young Croats in uniform. Reports were circulating that President Tudjman had deliberately sacrificed Vukovar, which never supported the HDZ, leaving it undefended in his quest for international support. With the Avis office in Graz clamouring for its car, I gladly left for Austria and thence to London. Ten days later, Dubrovnik suffered its heaviest bombardment of the siege.

11

Cry the Beloved Bosnia

Sarajevo, January to June 1992

'Anyone who has seen the streets of Sarajevo and its bazaar as sparkling as a mirror and compares these with what obtains in cities or countries held up as paragons of civilizations is inclined to use the term "Balkan" as a compliment as others tend to employ the word "Scandinavian", – *Claudio Magris, Italian travel-writer and historian*

'If I were a bird and had wings I'd fly all over Bosnia. I'd fly. I'd never stop until I'd seen all of it.' – *Bosnian folk-song*

Graffiti on Bosnian post office, summer 1992: 'This is Serbia.' *Graffiti underneath:* 'Wrong, dummy. This is a post office.'

'ALL QUIET IN the Balkans' runs an old German film title. When the histories are written of the collapse of Yugoslavia, the early 1990s will read like a breathless succession of tragedies for the Yugoslav peoples and of bungled mediation by the international community. However, as the winter snows of 1991/2 gave way to spring, briefly, tantalisingly it seemed as if the Balkan bloodbath was at an end.

For the first time in almost a year, far from needing support from their colleagues in Bucharest, the Belgrade stringers had time on their hands. On 3 January a UN-brokered ceasefire came into effect in Croatia. Twelve days later the EC recognized Slovenia and Croatia, and the fighting in Yugoslavia – or rather former Yugoslavia, as Tito's old federation was becoming known – died down. According to a UN peace plan, fourteen thousand blue-helmeted peace-keepers were to deploy in the third of Croatia captured by the Serbs. The principle enshrined in the Helsinki Final Act of 1975 that borders cannot be changed by force had, albeit belatedly, been upheld; the Serbs' bluff had apparently been called. By early February the UN vanguard was arriving in Croatia.

For two months, corresponding from the region was a languid affair, seldom disturbed by the urgency of hard news. I retired to Romania in early February to renew my acquaintance with the quiet side of the Balkans. In Bucharest the bright lights were coming on after forty years, in a hint at a rebirth of the old Paris of the East. Albania held its first democratic elections and dispensed with the old communists. It really seemed as if the darker impulses of the Balkans were at bay. The ultimate sign of this more mature spirit came in early March when Bosnia-Hercegovina tiptoed back from the brink of civil war.

Ever since the Bosnian elections of December 1990, when votes were cast on ethnic lines, with the electorate dividing between the national parties of the three communities (Muslims 44 percent, Serbs 31 percent and Croats 18 percent), Cassandras had predicted a bloodbath. Throughout the gloomy days in Croatia in 1991 they had warned of worse horrors to come in Bosnia. January 1992, when the Bosnian Serbs declared their own mini-republic with its own parliament, seemed to justify the alarmism. But in the first week in March, for once in the Balkans, the apocalyptic scenario was disproved. The day after a referendum in which Bosnia's Muslims and Croats voted for independence, shooting broke out in Sarajevo. Storm warnings were broadcast round the world and then a massive peace demonstration, led by the president, Alija Izetbegović, persuaded Serb gunmen to take down their barricades – a triumph, it appeared, for Bosnian reason over Balkan insanity.

I was in Bucharest at the time and I thought back to my own brief experiences of Bosnia, the delightful holiday in Sarajevo in 1990 and the Bosnian policeman outside Mostar in 1991 who had declined to fine me for speeding. That these eminently civilized people had managed to avoid plunging into ethnic conflict was only too plausible. I headed north towards Moldova and immersed myself in its copycat Yugoslav war, thinking no more about Bosnia.

It was, of course, a ridiculously naïve illusion, akin to Neville Chamberlain waving his scrap of paper. The March events in Sarajevo were merely a dress rehearsal for the war. Displays of public sentiment are irrelevant in a manipulative environment like the Balkans. Rather than canvassing the *Sarajlile*, the people of Sarajevo, journalists should have been up in the Bosnian mountains with the rural Serbs, whose stockpiles of weapons were almost complete, and who were merely waiting for the signal to begin.

At the start of April I slipped back to London to discuss extending my bailiwick further east. A culture of ethno-territorial brush-fires was sprouting in the former Soviet Union. The Balkans, I was told, were all very interesting when in flames, but when peaceful it was hard to distinguish one dusty town from another. It was while I was in London that Serbian gunmen in Sarajevo's Holiday Inn opened fire on a peace demonstration, erected barricades around the city and started shelling the centre.

By the time I flew into Belgrade in the middle of May, the Bosnian Serbs controlled over half of Bosnia and were laying siege to much of the rest. In the south-west, Bosnian Croats, backed by regular units from Croatia, were quietly carving out their own statelet. Bosnia was doing what it had always done – tearing itself apart. Or, to be more precise, it was suffering what it had always suffered – being torn apart.

Bosnia is the Balkans distilled and purified, all the best parts and all the worst parts rolled into one. Its history of treachery and heroism, bigotry and bull-headedness is quintessentially Balkan, as are its rugged topography, complex ethnic make-up and languid way of life. Ever since Emperor Theodosius split the Roman Empire in 395 along the River Drina, the eastern border of Bosnia, the territory known as Bosnia-Hercegovina (originally two kingdoms), has been in the no-man's land of the east and the west. It has, inevitably, a complicated past, but not as complicated as some in the early 1990s have tried to suggest.

Of all the truth-twisting Balkan fictions one of the most

egregious is the claim by revisionist Serbs and Croats that
Bosnia is an invention and that Bosnians are lapsed members
of their respective nationalities. There are no Bosnians,
runs this line of thought, only Slav Muslims, who before
the Turks invaded in the fifteenth century were Croat or
Serb. 'Look at the lack of nationalist iconography in Bosnia,'
continues the argument. 'This is not a real state. It's a
creation begun by the Ottomans and then retained by Tito
to keep us from our rightful heritage.'

As with most Balkan nationalist arguments, this 'Bosnia
doesn't exist' school of thought deploys a few selected
grains of truth to reach a wholly false conclusion. It's true
the people of Bosnia are of the same Slav stock as their
Serb and Croat neighbours. They all poured down from the
East Polish marshes together in the sixth and seventh
centuries. So, too, it's true that the Muslims of Bosnia, one
of the few nationalities in the world to identify themselves
by religion and not by language or race, indulge neither in
the baubles of national identity nor the historical myths so
beloved in young and immature states. It's also true that for
Tito, Bosnia played a crucial part as a neutral middle-
ground in his strategy of trying to balance the Serbs and
Croats.

However, the concept of an independent Bosnia is not
fiction. In the Dark Ages, when the Balkans was a shifting
maze of states and frontiers, Bosnia had a pedigree as
assured as Croatia and Serbia. The first Bosnian kingdom
was recorded in the ninth century, the last in the fourteenth,
three hundred years after Croatia disappeared.

The key moment for Bosnian identity came in the
twelfth century when their King Kulin sought to assert a
fuller independence from the encroaching Orthodox Serbs
to the east and the Catholic Croats to the north and west by
converting to Bogomilism, a dualist heresy better known in
the West as Albigensianism, which preached against material
wealth. Under King Tvrtko, who in 1377 was crowned
King of 'Serbs, Bosnia and the Croats', Bogomilism became
the official Bosnian state church. Tvrtko's Bosnia extended
over all of contemporary Bosnia-Hercegovina as well as

much of Dalmatia and a slice of modern Serbia – a fitting riposte to the proponents of Greater Serbia and Greater Croatia.

In a scenario familiar to Bosnian Muslims in the 1990s, in the Middle Ages the Orthodox and Catholic Churches tried to eradicate their tiresome neighbours who dared to preach against Church property. Consequently, when the Turks came roaring through the Balkans, the Bogomils proved the most enthusiastic to convert to Islam, taking refuge in the faith of their invaders. Under the Turks they flourished as an upper class, holding administrative positions in the towns. As part of the ruling system, they had no need to emulate the Serbs and Croats who nurtured their national identities on resistance to the Ottomans.

With the decline of Turkish power and the rise in Europe of the idea that nationhood and language are linked, in the nineteenth century Bosnian Muslims started to suffer an identity crisis. Their confusion lasted until 1974 when they were awarded nation status in the second Yugoslavia. The subsequent rise of a more assertive Islamic faith set alarm bells ringing in the minds of the more paranoid Serbian nationalists.

Those Bogomils-turned-Muslims are the lifeblood of the Bosnian state along with the many thousands of Bosnian Croats and Bosnian Serbs who identify with their location and their culture rather than their ethnicity, who see themselves as Bosnians first and Croats or Serbs second. Their homeland, Bosnia, was never a nation state. In a region still living out the nation-state fantasies of the nineteenth century it was always going to be vulnerable.

In 1992, with a rapacious Serbia to the east and a scavenging Croatia to the west, an independent Bosnia was only going to survive with firm international backing. The events in Croatia had shown all too clearly that Belgrade would use the fears of the Bosnian Serbs over their potential status in an independent Bosnia as a pretext to move for a Greater Serbia. But support the world was not prepared to give – as the Serbs, fresh from rampaging through Croatia, knew too well. After recognizing Bosnia in early April as a

fully-fledged independent state with a seat at the United
Nations, the world's leaders stuttered, decided they had
made a mistake and left Bosnia to be carved up by the
Serbs and to a lesser extent by the Croats. It was a
sickening display of political cynicism. In the spring of 1992
Bosnia briefly existed as a multi-ethnic state. I arrived in
Belgrade to watch it die.

It didn't take long to acclimatise to current Serbian thinking.
On my second night back in town I met up with Milorad,
my old journalist friend of the year before, and we disappeared into a beer cellar to rekindle old memories. With his
droopy moustache and long black hair, Milorad looked like
the stereotypical revolutionary of Balkan legend. He was in
many ways the best of Serbia, endowed with a liberal heart
and the dreamy romanticism which has long since disappeared from society in the West. Of all people, I had hoped
Milorad might be seeing sense. But it required only a few
glasses of thick Montenegrin wine to see that Milorad's
conscience was sorely troubled by his Serbian soul. He
would never support Milošević, the arch authoritarian, and
yet as a Serb he was caught up in his people's traditional
victim mentality, 'Serbia *contra mundum*', Serbia doomed to
suffer.

I willingly cut short the coffee and we drifted through
the back streets to meet some of his journalist friends.
Among their number was a Serb from Bosnia who laid in to
me with venom, spouting parrot fashion the official line.
Did I know about the fundamentalist Muslims? Why were
Western journalists only writing about Sarajevo and not
about the suffering of the Serbs?

There is an unwritten rule in war zones to smile politely,
whatever the circumstances, but on this occasion the wine was
making me combative and Belgrade was hardly the front line.

'What about the Croats?' I asked her.

'What do you mean, "What about the Croats?"'

'Well, last year when I was in Belgrade the government
media was talking about the fascist murderers in Croatia.
Now everyone talks about the fundamentalist Muslims.'

'But it's true. Izetbegović (the president of Bosnia) is a second Khomeini. The Muslim 'green berets' are butchering children. Every day bodies are floating down the River Drina.'

'So have you been there, as a journalist I mean, to check up? Have you seen the babies?'

'All my friends and relatives have. The Muslims have been preparing for this killing for years. For centuries they tried to eliminate the Serbs and now once again we face genocide.'

'Strange. On my two trips to Bosnia I found society there the most tolerant of all in Yugoslavia. The impression I had was that the Muslims were the ones facing genocide. I haven't heard of many Serb towns being shelled by the Muslims . . .'

My diary has a verbatim record of this conversation, spiced with a few gratuitous expressions of disgust at this Serbian Boadicea. I saw her again a few months later under very different circumstances in Pale, the mountain headquarters of the Bosnian Serbs. I was trying to negotiate a hire car with a friend of hers, when she walked in. The deal was off.

Serbia was in a poor way. In the centre of Belgrade a core of liberals was fighting the good fight for truth and freedom. Even in these bleak days Serbia was blessed with the most open-minded publication in former Yugoslavia. The offices of the news magazine *Vreme* became a second home for foreign correspondents looking for a breath of cynicism about Serbia's stance. Another favourite haunt was the independent B-92 radio station. The back wall of the edit-suite displayed a world map with its own alterations – 'Greater Serbia' was scrawled over North America and 'Milošević's Residence' over Florida. But these voices were a tiny minority, crying in the dark. Like a wounded beast, Serbia was wallowing in its misery and regenerating all its old historical grievances.

In the West, where history is the preserve of the appropriate scholars, it is almost impossible to comprehend the Balkan fixation with history. For Serbs, the past – or selected snippets of the past – is as real as the present. The battle of Kosovo in 1389, when King Lazar and the flower of Serbia's nobles died under Ottoman scimitars, is as relevant if not more relevant than anything in their own century. The only period that vies in importance with 1389 is the Second World War when hundreds of thousands of Serbs were killed by the Ustaše. The passing of the centuries (in the first example) and decades (in the second) is immaterial. Both 1389 and the 1940s are seen as the role-models for the present. That the Croats of 1991, while authoritarian, were not fascist and, more strikingly, that the Bosnian president in 1992, while Muslim, was not fundamentalist, were ignored. They were the enemies. The Serbs were the victims. Childlike in its simplicity, the state propaganda machine drummed out this line, with the implicit message that, unless the Serbs struck first, 'once again they faced genocide'.

A week after my arrival the UN imposed sanctions on the rump Yugoslavia, consisting of Serbia and Montenegro. The decision had little immediate effect on the economy but heightened Belgrade's siege mentality. 'I saved British pilots who were shot down in the war and now you turn against us,' one old man shouted at me. 'Does this mean I fought for nothing?' It was with a sense of relief that I left this recriminatory atmosphere and set off with John Holland of CBS Radio on a reconnaissance trip to Bosnia, to test the mood of the Bosnian Serbs.

We crossed the border from Serbia into the Bosnian town of Bijeljina on a sunny spring morning, six weeks after the area had been captured, or rather 'liberated', by the Serbs. Bijeljina is a light, airy town, less scarred than most Yugoslav communities by the drab conformity of communist architecture. Traders do very nicely from the traffic crossing the River Drina, the border with Serbia. The streets are lined with acacia trees. It is a prosperous place with a smug bourgeois ethos – or so Vlatka, our interpreter, explained as we waited beside the Drina for some goon to check our papers.

It would be presumptuous to say that we sensed the

horrors lurking beneath Bijeljina's facade. However, we were under no illusions about the brutality of the Bosnian Serbs' *blitzkrieg* through eastern Bosnia in April. Every street corner was patrolled by men in uniform. We decided the sooner we stopped driving aimlessly through the centre the better, although, as Vlatka wryly pointed out, the real giveaway was not our bright-yellow hire-car but our Anglo-Saxon features and contorted attempts at Serbo-Croat. We pulled up outside the Piazza Café.

Two young Serbian soldiers were sitting at a corner table and they shifted along to give us space. Their uniforms were crisply pressed. Their shoulders bore the insignia of 'Arkan', the *nom de guerre* of the most notorious Serb warlord, an ice-cream seller turned mass-murderer. While John and I acted dumb and uninterested, Vlatka flashed a beautiful smile and started gossiping. Full of triumphal rhetoric, Mladen and Zeljko were soon chatting away with her.

'It was my twenty-third birthday when we moved in here,' concluded Zeljko with a broad grin. 'And you know what? Instead of blowing out twenty-three candles I shot twenty-three Muslims.' His companion tittered and told him to shut up. We smiled politely.

A fat middle-aged man by the counter was looking at us suspiciously and asked Vlatka about our accreditation. We were outside walking towards the car when the waitress ran out of the back door. She spoke in staccato bursts for barely a minute. A few nights earlier the same two soldiers, smiling Mladen and blonde-haired Zeljko, had broken in, assaulted her and threatened to blow up the café.

'Whatever you hear, whatever you see, you cannot react to. You cannot ask any questions. You cannot catch anyone's eye for help. The curfew is at ten p.m. Then the real nightmare starts. People are just disappearing. One day they are there, the next they are not and a Serb soldier is sleeping in their house . . .' Two policemen wandered into sight at the end of the street. 'I must go back. My customers will get suspicious.'

The hyperbole of hyperboles, 'evil', is an untouchable for

journalists when writing reports. So, too, analogies with Nazi Germany rightly have to be used with extreme caution in newsprint. But in Bosnia in 1992 correspondents and UN officials struggled to find a lesser comparison. In Croatia in 1991 the flight of hundreds of thousands of refugees had been the inevitable consequence of the heavy fighting. But the exodus of the Bosnian Muslims in 1992 was not the consequence of the war, it was the intention. The Serbs were turning back the clock to the dark days of the 1940s and trying to create an ethnically pure state. All over East Bosnia the Muslims were suffering the closest thing to fascism in Europe since Adolf Hitler.

Before the war started there was a Bosnian-Serb point of view, albeit elitist and arrogant. The Bosnian Serbs were genuinely alarmed about their potential status in an independent Bosnia. In Yugoslavia the Serbs were the most numerous of the federation's six constituent nations. For them minority status was abhorrent and impossible to accept. When in 1990 the break-up of Yugoslavia looked inevitable, they made it quite clear that they couldn't belong to an independent Bosnia.

Aware of the hideous potential for war after the precedent in Croatia, the Bosnian government in Sarajevo did all they could to mollify the Serbs. In March 1992 they even agreed to an EC proposal to cantonise the state. But the Bosnian-Serb leaders never had any intention of compromise. It was all or all for them – unification with Serbia, all Serbs in one state, whatever the cost.

While in February and March the representatives of the Sarajevo government shuttled backwards and forwards between various international mediators, the Serbs planned their rebellion. Armed and funded by Belgrade, Dr Radovan Karadžić, the 'president' of the self-styled Serbian Republic of Bosnia-Hercegovina, stirred up the Serbian peasants in the hills with all the old nationalist poisons until they were ready to vent their most primitive and savage instincts against their old Muslim neighbours. Acacia-treed Bijeljina was a classic case. According to the census of 1991, the region was 60 per cent Serb and 40 per cent Muslim; in the town the figures were the exact reverse, the legacy of the old Ottoman days when Muslims monopolised Bosnia's civic positions. By June 1992 the waitress of the Piazza Café was one of the last Muslims left. A few months later I passed through the town. The café was closed.

A plate of Serbian beans is an excellent leveller, particularly when washed down with a glass of *slivovitz*. At the Ugljevik barracks twenty miles from Bijeljina, Colonel Nikola Dencić, a jolly ex-JNA officer in command of the assault on Tuzla, was so delighted at our alacrity to accept his hospitality, that he quite forgot his initial suspicion at our unsolicited arrival.

'We don't want any more land. We just want peace,' he explained genially. 'The Muslims keep hitting us with artillery. But we don't fight back. Yesterday they were blazing away and we didn't fire a single bullet in response . . .' He leaned forward intoxicated by his lies. 'We haven't burned a single house. We're against burning. We want peace. We need peace, so that all people can have their rights.'

Vlatka's father was a Croat and she had a Croatian identity card. By venturing into checkpoint territory she could have been shot out of hand. The previous week in Belgrade her mother (a Serb) had been beaten up by a neighbour who shouted 'I always wanted to do that to you, you Croat . . .' It was with this in mind that I refrained from arguing with the colonel. We listened in silence, occasionally prompting him in the hope that something interesting would emerge from the web of deceit, smiling sycophantically at the appropriate moments.

I suspect Colonel Denčić knew we didn't believe him, but he didn't care. It was as if he was mocking our capacity for outrage, daring us to do something, knowing that liberal sentiment counts for nothing in the Balkans where might has almost always been right. We asked his opinion about the sanctions. He guffawed.

'Sanctions? Pah, we don't care about them. We had sanctions in 1908 in the war with the Austrians and we survived. When our oil runs out we will use donkeys like we did in Tito's day.' It was bluster, and a bluster which I wasn't inclined to believe, but one which was not to be put to the test, at least in the following year. Sanctions on Serbia, the West's initial response to the crisis, conspicuously failed to slow the Bosnian-Serbs' war machine.

For some unexplained reason we were not allowed to go forward to see his men 'under fire'. Our safety apparently couldn't be guaranteed. One of the few certainties in the war was that whenever you were told that such and such a route was too dangerous, it was because there was something down it you were not meant to see. We returned to Belgrade to hear that Denčić's 'peace-loving' colleagues on the hills around Sarajevo had launched one of their heaviest bombardments to date.

The Hyatt Regency, Belgrade, has bath towels like sheets, a swimming-pool in the basement and piped Vivaldi in the lifts. They turn down your bed at night and put orange juice in your fridge in the mornings. The 'Signor Rossi' restaurant serves fresh pasta and crab. In short it is *the* hotel in the Balkans – and after a week in its air-conditioned and sanitised clutches I was craving to escape.

In the summer of 1992 there was one story dwarfing all others in Yugoslavia and arguably the world. The city of Sarajevo had been under siege since the 6 April. The bulk of the UN forces who were stationed there for the peace-keeping operation in Croatia had withdrawn five weeks later, along with most of the journalists. By the end of May water and food were reported to be running short. Still the Serbs' shells kept coming.

The consensus among the media was that Sarajevo had become too dangerous a story to cover. But at the same time most of the correspondents in Belgrade had a nagging guilt that by reporting the siege from Belgrade we were failing the people of Sarajevo. It was impossible to convey the intensity from two hundred miles away.

Then, a few days after my visit to Bijeljina, the United Nations announced that it was sending a convoy to Sarajevo to supply its rearguard and to negotiate opening the airport for humanitarian aid. Journalists could accompany it at their own risk.

The correspondent from Agence France Presse had a space left in his car. I borrowed a flak jacket from a departing CBS cameraman. He gave me a quick briefing.

'Ever worn one of these before?'

'Um, no.'

'Well, when you run across the street, link arms with your companions. That way, if you get hit, the others keep running and drag you clear . . . It worked well in Beirut. Oh, one more thing, keep the bullet-proof plates in. You'll need them.'

My acquisition weighed a good twenty-pounds. I lugged it upstairs convinced that the idea of walking in a flak jacket, let alone running, was ridiculous.

That night the comfort of the Hyatt beguiled as never before. Room-service delivered a bumper package of take away sandwiches. I raided the mini-bar for peanuts and miniatures. Unable to sleep, I wondered for the umpteenth time why I was going, suddenly aware that I had drifted into assuming I was Sarajevo-bound without considering my decision. Three hours later I was in the lobby waiting for my ride.

Nothing could prepare you for Sarajevo. After Dubrovnik I had somehow imagined I knew how to cover a war. Sarajevo was completely different. It was about panting on street corners before charging across junctions, wondering if a sniper had you in his sights. It was about praying that as you careered round an exposed junction on two wheels on the wrong side of the road there was no one coming the other way. It was about lying awake at night to the steady boom of exploding shells, unsure whether to blow out the candle, to put on your flak jacket, to lie under the bed, listening to the barrage creep nearer and nearer and closing the curtains to keep out the noise. It was about looking up at the hills which surround the city and realizing that nowhere was safe from the gunners' sights.

I was initiated into the Sarajevo routine almost immediately on crossing the Serbs' lines. The final moments of the journey from Belgrade had been fittingly dramatic. As the white UN vehicles trundled into the city a band of Serb irregulars pounced on the press cars trailing the convoy. Two bearded heavies, draped in bandoliers of ammunition, pounded at the door of the car in front. For a few moments we were stranded in no-man's land until Brigadier Lewis Mackenzie, the UN commanding officer, jumped out of his armoured vehicle and stood astride a crossroads beckoning us through. The irregulars, encountering, maybe for the first time, a real soldier, withdrew and we drove into the city.

As if on cue, the sun broke through the clouds to reveal the Bosnian capital, etched in the dramatic colouring of a Turner storm. I was still taking in the faces peering from the windows, the men and women running from doorways, waving, blowing kisses, in tears, throwing roses, when we reached the UN headquarters in the city post office (PTT).

The city centre was a mile down the open road. My AFP colleague disappeared in his car to find a friend who had broken his neck the day before. An Italian TV crew were setting up their satellite phone on the roof of the PTT. The hills all around were spluttering and fizzing with small-arms fire. When a car screeched to a halt and a voice shouted, 'Do you want a lift into town?' I came running.

Jana Schneider had a long black skirt, a brace of cameras hanging round her neck and the photographers' uniform of a khaki waistcoat. She had been among the half-dozen journalists who had stayed after the evacuation of the UN and the bulk of the media. Rumour avowed that she had abandoned a successful career on Broadway ten years before and had been roaming the world's wars ever since.

Dan Stetz from the *Philadelphia Enquirer* was allotted the front seat, a perk because he didn't have a flak jacket. I went in the back, twisting my legs around various packages of food, desperately trying to tuck as much of my body as possible under my flak jacket.

'You OK hons . . .? Hold on tight. The first hundred yards is OK. Then keep low as we hit one of their [by her tone of voice I assumed she meant snipers] favourite spots.

'You see that street; that's where George and Alfonso got caught out yesterday. They were turning away from hostile fire, tore across this junction and, boom, they hit another car going the other way. Lucky to survive. That's their car; beyond them in a straight line are the Serbs.'

George Gobet of Agence France Presse and Alfonso Rojo of *El Mundo* were lucky to be alive. The heap of twisted metal which Jana pointed to was barely recognizable as a car. A hundred yards further on was the body of an old woman, shot dead moments after George and Alfonso were dragged clear. There was time only for a glance over the windscreen and we were round a corner, past a row of burned-out buses, the only people on a long and seemingly endless road. Some joker had scrawled 'Welcome to Hell' on a wall. Jana kept up a running commentary.

'Woah, what the shit! That was never there before. Ah, yes, remember that bollard, that's where you jink left. Very important. Up there on the right, that's the Jewish Cemetery. The Bosnians took me there yesterday – great pictures, street battles every day . . . but, hons, you mustn't rush it. Better to take it slowly for a day or so . . . It all depends on where you want to stay, what you want to do.'

Half an hour with Jana was arguably the best possible introduction to Sarajevo – that night I wrote in my diary that I would leave at the first opportunity. Jana's generosity in ferrying us through the centre of town was unquestionable. But there was something disturbing about her apparent total lack of fear. When she announced she was going to Dobrinja, a south-western suburb which was cut off from the rest of the city, only her Slovene boyfriend, Ivo Štandeker, agreed to go. Jana came back twenty-fours later on a stretcher with shrapnel wounds in her stomach and legs. Ivo was dead. Jana had stood up as a Serbian tank approached to get a better picture.

I finished up at the Delegates Club, an old Habsburg staging post, sharing a candle-lit tin of pâté with WTN's Faradoun Hamani. In the communist days the Delegates Club, an elegant villa facing on to a secluded driveway and shrubberies, was reserved for visiting dignitaries. Its faded grandeur reminded me of the state bungalows in Pakistan. With running water for two hours a day and a kitchen providing basic meals, by Sarajevo standards it was luxurious. Most of the press corps based themselves there by day, but at night the complement dwindled.

Faradoun, another of the Sarajevo old-hands, explained that most journalists slept in the Military Hospital, returning to the Delegates Club for breakfast.

'So why don't they spend the night here?' I regretted the question even as I asked it. Faradoun cocked his ear towards the sound of shells outside.

'On our left is the headquarters of the Bosnian Army. On our right is a police barracks. Have you seen the thickness of the walls here? The Military Hospital is a nice big solid building . . .'

I groped my way upstairs through the darkness and fell asleep in an empty room, only to be woken at seven by the door slamming, a kick at my mattress and a heavily-accented – and irate – French voice.

'Who the hell are you? I don't like people sleeping in my bed.'

The *envoyé spécial* for *Le Figaro* had had a harrowing few days and was in no mood to listen to my stammering apologies. Unintentionally he exacted a swift revenge. He had undertaken to pack up the belongings of George Gobet, the wounded photographer, who was due to be evacuated by the UN that afternoon. When I returned to the Delegates Club in the evening, I found that my spare set of clothes, a packet of batteries and, worst of all, my Hyatt sandwiches were on their way back to Belgrade.

By the middle of 1992 Bosnia had become the benchmark by which the West judged ethnic and territorial disputes. In less than two months the tiny state had gone from being an obscure little country best known from yellowing maps and history lessons, to Europe's 'basket case', the apotheosis of political intractability. In London time and again the pundits intoned that only Tito had managed to keep the lid on the old passions, as if Titoism, Yugoslavism or communism, whatever you liked to call it, was all that had stopped Serbs, Croats and Muslims from killing each other.

The Bosnian Serbs lovingly peddled this line. 'We are like cat and dog, we can never live together,' explained Dr Karadžić, the only politician in the Balkans whose facility for deceit exceeded that of his lord and master, Milošević. It was an argument adopted with enthusiasm by Western politicians, who were desperate to find reasons not to involve themselves in the conflict.

However, not only is this false, it's an inversion of the truth. For much of its history Bosnia has been a model of a multi-ethnic society. Under the Ottomans it was one of the most tolerant states in Europe. Spain's 'Ladino' Jews fled to Sarajevo to escape from the Inquisition. When in the late nineteenth century the Serb and Croat peasants in Bosnia and Hercegovina rebelled against the Turks the issue was poverty not ethnic hatred, although Serbia with its pan-Slav backers in Moscow and the Habsburgs championing their fellow Catholic Croats portrayed and exploited the revolt as a struggle of national liberation.

Expounders of the 'Bosnia equals ethnic cauldron' philosophy upholster their case by referring to the Second World War when of the estimated 1.7 million people killed in Yugoslavia, half came from Bosnia-Hercegovina. This was indeed a dire warning of Bosnia's hideous potential for violence. But it was not a blueprint. The parallel crying out to be drawn from Bosnia's history is not that Bosnians have always killed each other, but that Bosnia has traditionally been coveted by its neighbours and that to survive as an independent state it needs the backing of a world power. Until the twentieth century Bosnia-Hercegovina was under the wing of first the Ottomans and then the Habsburgs. The horrors of the 1940s occurred when the only intervening great power, Nazi Germany, was actively involved in fanning the ethnic hatred.

The armchair strategists of the 1990s who trumpeted about Bosnia's dark history always seemed – conveniently – to forget the four decades following 1945 when over a quarter of Bosnian marriages were inter-ethnic, when imams paid courtesy calls to Orthodox churches at Christmas and when ethnic hatred was voiced only in the ravings of the drunk or the tortured memories of those who remembered the war.

On my first day in Sarajevo I heard a senior British cabinet minister on the BBC World Service warning about the dangers of over-simplifying the conflict. As I stood in Sarajevo's Lion's Park watching a drinking society, the Black Mamba Club, bury their dead, the war seemed peculiarly simple. An informal gathering of Serbs, Croats and Muslims, before the war the 'Black Mambas' larked around in the best Yugoslav tradition, strumming guitars, going to night-clubs, sipping cappuccinos on the banks of the Miljacka. When the shells started falling on Sarajevo they formed their own unit. Barely half were left alive. The latest to fall, Samir, Kenan and Mario, two Muslims and a Croat, lay wrapped in sheets on the ground – an artist, a waiter and an opera-singer. Their triple funeral lasted barely three minutes.

It was a bright, sunny morning and a rare lull from the sounds of battle. A few days previously Serb gunners had zeroed their sights on a funeral party, showering the mourners with earth, churning a crater beside an expectant grave. As the grave-diggers took advantage of the more favourable conditions and sweated over the clay-heavy earth, Dragan, a chubby-faced Serb student, blurted out sketchy biographies of his fallen friends.

'This one, here, had two sons . . . He had a voice like an angel . . . Kenan was barely twenty-four, unmarried, of course . . . a great one with the girls . . . Samir, well, he was a great fellow . . .' Two imams with purple-rimmed hats had arrived, the dead were thrust underground and the relatives clustered around, throwing in clods. In a few moments the service was over and people hurried down the hill.

'We all had cars. We all had money. We pledged eternal friendship,' said Dragan. 'Now we are made to run around like rats. They must love watching this. They hardly have to fire a shot and still we run.'

A week later a UN official explained to me that the

Bosnians were shelling the cemetery to draw attention to their plight. It was an argument I always found hard to accept.

Without a car I was reduced to covering the siege on foot, which was probably the safest way. Most of the material for my despatches was gleaned from traipsing the city with two archetypal *Sarajlile*, Branko and Milica Babić, husband and wife, a Croat and a Serb. Articulate, well-read, before the war they saw themselves as Yugoslavs first and Bosnians second – their 'Serbness' and 'Croatness' were irrelevant.

'And now?'

'Well . . .' Milica paused. 'Now, now we are Sarajevans . . .'

They lived only a few hundred yards from the Delegates Club and we would sit savouring the last few grains of their coffee, talking loudly when the shells intensified. On clear days we would gaze up at the hills while they reminisced about walking-weekends in the mountain-resorts, enjoying a break from Sarajevo's sweltering summer.

Milica and Branko seemed to know everyone, the manager of the bread factory which was keeping the city alive, the chief imam who explained to me the history of Bogomilism, even Juka, the debt-collector turned militia-leader, one of the few high-profile Bosnian fighters to emerge from the conflict. Jusuf 'Juka' Prazina, a former class-mate of Milica's, the devil incarnate in the Serbian press, was someone I was particularly keen to meet.

A small-time gangster, in the early stages of the war Juka masterminded the defence of Sarajevo. Wounded three times, he became a cult-figure for the city, a buccaneering hero for a community badly in need of a boost to morale. Despite the siege, his old contacts were clearly enduring. A minion served us Coke and biscuits – the first of either I had seen in Sarajevo. Juka, who was swathed in bandages after a car-accident, lobbed us a carton of Marlboro.

In Serbian mythology Juka became the incarnation of Bosnian evil, accused of roasting Serbian babies etc., etc. His ruthlessness was undisputed. After the interview Milica recounted that when she had visited him to arrange our meeting he was interrogating a suspected fifth columnist – with his metal crutch. But there was no comparison between the rough and ready justice of such as Juka and the systematic killings and expulsions of the Serbs. The Muslims were barely managing to defend themselves. Indeed one of the most remarkable elements of the siege was the forebearance shown by the people of Sarajevo towards the city's Serbs, most of whom stayed loyal to the Bosnian government. Milica and I were walking back from a dawn visit to a private bakery when we came across a volunteer police unit on a mission to track down Serbian spies. A more amateur and fair-minded posse I find hard to imagine.

The team-leader, Munib, a grey-suited professor of engineering, reminded me of a country parson with his quiet apologetic manner. Adnan, his number two, was a former croupier. Slobodan had only just left school. With an umbrella and a Kalashnikov between them, they had a list of suspect addresses. First house on the list was No. 55 Mohammed Adžudže Street. We paused in the porch for a whispered discussion on strategy before tiptoeing up to the first floor.

The landing was an excuse for another pause. They decided there had to be witnesses and Adnan was despatched in search of the block's caretaker. The man in question was out, but a walrus-shaped character from the floor above volunteered. He lumbered down the stairs waving a hatchet. The professor ushered Milica and me to the back:

'Sometimes the snipers stay in the apartment until the last minute and then jump out the window,' he whispered. 'But there's always the danger they will fight.' Nodding uneasily, Adnan unslung the Kalashnikov and took a swing at the door. With a final kick, 'to beware of booby traps', we were in.

The Miatović family had plainly left in a hurry. The beds were unmade. Cupboard doors were swinging off the hinges. Dirty crockery littered the kitchen. A stench of rotting food came from the fridge. Slobodan pointed to a pattern of bullet-holes scarring the window.

'Aha!' His attention turned to a knife half-hidden under a cushion. Half an hour later the sitting room floor was covered with books, papers and clothes as he leafed through schoolbooks and family photo albums, with a wad of 'suspect' material at his feet.

Amela and Edin, a young Muslim couple from the next-door flat, knocked politely on the door. They perched on a sofa-arm in amazement, recalling their many happy times in the Miatovićs' company.

'If someone had told me two months ago that I would be breaking in here I would never have believed it,' said Amela. 'I mean we used to get on so well. We were always popping in and out if we needed anything.'

Mr Stjepo Miatović had been a minor functionary in the Bosnian Serbian political machine – or rather in Dr Karadžić's political machine, as Milica quietly corrected me. He and his family had left Sarajevo without warning their neighbours. For six weeks his confrères had been blasting away at their apartment block and all his neighbours would say was what nice people they were. Such was the harmony of the old Bosnia.

With the inspection over, everyone filed out. The professor ticked his list and the door was carefully sealed.

Afraid, tired and suspecting my luck was running out, I left Sarajevo after a fortnight. Every day the catalogue of journalists' bizarre escapes from injury expanded. Slobodan Lekić, the Associated Press correspondent, was driving at speed through the centre when a bullet burst through the roof of his car, ricocheted around the inside and landed spent on the top of his head. A Danish free-lance photographer, Mikkel Ostergaard, was sitting in the passenger seat of a colleague's car, again travelling at speed, when his wrist felt as if it had been kicked by a horse – a bullet had impacted in his watch. Morten Hvaal, also of the Associated Press, was driving in a van which was hit by machine-gun fire. One of two people to survive, he walked away without even the proverbial scratch.

Such occurences were of course incidental for your average Sarajevan. Milica was late for a rendezvous one day; she had been at her best friend Angelina's apartment inspecting the new addition to the furniture. Angelina had been woken early by a crash in the roof, a whoosh of cold air and a shower of dust. A tank shell had landed in her wardrobe – it didn't explode. Day after day, week after week, the population endured this existence. Journalists could leave at any time. Later in the year a number of correspondents colonised Sarajevo as their own 'personal' story and stayed for months at a stretch. I could only admire their stamina.

The only reliable telephone was in the headquarters of the fledgling Bosnian army – possibly the Serbs' favoured target. Bosnian soldiers had a mischievous habit of imitating the whistle of incoming shells. I never grasped the old hands' appraisal of the difference between incoming and outgoing shells. After a week of throwing myself to the ground at the wrong time I was wincing at the backfiring of a car.

My final moment of decision came when a shell burst through a building almost on top of me. I had hitched a lift with Morten Hvaal, to the old parliament building where several hundred refugees were rumoured to be about to arrive. We were half-way there when the building in front of us sagged as if hit by two massive punches and then the outside wall erupted outwards. Morten screeched to a halt and did a U-turn. We retreated a few hundred yards, caught our breath and moments later again took to the road, not out of bravery, but rather stupidity and obsession with reaching the story. It was time to leave.

Journalists were now pouring into the city, including, ironically, a French photographer with my missing clothes. Crucially for Sarajevo, the world's television cameras had returned. If nothing else, our original contingent of journalists had shown that Sarajevo did not have to be abandoned.

For Milica and Branko my departure was a chance beyond their wildest dreams. I would drive their car behind the next UN convoy and Milica would come as my 'interpreter'. Branko, of course, had to stay – all adult males were banned from leaving the city.

When a distinguished British television correspondent adopted a child from Sarajevo there was endless debate in Britain over the ethics and motives of his act. I thought the furore was unfair. If they had had an escape route and somewhere to go, most Sarajevans would have left their city to start again. Aiding Milica to escape and to join her children was, I'm sadly convinced, of greater value than any number of my reports on the Bosnians' plight.

We took the wild-strawberry trail to Belgrade, high into the Bosnian mountains, twisting through the forests, at the whim of the various militias. Three hours out of Sarajevo, the accompanying UN armoured car fell into a ditch. The French detachment blamed the Canadians and the Canadians blamed the French. It took thirty-four hours to cover the two hundred miles − a fair reflection of the UN's dismal progress in the conflict.

Crown Prince Alexander of Yugoslavia was due to return to his father, King Peter's, old capital Belgrade. The previous year on his first visit to Serbia, Alexander had met a rapturous reception. His arrival boded to be a good Balkan tale. But Sarajevo had exhausted my curiosity. I left for Romania, passing the Karadjordjević limousine outside Timişoara.

My taxi driver had relatives in Belgrade and was keen to know about the war and the latest from Bosnia.

'Tell me,' he asked, 'why exactly are the Muslims shelling Sarajevo . . .?'

12

Off the Edge of Europe – 'This is Huambo'

August 1992–April 1993

They cut off his left arm
and his right arm,
one, then the other leg,
finally his head
and they planted his neck in the soil
– to grow.

children and scapegoats
hang on his stumps.

– *'The National Hero' by Gojko Djogo, a Serbian poet imprisoned in 1981 for 'subversive writing'.*

'History will record that the West stood by and watched as the Muslims of Bosnia were wiped away' – *Haris Silajžić, Bosnian Foreign Minister*

'Europe is like an old woman who doesn't see the flowers trampled in her garden' – *Emir Tica, Bosnian soldier and friend*

DATING WHEN THE BALKANS first started to fall behind West Europe is one of Europe's knottiest historical wrangles. Balkan historians blame the Ottoman occupation in a bid to assert their share in Europe's heritage and to emphasise their native pre-Ottoman roots. Turkish scholars counter that Ottoman rule benefitted the Balkan peasantry. Neo-Marxists look for a colonial interpretation and blame 'Western economic exploitation' in the eighteenth and nineteenth centuries. Within all the theorising there is one constant: the recognition of the extreme relative backwardness of South-East Europe in the last five hundred years.

In early 1990 there was just a faint hope that the end of these centuries might be in sight, that the post-communist order might be the start of a new spirit of co-operation between the West and its long-forgotten junior neighbours. Such a dream buoyed up the last federal Yugoslav prime minister Ante Marković, who, until war broke out in June 1991, continued to push for Western credits. It infected governments in Bucharest, Sofia and Tirana desperate for financial support to help them to tackle the grim task of dismantling the economic quagmire left by the commissars. Most strikingly of all it was the last hope of the Bosnian government who for month after month in 1992 refused to descend to the level of the Serb and Croat aggressors, in the belief that the West would come to help a kindred spirit.

However, the brutal truth is that the Balkans no longer count. During the Cold War, while the West propped up Yugoslavia, Moscow funded its Balkan neighbours – bar Albania which remorselessly steered itself back into a medieval wooden-cart economy. After communism there were other priorities. The Central European countries, Czechoslovakia, Hungary and Poland, are further down the road towards the free-market, closer to the West and have a more developed pre-communist history. Russia, by virtue of strategic importance, demands first tug at the West's purse-strings. The Balkans are marginalised.

There are, Western governments stoutly insist, limits beyond which the Balkans cannot pass. A pan-Balkan war is considered too much to accept. Hence in 1992 the EC and the US drew a line along the Serbian border with Macedonia, warning Belgrade that their aggression could go no further south. But this pre-emptive play in Macedonia is a special case, stemming from the fear of a war which could drag in two NATO countries, Greece and Turkey. The prime reason to intervene in Bosnia was moral – and this was never enough. It took me one more visit to Bosnia to realise that for the West the Balkans was pre-eminently 'a faraway place'.

For correspondents, the sweltering summer months of 1992 passed in feeding a seemingly insatiable public appetite

for Bosnian atrocities. When interest in the sieges was
waning, 'ethnic cleansing' hit the headlines, closely followed
by the barbed wire and emaciated frames of the Serb-run
detention camps. Each horror brought more and more
outrage from the public and consecutive sterner reprimands
from the politicians. In August President Bush, in the
closing stages of his re-election campaign, was drawn into a
few bellicose comments. There was still the belief that
maybe someone in the West would decide that something
had to be done whatever the cost. It was with this in mind
that Maggie O'Kane and I decided to make a try for
Goražde, the east Bosnian town which had been cut off by
the Serbs since April. I hadn't seen Maggie since our
departure from Dubrovnik, since when she had become the
indefatigable star of the Yugoslav beat, determined to ram
home the full horror of the situation. No one had been to
Goražde since the siege began. It was, we said, going to be
the killer blow.

For once in Bosnia, travel arrangements were straightforward. Maggie had a letter of welcome from a local Serb
warlord, Commander Dušan 'the Turtle'. A journalist from
the Bosnian Serb television had a Golf which he was willing
to hire. It was in poor shape, with a collapsed front seat
which slid freely over the floor, compelling me to drive
with my head barely visible over the dashboard. But for
fifty dollars a day it was a good deal.

　　Along the road which winds above the Bosnian capital
the Serb gunners were lounging in the sun, heeding, for the
time being, yet another ceasefire. Below them Sarajevo was
spread out like a toytown. Looking through their gunsights
at the distinctive yellow and green of the Holiday Inn, the
journalists' headquarters, was a chilling experience.

　　'We only fire in self-defence,' said one bearded irregular,
pointing to his empty magazine as the ultimate in proof.

　　'Oh, really? So they attack you?'

　　'Yes, they pour up the slopes in uncontrolled hordes.
We're hard pushed to keep them back . . . The Holiday
Inn? Oh, no. This gun couldn't reach that far.' Once again

it was the one-track language of the miners in Bucharest. Once again it was not the time to differ.

We decided to take advantage of the lull for a reconnaissance to the front lines. A UN convoy of humanitarian aid was due to try to negotiate safe passage into Goražde the following day. We would spend the night at the Serbs' forward position and join the UN convoy into Goražde. Maggie, who was learning to drive, took the wheel. I put on my canary yellow *Antiques Roadshow* sunhat, saved for just such an occasion, and practised my goofiest grin. One thing we were not trying to be was subtle. No true red-meat-eating Serb would take seriously a car driven by a woman and accompanied by a man in a bright-yellow hat.

As we approached Rogatica, just twenty miles from Goražde, the clouds gathered and unleashed a ten-minute burst of impenetrable rain. Water was coursing down the back streets, which looked suspiciously as if they had been the scene of recent fighting. Surprised that there was no Serb checkpoint, we continued, emerging a few miles later into the sun and an increasingly brooding Bosnian landscape. Sheer scree-slopes rose on either side. A succession of mini-rockfalls forced us to slow to a walking pace. Finally we rounded a corner and came to an abrupt stop. A landslide had cut the road. We got out and walked to the obstruction. It was hard to tell if it was natural or man-made. Somehow I had the feeling we were being watched.

Half a mile back the way we had come, a lanky teenager was fishing by the river and we scrambled down the bank to ask him the way. We waded through a stream and I kept my eyes on the ground until we were barely ten yards away.

'*Dobardan.*' I started and stopped and stared. The fisher-boy's faded beret bore the blue and gold *fleur de lys* badge of the Bosnian government. It couldn't be . . . but it was. Inadvertently, under cover of the storm, we had crossed the lines. We were in free Bosnian territory.

Later friends and colleagues queried our judgement in deciding to continue into the valley. But at the time we didn't have a choice. We had stumbled upon a lost region which we didn't know existed. Even the Bosnian authorities in Sarajevo thought the area had long since fallen to the Serbs. We were committed too far to turn back – besides, to retrace our steps would be to approach the Serb lines from the wrong side.

Communicating by sign-language, we persuaded Emir, the fishing lad, to take us to his village. We were walking towards the car when a man materialised out of the trees, and another, and another, until suddenly there were twenty or thirty, mainly in their late teens, festooned with an array of antiquated weaponry, distinguished by their blue and gold scarves. It was a magical moment. There was something wonderfully beguiling about this buccaneering band who pranced up and down, pawing us like exotic birds, appealing for cigarettes and news from the outside. When I produced my yellow cap they burst into laughter: our inspection of their barricade had, I gathered, been observed. Electing Emir as guide, they melted back into the hills, dragging a sheep in their wake.

One of the classic H. G. Wells short stories recounts the tale of a man who stumbles upon a valley of the blind and finds to his consternation that his sight is no advantage and that he is treated with intense suspicion. So it was for Maggie and me arriving in our forgotten valley, which for three months had been cut off from all contact with the outside world. Stretching east from Goražde by about thirty miles, barely ten miles wide, it was one of the last sanctuaries of the Bosnian Muslims, home to forty, maybe fifty thousand refugees from the surrounding region. Apart from refugees, we were the first to have crossed the Serbs' lines since April – understandably something of a curiosity.

In this uncertain atmosphere I almost made a terrible mistake. After leaving our car hidden down a track, Emir escorted us to the local policeman, who was to provide a roof for the night. Nihad Devlić, whose bushy moustache and swarthy face were unmistakable evidence of his Turkish ancestry, gave us a warm welcome. Determined to prove what good friends we were of the Bosnians, I rummaged in my wallet for a receipt from the Holiday Inn. A green

Bosnian Serb press card fell to the floor. The cyrillic script caught our host's eye, the letters of the hated aggressor . . .

'Srbski, Pale,' (the headquarters of the Bosnian Serbs), he muttered, aghast. In a moment the mood had changed. We were no longer the visitors from the West, we were the friends of Serbian television, almost certainly spies. Inwardly cursing, frantically apologising to Maggie, while Nihad summoned his family for a consultation, I cast around in my bag for a counter charm. It had to be something good. Bits of loose change, sundry Balkan visit-cards, the remains of a UN ration pack, none of those would do. Then, at the bottom of my bag, I saw a little white badge.

I had picked up the badge from some street-children in Sarajevo the previous afternoon. It bore the symbol of 'Juka', the debt-collector turned militia-leader whom I had met earlier in the summer. His fame had clearly spread. The Bosnian Serbs' press-card was forgotten and the Devlić family examined my present with a religious devotion. We spent the next hour with Nihad plotting our approach into Goražde. It would be a good day's walk – within easy range of the Serbs' guns.

For a blessed half hour the next morning it was possible to forget the war and we could have been on holiday in any remote part of the world. Nihad's wife roused us at dawn with a jug of hot milk and sweet bread. From the balcony you could see ripening plum trees. Woodsmoke twisted through the village square. With the early-morning mist swirling around the mosque, I was reminded of the simple life in rural Turkey. But as the sun rose, so the delusion faded. The Serbs had stormed through the village of Ustiprača in April, leaving many houses charred ruins. As we started the ten-mile trek west towards Goražde, it was clear that the Serbs' territorial aspirations were by no means over.

'Come, look at this!' shouted Mehmet Mehovići, a farmer at the next village up the valley. 'It landed in June, I'm not sure exactly when . . . just mind where you throw your apple core . . .'

Embedded in the front of his orchard, neatly draped in apple boughs, was an unexploded cluster bomb. On the track outside was the casing of a second. There was barely time to look. Two loud explosions signalled the start of a new barrage and we ran for shelter.

'Every day we get this stuff,' said the village head from his prostrate position on his sitting-room floor. 'But we like this, it's 105 mm – not so bad. It could be 155 and that's really heavy, takes a house away just like that.' His wife, greying and head-scarfed, was crouched behind the kitchen door, clutching a coffee grinder, whimpering with fear.

Even though the Bosnians technically controlled the valley, the Serbs' gun emplacements commanded all the approaches to Goražde, making movement in and out impossible except under cover of darkness. We finally slipped into the town two hours after the departure of the UN convoy – an hour after the heaviest barrage of the week. The Serbs had waited just half an hour.

We spent twenty-four hours in Goražde, running, scrambling, dodging and trying not to think what would happen if either of us was hit. Death was at hand on all sides. Wooden crosses littered the back gardens. Dada Tatarević, a French teacher who volunteered as a guide, took us on a guided tour of her apartment block. In the old days No. 35 Sandzački Brigada was a coveted address. It had become a symbol of the fragility of life in Bosnia – every floor bar Dada's, the fourth, had lost someone in the siege.

'It makes me a little worried,' she confided. 'My floor must be the next to suffer.' It was hot that afternoon, real siesta weather, and overnight we had slept for barely an hour in the hospital. While we were dozing in Dada's sitting room, her neighbour slipped into the garden to pick some plums. A shell hit the tree. He was killed outright.

It was so easy for the Serbs up on the hills with their bottles of *slivovitz* and hunks of pork, lobbing down shells as and when they liked. It was also so easy for the pundits in the West to talk dispassionately about Bosnia's warring factions. But there were no warring factions in Goražde. There was a community of thirty-seven thousand people, doubled in size by refugees, in thrall to relentless thuggery. A month earlier Maggie had been up on the hills with Colonel Slavko Gub, the commander of the besiegers. These were not a professional army. They were drunken bullies. Every Friday night their attacks intensified with the arrival of the 'weekend warriors' from Montenegro – part-timers, out for a spot of raping and pillaging. Among them there were genuine Serb nationalists, who believed passionately in the 'Serbian Question', in the need for all Serbs to be in one state. But most of the fighters were the flotsam of society. It was the philosophy of football hooliganism magnified a hundredfold, against which the people of Goražde were fighting with homemade arms. 'Bosnia is awash with weapons,' said Douglas Hurd, justifying the retention of the UN arms embargo against the former Yugoslavia. It was yet another memorable line about the war – true enough, but all the arms were with the Serbs and the Croats.

We left Goražde in a blacked-out car, weaving between the lines, shaking with fear at the impact of each falling shell, haunted by the closing words of the town's commander: 'Send a message to your governments. Thank them for their food and medicines. Tell them that at least we'll die with full stomachs . . .'

It took us another two days to leave the valley. On reaching Ustipraca we learned that our car had been stolen and destroyed in a Serb ambush – or, at least, that's what we were told. In itself this was a minor inconvenience. We felt no obligation to the Bosnian-Serb owner. Indeed for a few moments we amused ourselves with a vision of the battered white Golf spearheading a Bosnian assault. Our problem was how to convince the Bosnians that we had to leave their valley. The survivors of the Serbs' ethnic cleansing, they couldn't conceive of the idea of anyone crossing into Serb-held territory. They were people like Zehra Turjahija, whose head was blackened, whose ears were melted, whose arms were covered in yellowing bandages – the only survivor of a human bonfire. To such people the security of Sarajevo, where no one had been 'cleansed', was a dream.

Amazingly, Zehra could still talk. As if reciting a shopping list, she described how on 25 June her family and many of her friends were burned alive in the town of Višegrad. 'Seven Serbs, led by a man called Milan Lukić, knocked on our door and escorted us to another house up the road. The door was blocked with furniture and they took us round the back via the balcony. First they started shooting then they lobbed in grenades.'

A fly settled on her right arm. She paused. 'They pulled back and watched, blaring out music to hide the screams. It was all so quick. Moments before, Mum told me not to worry and then we were all choking. They'd blocked the balcony with a garage door but there's a small window and I pushed my way through. They told me to stop but they were rather drunk. I went to an army officer and asked him to kill me. But he got a doctor and I later escaped.'

One of the difficulties of reporting wars is sifting reality from myth, disseminating the truth from ritual. But confronted with Zehra's hideously mangled features we could have no doubt in her story. On the same morning as we sat under a plum tree in the village of Medjedja, listening to Zehra, we heard on the BBC World Service news of the West's threats to blockade southern Iraq. 'John Major has warned Saddam Hussein that his attacks against Shi'ites are unacceptable,' said the announcer. 'Britain, France and the United States are ready to impose an exclusion zone for Iraqi aircraft.' Here was George Bush's New World Order: evil will be punished. Somehow it was a little hard to explain to Zehra and our new Bosnian friends.

The mayor of Medjedja thought he had the solution to our problem. We could transmit our pieces by courier to Goražde, thence by radio ham to Sarajevo and thence to London. We would stay in the valley until the end of the war, avoiding the danger of crossing the lines. The more insistent we were that we had to leave the more dogged he became that we had to stay. It took several hours of alternate wheedling and shouting to make him change his mind. I'm still not sure which argument won the day. But in the early afternoon five young men presented themselves before his house, volunteer guides to the far end of the valley.

With a pistol and a Tommy gun between them, our escorts chattered all the way, like boy scouts on an outing. For the final stretch they thinned down to a daredevil duo who had us running down a hillside, ducking from bush to bush. Suddenly they came to a stop, put their fingers to their lips and pointed through the undergrowth. Five feet away was a tarmac road, the highway to Višegrad.

Praying no car was coming, we jumped on to the road, expecting a shout or even a shot. There was only one way to do it. Covering our flak-jackets with our shirts, stuffing our notebooks against our bodies, we marched down the road, singing at the top of our voices.

Višegrad's fifteenth-century bridge, immortalised in the work of Ivo Andrić as a symbol of Bosnian harmony, had become a symbol of fascist terror. After all the forebodings, we found it unmanned and we strolled into the Serbs' stronghold like regular visitors. Before the war Višegrad was 70 per cent Muslim. Not one remained. The mosques had been dynamited. Muslim homes and businesses had been looted. A hundred yards from the home address of Zehra there was, as she had said, a blackened pile of rubble. We were walking down the main street when we were accosted from behind. Two minutes later we were in the police station.

'You see, we got a bit lost,' said Maggie. 'And ended up wandering down the road . . . Yes, we did know there was a war on when we came. But we didn't really know what it was like. You know, all we really want to do is to go home.'

I'm not sure the militia believed the story. But for once our interests coincided with theirs. They wanted us out of there and we desperately needed a phone. We had been out of touch for four days. Alarm bells would, I knew, be ringing in the offices of the *Telegraph*, not to mention with Sophie in Bucharest. The police chief personally gave us a lift to a village a few miles short of the border with Serbia.

'Come back and write about the Muslims massacring the Serbs,' he said. We nodded weakly.

There was just one more Bosnian-Serb checkpoint to pass. In my excitement I gave the commanding officer a friendly pat on the back. He thought for a moment, swivelled and punched me in the chest. It was the time for silent submission and downcast eyes, not for the 'Hail, fellow, well met' routine and the *Antiques Roadshow* hat. Twenty minutes of grovelling later we were in Serbia.

Journeys' ends tend to be fraught with disappointment. Cumulative fatigue rapidly overwhelms any initial triumph at reaching a goal. Pride in personal achievement plummets in the context of the wider world. Emerging from the Goražde valley – which was taken and 'cleansed' by the Serbs six months later – was to arrive in an *Alice in Wonderland* world where the great and good of the Western world had an argument tailored to discount everything we had seen.

On our first night back in Belgrade we had dinner with the resident British diplomat. For two hours he steadfastly highlighted misdoings by the Croats and Muslims. The Croatian offensive in western Hercegovina was arguably receiving less coverage than it merited. Before the war began the Bosnian-Serb and Bosnian-Croat leaders had held a secret meeting in Graz discussing a possible carve-up of Muslim-dominated territories. As the war developed, so the Croats' audacity grew. In places they started to match the Serbs for inhumanity. But on a strictly utilitarian principle this was at least initially small pickings compared with the horrors of northern and eastern Bosnia under the Serbs. It was the hyena devouring the scraps left by the big cats. The more the diplomat talked, seemingly treating the Serbs' aggression as a given factor, the more credence I attached to a prevalent conspiracy theory that early in the conflict the Foreign Office took a conscious decision to back the Serbs.

For Western politicians, by the late summer of 1992 there were many sound reasons for cautioning against intervention. Bosnia's mountainous terrain negated many of the advantages of a modern army. There would inevitably be casualties. A force of peace-makers, such as was mandated to liberate Kuwait in 1990, could be tied down in Bosnia indefinitely, at huge financial cost. To weigh these factors against the moral argument that we were sitting and watching Europe's most terrible massacres since 1945 was the duty of any responsible government. Morality versus pragmatism has been the dilemma faced by foreign ministries down the centuries. However, one of the most agonising parts of the months which followed our sojourn in the valley was listening to the Balkan debate being obscured by a welter of misleading and plainly false arguments, trotted out to bolster the anti-interventionist case.

A favourite line among the armchair strategists was to invoke the memory of Tito's Partisans. 'Plucky guerrilla-fighters, these Yugoslavs. Tied down scores of Hitler's divisions,' ran the argument, leading to the conclusion that no outside force could ever prevail in the Balkans. The 'Partisan analogy' was wrong on two counts. Firstly, in April 1941 the *Wehrmacht* took Yugoslavia with half a dozen divisions in three days. Secondly, while the Partisans were a mass movement of national liberation, the bulk of the Bosnian-Serb forces were drunken bullies who specialised in shelling defenceless civilian communities. Not once in the first two years of the Yugoslavia war were they confronted with a serious military challenge.

A second pet-argument of the anti-interventionists was that of moral equivalence. Again it resounded glibly in London clubs but bore no relation to recent history. In Goražde, Sarajevo and a score of other towns, Bosnians were one day sitting drinking coffee in the sun, the next they were under attack from the Serbs on the hills. As the Bosnians in their under-armed way started to defend themselves, the 'they are all as bad as each other' theorists felt emboldened to say 'I told you so'. It would be interesting to see what the same theorists would have said about the Jews in the Warsaw Ghetto defending themselves against the *SS*.

Possibly worst of all was the attempt to talk up the case of the Bosnian-Serbs. A vociferous pro-Serbian lobby in London pumped out their propaganda, pandering to a UK public which is conditioned to distrust Muslims and which has a folk memory of plucky Serbs on our side in the World

Wars. An interview was published in a prominent Sunday newspaper in which Dr Karadžić, the Bosnian-Serb leader, was recast as a saintly man of peace. 'His voice is gentle and his eyes are kind,' wrote the London-based journalist. 'He appears utterly devoid of the hatred and foxy mind-games favoured by lying leaders. He just seems eaten by a quiet anxiety.' The interviewer strangely forgot to mention that earlier in the year Karadžić had denied his men were besieging Sarajevo and had also denied the existence of the detention camps. This piece and others like it make interesting comparison with the fêting of Goering in certain London circles in the late 1930s.

Ultimately the more the outside world dithered, the more inevitable became the radicalisation of the Bosnians. By late 1992 the Muslim crescent was starting to replace the *fleurs de lys* as the more commonly-seen Bosnian standard. By the spring of 1993, a full year after the war had started, the Muslim-led Bosnian forces launched a pre-emptive strike against Croats, carving out a patch of disputed territory and cleansing it of non-Muslims, just as had been done in hundreds of mainly-Muslim communities by Serbs and Croats. With the Croats of Hercegovina killing and cleansing away, the argument of the Foreign Office was becoming a self-fulfilling prophecy. Bosnia had at last become a place where village fought village – but only because we had sat on the sidelines while the anarchy gathered pace.

For the Western politicians, Bosnia's final descent to tribalism could give them a sense of satisfaction that they hadn't committed large forces. But in the long term the verdict of history will be more damning. In the Croatian conflict of 1991, while the Serbs were doing the bulk of the killing and destruction, in short, winning the war, there was, with a stretch of the imagination, a sense of balance to the fight. President Tudjman made his push for independence with a crass and calculated disregard for the sensitivities of the Serb minority. His people, while unready, were bolstered by their own strand of rampant nationalism. But in Bosnia there wasn't the slightest hint of such balance. For months the Bosnians restrained themselves in the

lingering hope that they would be rewarded for their decency and civilisation. 'We are Europeans first, Bosnians
second, Muslims third,' they would say. This wasn't a war.
This was the triumph of fascism, a defeat of decency.

While I was a committed interventionist for most of
1992, by spring 1993 I reluctantly had to agree that it was
too late for action, that Bosnia was dead, that its Serb and
Croat aggressors had won, that it was a case of picking up
the pieces and learning from the mistakes, that the Palmerstonian principle of foreign policy was now correct. However,
this does not excuse the catalogue of errors made by the
international community and their knee-jerk reaction to the
Bosnian suffering. From the outset of the war the Bosnians
received endless diplomatic posturing which merely prolonged their agony. For six months the West touted a peace
plan drawn up by Cyrus Vance and Lord Owen. The plan
looked great on paper, a unitary state with strong regional
government. But on the ground it was always doomed to
fail unless someone was prepared to enforce it with military
might. The Croats in the south-west saw the plan as
a blueprint to enforce their rule on Muslim areas. The
Serbs had had their own way for eighteen months. Why
should the men who had destroyed Vukovar suddenly start
coming to heel at a new piece of paper?

When we emerged from Goražde much of this political
see-sawing and diplomatic wringing of hands was still to
come – as well as the empty gestures, the announcement of
a 'No-fly Zone' when virtually no planes were flying, the
pronouncement of 'safe havens' which were left unprotected.
But even then the signs were clear enough. These were
gloomy days in the corridors of the Hyatt Regency, Belgrade. It was time to leave.

On the eve of my departure for Romania, I bumped into
Marcus Tanner of the *Independent* in the foyer of the
Hyatt. Like many of us, he had been listening to the BBC's
intensive coverage of the siege of the south Angolan city of
Huambo, with a pained expression, as if to say, 'the siege of
where? But what about Bosnia?' Then a wry smile crossed
his face.

'I have it now. This is Huambo. Sarajevo is Huambo. All of Bosnia is Huambo. The whole Balkans is Huambo.'

In January 1993, three years after my arrival, there was time for a last visit to Timişoara. On the streets there were food queues, lines of squat, grey people, shuffling along the pavements with their string shopping bags. Outside the petrol stations vehicles stretched for a mile in each direction, just as I remembered. However, the queuers were Serbs not Romanians, crossing the border to buy up cheap Romanian goods to offset the effect of international sanctions. The petrol lines were Romanians flogging fuel across the border.

In the old Central Committee building, where I had been proposed for associate membership of the government, the prefect Dorel Borza remembered me from January 1990. George Ardelean, an old friend from those early days, came rushing up to me. He could get some petrol – for a price.

'Do you know,' he asked, 'where the petrol came from?' I shook my head. He put his finger to his lips. 'The CIA . . .'

'CIA?'

'And the KGB . . .' He laughed and talked of his plan to ship Chinese silk into Romania. 'Maybe you would like to be the London broker . . .?' We stayed up late over a bottle of *ţuica* and talked of the changes since the Ceauşescu regime and the new opportunities. It was a ray of light in the gloom and it is how I would like to remember the Balkans.

Balkan Chronology

1989

16 December   Uprising breaks out in Timişoara

22 December   National Salvation Front takes over in Bucharest after flight of Nicolae Ceauşescu

25 December   Nicolae and Elena Ceauşescu executed

1990

20–21 January   Last session of Yugoslav Communist Party – Slovene delegates walk out

29 January   Coal miners beat up political opposition in Bucharest for first time

13–15 March   Five killed in fighting between Romanians and ethnic Hungarians in Tîrgu Mureş

4 April   Slovenia's first post-communist elections

22 April   Croatia's first post-communist elections – Franjo Tudjman elected president

20 May   Romania's first democratic elections since the Second World War

14–15 June   Club-wielding miners take over Bucharest after day of anti-government riots

17 August   Croatian police have armed confrontation with Serb minority of Krajina

	with Serb minority of Krajina
18 November	Elections in Bosnia-Hercegovina – vote split down ethnic lines
9 December	Serbian elections return Slobodan Milošević as president

1991

9 March	Two killed in anti-Milošević protests in Belgrade
25 June	Croatian parliament declares independence
26 June	Slovenian parliament declares independence
27 June	Federal army tanks move against Slovenia
6 September	Opening of abortive EC Peace Conference for Yugoslavia in the Hague
1 October	Federal forces start to besiege Dubrovnik
17 November	Fall of Vukovar to Serb irregulars and federal army

1992

3 January	UN-brokered ceasefire in Croatia
15 January	EC recognizes Croatia and Slovenia
9 January	Serbs in Bosnia-Hercegovina declare own republic
28 February	Referendum in Bosnia. Muslims and Croats vote for independence. Boycotted by Serbs
6 April	Serb snipers fire on Sarajevo peace demonstration for second consecutive day. Siege of Sarajevo begins
7 April	EC recognizes Bosnia
16 May	UN evacuates bulk of troops from Sarajevo
31 May	UN imposes embargo on rump Yugoslavia (Serbia and Montenegro)
6 August	World alerted to Serb-run detention camps

26 August	London Peace Conference sets up Geneva Peace Conference
28 October	Vance/Owen Peace Plan unveiled for Bosnia

1993

3 April	Bosnian Serbs reject peace plan

Sources

For material I relied primarily on my own roamings. But I also plundered freely from various Balkan classics. Many of my historical references were gleaned from R.W. Seton Watson's *History of the Roumanians*, published in the 1934, still the pivotal work on Romanian history. Ivo Porter's *Operation Autonomous*, Sir Sacheverell Sitwell's *Roumanian Journey* and Patrick Leigh Fermor's *Between the Woods and the Water* gave an incomparable glimpse into Romania's heyday in the 1930s. Hannah Pakula's *Queen of Roumania: The life of Princess Marie, grand-daughter of Queen Victoria* was an endless source of off-beat anecdotes and delightful detail about the royal family. Richard Wagner's taut novelette *Exit* about Timişoara in January 1990 made interesting comparison to my own initial impressions. Mark Almond's *The Rise and Fall of Nicolae and Elena Ceauşescu* provided impeccably-researched background material on, and insight into, the career of the Ceauşescus as did John Sweeney's *The Life and Evil Times of Nicolae Ceauşescu*. For scholarship on the Iliescu era, Martyn Rady's *Romania in Turmoil* excellently combines dispassionate assessment with an appreciation for the nuances of the Balkan conspiracy.

To lend historical depth to the fruits of my forays the other side of the Danube, Barbara Jelavich's two-volume *History of the Balkans*, published in 1983, proved ideal, thorough and yet immensely readable. Chris Cviic's *Remaking the Balkans* provided a crisp analysis of the countdown to war. Misha Glenny's seminal *The Fall of Yugoslavia* and Mark Thompson's *The Paper House* added much-needed learning and insight to my impressions from the road. A range of miscellaneous historical and literary works have topped up the politics. Ernle Bradford's *The Great Siege*, source of the Balbi da Correggio material, helped me to put my feelings about Dubrovnik in context. Claudio Magris' *Danube* was irrepressible on the soldiers of the Military Frontier and, indeed, on a range of Balkan people and places. But without a doubt the most inspiring Balkan work of all time is Ivo Andrić's *The Bridge Over the Drina*, a haunting account of Bosnia through the centuries, a poignant epitaph to a society the West has watched disappear.

Index